RUSKIN
AND
SOCIAL REFORM

For
Alexandra and Georgina

RUSKIN
AND
SOCIAL REFORM

Ethics and Economics in the Victorian Age

GILL G. COCKRAM

Tauris Academic Studies
LONDON • NEW YORK

Published in 2007 by Tauris Academic Studies, an imprint of I.B.Tauris & Co Ltd
6 Salem Road, London W2 4BU
175 Fifth Avenue, New York NY 10010
www.ibtauris.com

In the United States of America and Canada distributed by
Palgrave Macmillan a division of St. Martin's Press
175 Fifth Avenue, New York NY 10010

International Library of Historical Studies 47

ISBN: 978 1 84511 349 0

A full CIP record for this book is available from the British Library
A full CIP record for this book is available from the Library of Congress

Library of Congress catalog card: available

Printed and bound in India by Replika Press Pvt. Ltd
camera-ready copy edited and supplied by the author

CONTENTS

ACKNOWLEDGEMENTS

During the writing of this book, which began as a doctoral thesis, I have become indebted to many people. My first thanks must go to my supervisor at Royal Holloway, Professor Gregory Claeys, not least for encouraging my interest in Ruskin and in helping centrally to delineate the scale of the project. I am also very grateful to my back-up supervisor, Professor Penelope Corfield, for support and encouragement during the long haul of finishing a PhD. I would also like to thank the staff of the many libraries I have visited. These include the very helpful staff at the London Library, the archives of the London School of Economics, the Ruskin Library at Lancaster University, the British Library, Senate House Library, the Marx Memorial Library, the People's History Museum and many other people who have answered my queries with great patience.

My thanks must also go to the Rev. Peter Thomson, for taking the time to talk to me about the tradition of Christian Socialism within the Labour movement, and to Dr. Ian Donnachie for expanding my knowledge of Robert Owen. And for practical help in putting this book together, the calm expertise of Richard Williams, Audrey Daly, Carolann Martin, Meg Davies and Elizabeth Munns has proved invaluable.

Two further debts must be acknowledged. The first, to my friend Thelma Stollar, for her constant encouragement and for introducing me to the London Library. The second, and most important, to my family, for their patience and wholehearted support during my research.

CONVENTIONS

B.L.   British Library
L.L.   London Library, St. James's Square, London
L.S.E.   London School of Economics, University of London
M.M.L.   Marx Memorial Library, Clerkenwell, London
R.L.   Ruskin Library, Lancaster University

Fors   J. Ruskin, *Fors Clavigera* (1871–84)

Notes:
Place of publication of all works cited is London, unless otherwise specified.

The standard Cook and Wedderburn publication of Ruskin's works has been consulted throughout this thesis, and the select works are listed in the bibliography. Original and variant editions have been used, however, as appropriate in a study of reception. These alternative citations are recorded in the relevant footnotes.

1

INTRODUCTION

Ruskin was repudiated and attacked by every circle and school. The Bishop repudiated his theology; the political economist his social teaching. But one vital fact soon emerged above the sea of criticism. That was the reception of his teaching by the working classes of this country. The appeal to their hearts and imagination was undoubted. They soon realised that one with sympathy for the lives they led was speaking to them, and that he wished to create for them here and now a new and happier world.[1]

J.H. Whitehouse (1920)

Ruskin directed public attention to this evil sixty years ago. The world would have been much happier would it only have listened to him.[2]   A.J. Penty (1917)

Everyone with any knowledge of nineteenth century history knows something about John Ruskin. Some think of him as the art critic who famously insulted Whistler, others remember that he had a penchant for Gothic architecture, and a small number indulge in anecdotal ribaldry concerning the circumstances of his divorce. Few, however, are aware of the extent and depth of his influence as a social and economic critic. Yet Ruskin's impact in this area was profound, a factor which has been largely overlooked by historians of the nineteenth century. Those writers who have studied his social thought are conscious of this gross anomaly and have acknowledged the requirement for a reassessment of his importance. It was with this aim in mind, that I undertook to examine Ruskin's reception and influence as a social critic in the second half of the nineteenth century.

My investigation begins around 1850, a time that marks the emergence of Ruskin's serious incursion into the field of economic criticism, and ends in 1906, the year of the first Labour representation in the House of Commons. It was during this period that Ruskin became increasingly antagonistic to the instrumental values of industrial capitalism, a theme that resonates through most of his later writings. In *The Stones of Venice* (1853), he strongly criticised the division of labour, and in *Unto This Last* (1860–2), using a basic Christian ethic of cooperation, he scathingly attacked the whole *laissez-faire* philosophy which underscored the Liberal interpretation of classical economics. The central ideas of *Unto This Last* were then further developed in *Munera Pulveris* (1862–3), *The Crown of Wild Olive* (1866), *Time and Tide* (1867), and *Fors Clavigera* (1871–84).

The initial response to Ruskin's early social critique has been well documented. As can be seen in contemporary reviews and notices, it was a combination of fear and incredulity. What is less well known however, is that some twenty years later Ruskin was hailed as a major influence, especially among socialist sympathisers. This dramatic change in his reception in Britain demands a closer look at the social and intellectual background. During this transitional period much of Ruskin's original economic analysis, as it was assimilated and diffused by other major reformers, became increasingly plausible. In this context the reception of Ruskin's social critique takes on a new significance.

The publication of the critical essays, which formed *Unto This Last* in 1862, had a dramatic effect on Ruskin's reputation. Opposition to this work was violent, multifaceted, and came from a variety of political persuasions, as indeed did his later support. Written at the high tide of individualist idealism, it was, commented Ernest Barker, published when '*laissez-faire* was as much a political dogma as it was an economic doctrine', and Ruskin's writing had 'undermined the doctrine in both of its applications'.[3] It was therefore seen as much as an attack on liberalism as a concession to socialism. In the reforms that Ruskin advocated, he transgressed all the rules of the non-interventionist economic system, and, in so doing, reinforced an important principle of socio-economic interaction which initially gained him many enemies. He never lost faith in the right-thinking of *Unto This Last*, however, and republished it independently in 1877 when sales were already beginning to escalate. By that time, many intellectuals were reconsidering the nature of orthodox political economy and Ruskin must be given strong credit for assisting this process.

The reaction to Ruskin's thinking, which often matched the passion of his own critique, is important on two counts: not only as an indicator of his competence as a social critic, but also as a benchmark in the dynamics of the movement toward collectivism. Those who were initially antagonistic to his social criticism tended to fall into two groups: the businessmen who would almost certainly suffer financial loss if they followed his humanitarian economics, and those who genuinely believed that his proposals for reform were unworkable. As will become apparent, his reception changed, but then so to a large extent, did his audience: from mid-nineteenth century middle-class liberal entrepreneurs to a preponderance of labourers and trade-unionists, who ultimately became the greatest purchasers of Ruskin's books. Yet despite this later left-wing reverence for his writings, it has proved difficult to place Ruskin accurately within the tradition of working-class radicalism. His insistence on state intervention and social stratification makes him a 'destroyer of liberalism', as Raymond Williams suggests,[4] but this does not make him a socialist. And Ruskin is equally removed by his radicalism from the 'enlightened Tories' of the first wave of Christian Socialism, led by F.D. Maurice in the middle of the nineteenth century. Much of this confusion resides in the erratic development of socialism itself. When Ruskin wrote *Unto This Last* in 1860, socialism was, as Royden Harrison notes, dependent on the support 'of a few scattered individuals'.[5] Ruskin's true position therefore has remained ambiguous not only because of his own complexity, but also because of the timing of his most effective social critique. This has led to confusion over his role. A recent primer by H.S.Jones, *Victorian Political Thought* (Basingstoke, 2000), for example, makes no mention of Ruskin, whose name does not even appear in the index. Whatever the answer to Ruskin's political persuasion may be, it is to be found in the pages of *Unto This Last,* which contains the essence of his social thought, and yet has been too readily dismissed as economic fantasy.

This small book was not a utopian socialist manifesto, although many perceived it as such at the time of its first publication.[6] Instead, it was an attempt to redefine the whole language of political economy, at a time when opposition to *laissez-faire* was mounting from all quarters. Yet although *Unto This Last* ultimately received an endorsement by many Labour MPs, Ruskin's social criticism has been frequently misunderstood. Despite the availability of excellent secondary sources, there are problems in trying to assess the influence of a man who was by nature full of contradictions, and who professed so adamantly to be anti-partisan throughout his life.[7] While William Morris continues to be applauded for his active political radicalism, Ruskin's stance remains equivocal, and it is difficult to assign him to any specific political ideology other than through the orientation of his disciples. Those influenced by Ruskin, moreover, were not in any sense organised into a cult or anything as clear-cut as a Ruskinian 'school'.

Modern critics are not unaware of this dilemma. In his book, *John Ruskin's Labour* (1983), P.D. Anthony admits to a great admiration for Ruskin, but nevertheless gives a thorough and intellectually detached examination of his merit as a social critic, with a particular emphasis on his significance *vis à vis* Marx. Anthony draws interesting parallels between Ruskin and William Morris, whose 'canonisation coincides with the argument that he is a Marxist'.[8] Indeed, Morris was not taken seriously until he acquired this political label. No one, however, could label Ruskin a Marxist[9] and, since 'seriousness and significance have come to be acquainted with Marxism, Ruskin's social theory has remained a subject of considerable condescension.'[10] Yet, writes Anthony, 'Morris followed a trail laid by Ruskin. Morris's famous denunciations are remarkably similar to Ruskin's, except that Ruskin's are more savage, sometimes coarser, and were made first.'[11] Yet this link is a factor which seems subsequently to have been either forgotten, or else relegated to the status of polite academic deference. Anthony attributes this deficit largely to Ruskin's opposition to Marxist political activism and comments, 'It is the utopian moralist in Morris, not the political activist, that provides the decisive link between Ruskin and the practical possibility of a revolutionary change in the world's values.'[12] In fact, Anthony considers, it has proved to be the moral appeal of Morris which has endured rather than his political activism and this moral stance undoubtedly came largely from Ruskin.

Anthony's respect for Ruskin is further endorsed by J.C. Sherburne, who, in *John Ruskin or the Ambiguities of Abundance* (1972), concentrates also on Ruskin's social critique, giving an extremely erudite analysis of his plausibility as an economic critic. Sherburne, however, comments in his epilogue:

The degree of Ruskin's influence . . . remains to be determined. So does the question of whether the wholeness and aesthetic quality of his perception survived the secular, sociological, and scientific sea change which the language of social criticism underwent around the turn of the century. Hobson's work would be an excellent test case, but this lies in the future.[13]

It is hoped that this book, which places great emphasis on Hobson's role, will go some way to addressing this requirement. To give historical perspective to Ruskin's attack on classical political economy, it is useful to look briefly at criticism of *laissez-faire* prior to 1860. When Ruskin began his critique in the late 1850s, Adam Smith's teaching, as amended by Ricardo, still provided the inspiration for British economic policy. *An Enquiry into the Nature and Causes of the Wealth of Nations* (1776) was at the heart of the system which dominated the long process of industrialisation in England from the late eighteenth century until the mid-nineteenth century, when *laissez-faire* began to face mounting opposition from reformers.[14] This antipathy to *laissez-faire* was tempered by the fact that some intellectuals still persisted in regarding the problems of indigence as the fault of the individual. Many reformers, while not endorsing Malthus' depressing conclusions on the inevitability of an economic underclass, felt that the causes of social distress lay more with immorality than with classical economic policy. Benthamite utilitarianism, allied with a revival of evangelicalism, had dictated that the individual was responsible for his or her own fate. This view endured despite a strong undercurrent of discontent among the labouring classes and their sympathisers over the relationship between labour and capital, and the role of the state in addressing social issues.

The apparent synthesis between *laissez-faire* economics and the doctrine of personal salvation, preached by an evangelical clergy, was not lost on those capitalists who had everything to gain under the existing system,[15] but it increased the anger of reformers as disparate in their views as Southey and Marx, and of course, later, Ruskin as well. Indeed, the continuing dominance of *laissez-faire* economics caused an undercurrent of opposition from people of often widely divergent political persuasions. As Raymond Williams has commented on 'the complexity of this difficult period':

Where Cobbett sneered at Owen's 'parallelograms of paupers', Southey, with very many of the new generation of English industrial workers, approved. In a movement like Christian Socialism, the influence of both Southey and Owen can be clearly discerned.

Yet Owen, in his main bearings led to socialism and the cooperatives; Southey, with Burke and Coleridge, to the new conservatism.[16]

Opposition to the principle of *laissez-faire* also entered the national
consciousness through much of the literature gradually becoming available
to a wider reading public. Dickens, in *Hard Times* (1854), posed the
individual against 'the system', a covert attack on utilitarian 'gradgrindery'
and Millite individualism; and there were many tracts of a radical nature
which predated Ruskin's critique. In *Ambiguities of Abundance*, J.C.
Sherburne acknowledges that Ruskin's eclecticism rendered the extent of
his debt to previous critics of classical economy unclear. Nonetheless,
Sherburne indicates some of the most likely influences upon Ruskin.

One strand came from the work of Simonde de Sismondi (1773–1842),
who, in his *Nouveaux principes d'economie politique* (1819), 'warns against the
economists' tendency to simplify and generalise'.[17] As with Ruskin, notes
Sherburne, Sismondi's 'attack on method is a way of injecting ethics into
economic analysis'; but, unlike Ruskin, Sismondi 'retains a strong interest
in making economics more accurate as a science'.[18] Ruskin's true antece-
dents, however, were to be found less in the field of economic history than
in more Romantic sources. Also important was Robert Southey,[19] who
along with Wordsworth and Coleridge condemned political economy for
defining man as a purely rational and mechanistic being, devoid of all
sentiment. To this list of influences upon Ruskin must be added Carlyle,
Hazlitt, and, of course, Dickens. Above all, no one who reads Ruskin
extensively can doubt his affinity with Carlyle.[20]

Carlyle's vociferous social criticism had a considerable impact in the
middle years of the nineteenth century. That stemmed especially from his
series of historical writings and works of social criticism, in which he
attacked the 'mechanical' nature of industrialised society, which precluded any reference to spiritual causes. In *Signs of the Times* (1829),
Carlyle complained explicitly:

> It is no longer the moral, religious, spiritual condition of the
> people that is our concern, but their physical, practical, economical
> condition as regulated by public laws.[21]

As Michael Levin points out, Carlyle was not against 'industrial transformation' but was opposed to 'the way society had downgraded

spontaneity and community'.[22] In this, too, he influenced Ruskin, who shared with him an abomination of vulgar materialism such as they both considered to be celebrated by the Great Exhibition. But when Ruskin was beginning in the 1850s to establish himself as a social critic, Carlyle's influence was diminishing.

One of the reasons for this was the fact that the economic optimism of the mid- nineteenth century did nothing to endorse Carlyle's earlier expressions of gloomy foreboding. But as A.L. Le Quesne comments, 'The divergence between Carlyle and his leading disciples can be traced back before 1848.'[23] Carlyle's growing emphasis on the role of the 'hero' proved unacceptable to his followers; despotism was not considered a plausible solution to social ills.

Ruskin may have been influenced by Carlyle's anti-democratic stance, but ultimately Ruskin was far more radical and far more analytical and accessible to the working-man in his critique of *laissez-faire* economics. Carlyle had exposed social evils, but he had not offered any workable alternatives. This was reflected in what A.L. Le Quesne terms 'a progressive coarsening in the fibre of Carlyle's thinking and writing from the early 1840s onward'[24] which indicated a 'change in attitude to the mass of mankind'.[25]

Ruskin gained much from Carlyle in terms of opposition to individualistic rationalism; both feared that a breakdown of natural relationships would be the outcome of an increasingly industrialised society. Ruskin, however, showed a much greater humanitarian concern for the plight of the working man, and, especially in *Unto This Last,* tried to offer an alternative to economic exploitation.

There is another possible source of influence, however, which it is helpful to analyse both in order to evaluate Ruskin's originality and to understand the parallel strands that certainly augmented Ruskin's popularity in the socialist revival at the end of the nineteenth century. Ruskin's eclecticism, claims Sherburne, meant that he could 'incorporate into his criticism of economic man elements from a very different tradition, that of Robert Owen and the "Ricardian socialists"'.[26] Ruskin gave no credit to Owen, but agreed with him on many social issues which were certainly picked up by the emergent labour movement at the end of the nineteenth century. As with Ruskin, Owen's paternalistic, anti-democratic stance makes him a dubious sort of socialist, but his emphasis on community and his refutation of *laissez-faire* economics secured his influence on a working-class audience. Indeed, themes from early socialism, inspired by Owen's ideas, were translated into later forms, notably in the field of cooperative economics.[27]

One of the men who expanded Owen's ideas was William Thompson, who foreshadowed Ruskin's view of man as a complex organism – a factor which both Thompson and Ruskin considered should be recognised and acted on by economists in the interests of promoting general well-being. Thompson advocated 'the utmost possible, nearly approaching to a perfect, equality of distribution of wealth, and thus to the greatest happiness desirable from it'.[28] He set out three rules of action[29]:

> First. All labour ought to be free and *voluntary,* as to its direction and continuance.

> Second. All products of labour ought to be secured to the producers of them.

> Third. All exchanges of these products ought to be free and *voluntary.*

Thompson thus opposed the principle of individual competition with one of mutual cooperation. He recognised that there were some benefits in competition with regard to endeavour but these were outweighed by the evils. Competition, in his view 'retains the principle of selfishness as the leading motive to action in all the ordinary affairs of life.'[30]

Thompson's Owenite views were endorsed a year later by John Gray, who in his *Lecture on Human Happiness* (1825) attacked the current system for inadequately treating the effects, rather than the causes, of human misery. Gray's concern, like Ruskin, was that 'the greater proportion are led to seek for happiness in the pursuit of wealth' but, if they are not educated to make good use of it, 'it commonly happens that they convert it to the destruction of their own peace.'[31] Years later, Ruskin was to emulate these sentiments in many of his works.

There are thus many sound economic and social reasons why it is important not to neglect Owen's influence in any consideration of Ruskin's thinking. And this is reinforced by Ruskin's association with the early Christian Socialists at the Working Men's College.[32] However much Ruskin may have wished to distance himself, in his flirtation with the first wave of Christian Socialism in the middle of the century, he was exposed to those who in principle upheld the Owenite philosophy of economic cooperation, even though their acceptance of this concept was gradual.

The Christian Socialist movement also serves to 'situate' Ruskin, both in his context and in his originality. In the early nineteenth century, Christian political economy was, as A.M.C. Waterman points out, strongly favourable to: private property rights, free and competitive markets, the institutions of marriage and wage-labour, and a high degree of social and economic inequality.[33] Under the leadership of F.D. Maurice, the first Christian Socialists opposed this orthodoxy in principle, but remained largely anti-democratic. Their promotion of cooperative enterprise was, as E.R. Norman comments, 'ethical' and 'educative' rather than political, and 'distinctly lacked a socialist economic base'.[34] But the Christian Socialists were not completely homogeneous, and where Kingsley echoed Ruskin's plea for practical reform, Ludlow foreshadowed his economic concerns.

In his work, *The Victorian Christian Socialists* (1987), Norman refers to the economist J.M. Ludlow as 'arguably the most important of the Christian Socialist leaders of the whole century'.[35] Ludlow, writes Norman, produced a collection of papers and reports on social issues which became 'a major resource for Church and cooperative reformers.'[36] Certainly, Ludlow was very outspoken in his denigration of the inactivity of both church and state in addressing the problems of poverty. He also attacked the political economists directly, finding their 'let-alone' system devoid of humanitarian concerns. He deplored the existing state whereby 'every partner [seeks] his own gain at the cost of every other's loss by what is termed competition.'[37] The remedy, claimed Ludlow, lay in opposing competition with 'combination' or cooperative enterprise.[38]

In reaching this conclusion the influence of the French visionary, Fourier, was paramount.[39] Ludlow had spent his formative years in France and was impressed with the methods and ideology of the Fourierists. Although he was not initially sympathetic to socialist thinking, seeing it as a challenge to the church, he later realised the possibility of a Christian form of socialism which incorporated the cooperative ideals of Fourier. Indeed, it was Ludlow, writes Norman, who introduced the 'French cooperative method' to Maurice and others of his circle, thus adding a new dimension to the radical socialist tradition, which in England had largely begun with Owen.[40] Ludlow was rather suspicious of Owen's communitarian experiments and disliked his unorthodox religious stance, but nevertheless Owen's emphasis on cooperation and his example of the exchange of equivalents of labour seemed to have its effect on the newly-formed Christian Socialists in the 1850s, even though their individual interpretation was different. As Norman points out: 'The Christian Socialists did much to encourage cooperative economic enterprise, and in the process forged an enduring link with at least one aspect of the emergent labour movement.'[41]

There were, then, many precursors to Ruskin's social critique, but no critic in the mid-nineteenth century managed to generate the same antipathy and controversy as did Ruskin in the 1860s. It is indeed, a measure of his effect that he was very rapidly suppressed in the most effective way possible – by the curtailment of publication. It is also significant that by the 1870s, it was much easier for others to follow his lead.

The nineteenth-century interpretation of classical economics was becoming a very contentious issue. Certainly, by the 1870s the whole concept of non-intervention and its plausibility in the context of nineteenth-century industrialism was being closely questioned. J.S. Mill fiercely defended the liberty of the individual; but this was at odds with many of the assumptions of utilitarianism and his detractors were quick to point this out. Robert Williams commented in 1870:

> It is a misfortune, that that portion of the community which makes its living by the poverty, the misery, and often by the sin of its fellow-creatures, should be able to quote the utterances of our great political philosophers in its favour. It is easily to be understood that there are certain persons and certain classes who will always deprecate the least interference on the part of the Government, and will raise the cry that commerce is paralysed, and that the liberties of the subject are in peril. These gentlemen owe their best thanks to the *laissez-faire* philosophy.[42]

By the 1870s, *laissez-faire* was being denied scientific respectability by some; and furthermore, its all-pervasive principal claims were increasingly viewed by reformers as being responsible for most of the social ills of the day. It will be seen that the avenues of attack used by these later critics mimicked those for which Ruskin was ridiculed in

1860. This was interpreted by many emergent Labour members as a vindication of Ruskin's argument, which endorsed his moral and economic credibility. Almost a century after Owen had established his factory system in New Lanark, socialists were again linking his name with Ruskin. Moreover, with the obvious proviso that Owen was a secularist, there were further plausible reasons for this conjunction. The most obvious correlation is that Ruskin mimicked Owen's communitarian experiments in his Guild of St George, established in 1871. But this is less important than the fact that Owen and Ruskin were united in their opposition to *laissez-faire* competition on both moral *and* economic grounds. Theirs was a morality free from the dogma of evangelicalism, and its central message of cooperation was further endorsed by the humanitarian ethos of the English positivists, many of whom were very pro-Ruskin.[43] Royden Harrison writes:

By the Religion of Humanity [the English positivists] expected to resolve the conflicts of capital and labour; order and progress; religion and science. Through Saint Simon and Robert Owen, John Francis Bray, Colin and Comte; the tradition of secular religiosity is joined to the formative stages of Labour and Socialist evolution.[44]

While English positivism largely lost its influence after 1880[45] however, Ruskin's quasi-religious economic critique endured. It endorsed Owen's plea for cooperation and added that extra spiritual dimension, which was so appealing to many reformers in what they felt to be the moral vacuum of capitalist society.

By the end of the nineteenth century, *Unto This Last* was certainly selling at the rate of two thousand copies per annum, and it has subsequently been translated into many languages. Ruskin had made a seminal contribution toward the moralisation of political economy, his onslaught on capitalist exploitation rivalling that of Marx. He has been an inspiration to men as culturally diverse as Proust and Gandhi. Closer to home, Ruskin also influenced William Morris, who publicly acknowledged his tremendous debt, the positivist writer Frederic Harrison, the economist J.A. Hobson, both of whom wrote books about Ruskin, and many more. In 1906, despite Ruskin's denial of any political affiliation, it will be seen that his particular form of Christian Socialism was quoted as being the main source of inspiration for many newly emergent Labour members. Yet this is not generally recognised. Indeed, Ruskin's contribution toward socialist/collectivist thought is often totally neglected or at best marginalised under the pejorative heading of 'literary influences'.[46] That is the reason for this book: to give a new view of Ruskin's reception as a social critic, to illustrate his profound influence on other prominent thinkers, and thus to restore his social thought to centre stage.

2

JOHN RUSKIN: THE EMERGENCE OF A SOCIAL CRITIC

There is hardly one aspect of modern life or of modern thought against which Mr Ruskin has not at one time or another poured out the vials of the wrath of God.[1]　　　　　E.T. Cook (1894)

Early Influences

While it would be travelling a well-trodden path to retrace Ruskin's journey from aesthete to social and economic critic, it is necessary before investigating his reception and influence to say something about those factors which combined so uniquely to formulate his later opinions. As Ruskin was by nature both eclectic and paradoxical, this renders the task simultaneously both more interesting and less easy.

Perhaps the first thing which should be established is that Ruskin was born into the commercial class. His father was a wine merchant, his grandfather was also a merchant, his mother was the daughter of a herring fisherman, and her sister had married a baker in Croydon. In the same town, his maternal grandmother was landlady of the Old King's Head. Ruskin's lineage was, then, the commonly accepted one of a commercial gentleman.[2] He was born on 8 February 1819, in a small house at 54 Hunter Street, Brunswick Square. At this time massive economic and industrial development was already creating urban wealth and poverty on an unprecedented scale. And, even though as the only son of a successful wine importer Ruskin was never himself exposed to want, as a sensitive child he must have assimilated some *frisson* of social friction from the outside world. Beginning with his early development, however, it is not difficult to see that any signs of an embryonic awareness of exploitation in those days touched his mind rather than his heart. His autobiography, *Praeterita* (1885–9), was obviously a retrospective viewpoint, but it nevertheless gives an illuminating insight into the Ruskin household.

The nature and demeanour of his parents and the tenor of the daily routine were the formative influences in Ruskin's life. The family seems to have been very self-contained. 'We seldom had company, even on week days,'[3] wrote Ruskin, and his mother was obviously very much in control where his upbringing was concerned. He was raised kindly but strictly, with few toys and fewer friends, but not, he commented later, as strictly as was sometimes alleged. He wrote in *Praeterita* that there was one aspect of his mother's character which 'must here be asserted at once, to put an end to the notion of which I see traces in some newspaper comments on my past descriptions of her, that she was any wise like Esther's religious aunt in *Bleak House*.'[4] On the contrary, he maintained, 'There was a hearty, frank, and sometimes even irrepressible, laugh in my mother!'[5] It was she who encouraged him, however, as befitted a true evangelical household, in daily Bible study, and he wrote with some resignation of her earnest endeavour to 'make a clergyman' of him. Indeed, Ruskin exhibited an early talent for this vocation by occasionally imitating their local preacher at home, which was regarded by his mother's friends as 'the great accomplishment' of his childhood.[6] He never, however, shared her enthusiasm for the ritual of Sunday worship.

Being kept from the normative peer group development engendered by regular school attendance, church and home were thus the predominant influences upon Ruskin's early life and his only exposure to social intercourse. The Ruskin household, which was transferred when Ruskin was about four to leafy Herne Hill, was obviously a well-ordered hierarchy where the servants, despite their lowly status, were treated with respect and affection as human beings. He recalled the servant Anne who remained 'very servile in soul all her days', and spent her whole life 'doing other people's wills instead of her own, and seeking other people's good instead of her own.'[7] How far the young Ruskin took this situation as the acceptable norm at the time is debatable, but there is little doubt that memories such as these caused him some distress in later years. In summing up dispassionately what, with hindsight, he later considered to be the shortcomings in his early training, he quotes the 'chief evil' as being that his 'judgement of right and wrong, and powers of independent action, were left entirely undeveloped.' His education was 'at once too formal and too luxurious', leaving his character 'only by protection innocent instead of by practice virtuous'.[8]

Ruskin certainly had a very pampered childhood, reinforced by frequent and very agreeable foreign tours with his parents, and whether this regimented over-indulgence was the primary cause or not, there is little doubt that he suffered from acutely sensitive feelings of social obligation in later life. When he came to write *Praeterita* it was in many ways as a form of palliative, an antidote to the bouts of madness induced by those aspects of contemporary life he deplored, but felt powerless to change.[9]

The special combination of discipline in religious matters inculcated by his mother, and the more secular, although nonetheless erudite taste of his father for Scott, Byron, Shakespeare, and for the visual arts, engendered in the early and rather solitary young Ruskin a propensity not only for erudition, but also for a solipsistic form of imaginative fantasy. The sad fact was that Ruskin's acute artistic sensitivity, which was at the core of his genius, made it increasingly difficult for him to identify with the bulk of the population. Having inherited his father's wealth, Ruskin's own intellectual development was never hindered by the mundane task of having to earn a living, and this fact tormented him in later life. His sensitivity to social deprivation, which was both acute and profound, was not based on personal experience, but on an aesthetic principle which acknowledged that the evidence of a debasement of style and taste was indicative of a sick society. He was thus distanced by both intellect and lack of acquaintance from those whom he sought to protect. Why is it, wrote E.T. Cook in 1894, 'that the writer whom so many readers find helpful, yet proclaims himself helpless?'[10] He concluded that the problem lay in Ruskin's 'morbid sensitiveness'.[11] But while a morbid sensitivity is probably not the best precondition for effective social and political criticism, in Ruskin's case his weakness was also his strength. No one was better equipped to be such an accurate barometer of the social and economic atmosphere, and no one could so eloquently articulate the deficiencies of existing economic practice.

Ruskin's literary richness is legendary, and the factors which contributed to the development of his style are as diverse and paradoxical as the man himself: a mixture of innate talent, the arrogance of Byron and Carlyle, both of whom he admired, the rhetoric of the scriptures, and the mythological language of the classics. Shortly after Ruskin's death in 1900, Leslie Stephen wrote the following acknowledgement of his poetic style:

There should be no cumbrous verbiage: no barren commonplace to fill the interstices of thought: and no mannerism simulating emotion by fictitious emphasis. Ruskin has that virtue in the highest degree. We are everywhere in contact with a real human being.[12]

But Ruskin was not only a gifted writer, he was also a powerful speaker. And the gift of rhetoric, which he so obviously possessed in abundance, was in part due to his evangelical upbringing. He was witness from an early age to the power of the spoken word and, although he later became disenchanted with evangelical religion, speaking drily of 'that slight bias' against it which is 'sometimes traceable' in his later work, he nevertheless remained aware of its positive and powerful aspects. He remarked upon having seen, at the age of seven on a visit to relations, 'the Scottish Puritan spirit in its perfect faith and force', which he says he later realised was 'instrumental'[13] in Scotland's reforming policy.

This tradition was reinforced by Ruskin's weekly and somewhat reluctant attendance with his parents at the Beresford Congregational Chapel, Walworth.[14] There, he remembered that the Rev E. Andrews 'preached, regularly, a somewhat eloquent, forcible, and ingenious sermon, not tiresome to him.'[15] Dr. Andrews also instructed the young Ruskin in Greek, despite an apparently inadequate knowledge of the language. Nonetheless, Ruskin recalled that Dr. Andrews 'wrote the letters prettily, and had an accurate and sensitive ear for rhythm'.[16] If there was irony in these retrospective remarks regarding the ecclesiastical orientation of Ruskin's early education, there was also a basic truth; religion never ceased to matter to Ruskin. Despite the growing scepticism of the nation, Christianity gave him his code of morality and underpinned all his later social and political criticism.

Identifying Ruskin's particular interpretation of Christianity, however, is also a complex exercise. He left home for Christ Church College, Oxford in 1837 at a time when Newman was at his most influential, yet Ruskin seems to have remained totally detached, even unaware of the admittedly esoteric impact of the Tractarians.[17] The evangelical movement was in full swing in the 1830s and 1840s, and certainly contributed to the ethical earnestness which characterised the middle-class psyche.[18] As the son of a successful evangelical merchant, Ruskin probably saw no reason at this stage of his life to question his religious inheritance. His mind was quite simply on other things.

His parents had contributed in no small measure to this initial narrowness of outlook. Both the elder Ruskins had him marked down for the church; Oxford was to expedite this aspiration. As Ruskin later wrote of his father in *Praeterita*:

> His ideal of my future – now entirely formed in conviction of my genius – was that I should enter at college into the best society, take all the prizes every year, and a double first to finish with; marry Lady Clara Vere; write poetry as good as Byron's, only pious; preach sermons as good as Bossuet's, only Protestant; be made, at forty, Bishop of Winchester, and at fifty, Primate of England.[19]

But this was not to be. Despite Ruskin's continuing affection for his college and the friends he made there, Oxford was not the major influence in his life. He felt the natural world had far more to teach him than any formal educational establishment. His love of nature meant that his early religious belief often took on a form of Wordsworthian pantheism, which is inextricable from his theories of aesthetics. In volume one of his first work, *Modern Painters* (1843), he declared his intention to prove 'that the truth of nature is a part of the truth of God: to him who does not search it out, darkness, as it is to him who does, infinity.'[20] Thirty years later, however, he had a more cynical viewpoint. In 1871, he wrote to his friend Charles Eliot Norton that:

> Of all the things that oppress me, this sense of the evil working of nature herself – my disgust at her barbarity – clumsiness – darkness – bitter mockery of herself – is the most desolating.[21]

Ruskin's early love of nature, as a divine concept fuelled and manifested in his celebration of Turner's art, seemed later to turn to the Rousseauesque notion that natural man had become brutalised by scientific development. These vagaries of Ruskin's thought were all part of the same man, as the romantic aesthete struggled with the realist in him. His first identification of nature with religion made nature inseparable from what he interpreted as the intrinsic morality of art. It was therefore not surprising that, in the dark shadow of industrialisation, Ruskin's theories suffered a shift of emphasis: from the beauty and divinity of the natural world to the greed and ugliness of a society in the grip of capitalist ideology.

The inevitable corollary of this growing condemnation of contemporary man was an eventual loss in Ruskin of that early evangelical optimism, which held each individual responsible for his own fate, and also a declining belief in the possible redemption of society through the moralising properties of art. On the contrary, he came to fear that the lack of a common aesthetic ideal would precipitate the demise of any form of good national art, thus leading to a society devoid of moral standards. An editorial in *The Times* on 12 February, 1878 commented wryly:

> Mr Ruskin has finally given us up. Replying to an invitation addressed to him by the committee of a provincial school of art, he writes: 'Nothing can advance art in any district of this accursed machine – and – devil-driven England until she changes her mind in many things, and my time for talking is past.[22]
> And, he added, I lecture here, but only on the art of the past.[23]

Ruskin was born and educated in a climate temporarily characterised by the evangelical values he later came to despise. This cluster of values, which reached its *apogee* at the time of the Great Exhibition of 1851, had been generally adopted by middle-class industrial capitalists; however, Ruskin's interpretation of these factors ultimately provided the trigger for his critique of classical economic theory.

While he turned against evangelical values, Ruskin was nonetheless intolerant of religious doubt. After his personal crisis of faith in 1858,[24] he embraced a broader form of Christianity which sought to tackle the problems of poverty with more emphasis on moral and physical welfare than on spiritual salvation. He was never officially a member of the Christian Socialist movement but his sympathies were similarly conceived and directed. His critique of capitalism was a combination of the English radical tradition, filtered through his aesthetic theory, and energised by non-conformist zeal. His vision was the re-establishment of moral relationships in a commercial society, where considerations of greater profit are secondary to the health, happiness, and welfare of the employee. The manifestation of this vision began, for Ruskin, with a celebration of Gothic architecture.

Ruskin's intense and systematic studies of Venetian Gothic architecture led him to some startling conclusions concerning the ethics intrinsic to methods of construction. His analysis in *The Nature of Gothic* (1853) of the division of labour indicated a serious incursion into the realms of

social and economic criticism. In contrast to nineteenth-century construction methods, medieval cathedrals were, he maintained, essentially
the product of spontaneity and cooperation, with each craftsman playing
his part with little regard for self-interest. Contemporary society had
destroyed this ethic by replacing cooperation and unity with competition
and fragmentation. Modern architects, Ruskin claimed, were motivated
by self-advancement rather than by a common ideal, resulting in
conflicting styles and demoralised and alienated labourers. 'It is not,' he
wrote when attacking Adam Smith, 'truly speaking, the labour that is
divided; but the men – broken into small fragments and crumbs of life.'[25]
And although the desire for wholeness was a romantic concept which can
be traced directly to Wordsworth, it was Ruskin who reinforced this idea
of architectural style and construction as being an important historical
record of the moral temper of a nation.[26]

   This notion was not without its opponents. There were inherent
difficulties in using the principles of medieval construction as a criterion
of social organisation. The qualities which Ruskin admired had their
foundation in a realistic society, but he was going beyond the bounds of
accepted historical analysis in formulating a theory based on an ethic he
claimed to have located in Venetian architecture. Gervase Rosser
observes:

> The belief that work in the medieval urban context was concep-
> tually unproblematic – that it simply happened – has encouraged
> an oversimplified understanding of those who performed it.[27]

Like any residual ideology, the principles of organisation in medieval
society must first be assessed accurately in their original context for a
correct evaluation of their present relevance.[28] Medieval scholars have
since established that Gothic construction sites had their own hierarchy
of labourers, many of whom were pressed into service under threat of
imprisonment and had little, if any, opportunity for self-expression.[29]
But if Ruskin's Gothic ideal was indeed based on myth, it had its origins
in a realistic community and the qualities he admired were those that he
considered to be patently absent in the processes of nineteenth-century
industrialisation. He thus established that all-important link between
morality, government and artistic style. As he said to the businessmen of
Bradford in 1866:

The book I call *The Seven Lamps* was to show that certain right states of temper and moral feeling were the magic powers by which all good architecture, without exception, had been produced. *The Stones of Venice* had, from beginning to end, no other aim than to show that the Gothic architecture of Venice had arisen out of, and indicated in all its features, a state of pure national faith, and of domestic virtue; and that its Renaissance architecture had arisen out of, and in all its features indicated, a state of concealed national infidelity, and of domestic corruption.[30]

While the last sentence is highly contentious – as good art has been produced at the worst of times and *vice versa* – there is little doubt that the location of 'right states of temper and moral feeling' is pivotal to Ruskin's philosophy. This was the condition he felt was being systematically eroded by the processes and ethos of industrial capitalism.[31] Thus the seeds of his social criticism began to flourish. The qualities he admired in Gothic architecture took their forms from nature, and by 1859 his original aesthetic theory had developed into an appraisal of 'Organic Form', which he said was the 'vital law', not only in architecture, but in every subject:

> We are all of us willing enough to accept dead truths or blunt ones; which can be fitted harmlessly into spare niches, or shrouded and coffined at once out of the way; we holding complacently the cemetery keys, and supposing we have learned something. But a sapling truth, with earth at its root and blossom on its branches; or a trenchant truth, that can cut its way through bars and sods; most men, it seems to me, dislike the sight or entertainment of, if by any means such guest or vision may be avoided.[32]

It was but a short step from this realisation to his attack on the people he held responsible for most of the ills of his contemporary world: the classical political economists. In rejecting what he considered to be the *a priori* methodology of the classical economists, he was attacking the spectre of Smith, Ricardo, Malthus and Mill, and also hoisting himself with the task of providing a workable alternative.

Although Ruskin was by no means the first to make an indictment of the classical economists, previous critics had rarely posed a serious threat to the *status quo*. Prior to 1860, no one had succeeded in seriously rattling the complacency of the triumphant political economists. Ruskin did exactly this with *Unto This Last*, and he was totally unrepentant at its initial violent and scornful reception. His attack was essentially moral, but that is not to say it should be dismissed as unscientific. The habit of erudition that Ruskin had acquired as a child, and the discipline of close analysis he pursued in his studies of the natural world, and in art and architecture, stood him in good stead as a critic of what he termed as a 'pseudo-science'. The Italian philosopher Mazzini had, after all, credited Ruskin with having 'the most analytic mind in Europe'.[33] And if he did have an unusual intellectual background for his entrance into the world of political economy, it was that specific and unique coalescence of influences, combined with his mastery of prose, which so ably equipped him for his task.

So, out of these disparate yet enduring factors, where does one look for the real motivation behind Ruskin's violent onslaught on social injustice? Some have been quick to quote sexual repression,[34] but then many Victorians suffered from a surfeit of repressive religion and few, if any, achieved Ruskin's intellectual stature. It is surely because he was so eminent that the circumstances of his divorce and subsequent relationships aroused such public interest. Carlyle was certainly a powerful influence and Ruskin was devoted to him, but did not follow him in everything. Indeed, Ruskin was often irritated by accusations of plagiarism. In a letter he wrote to Carlyle, dated 23 Jan 1855, he said:

> People are continually accusing me of borrowing other men's thoughts, and not confessing the obligation. I don't think there is anything of which I am more utterly incapable than of this meanness; but it is very difficult always to know how much one is indebted to other people, and it is always most difficult to explain to others the degree in which a stronger mind may guide you, without your having at least intentionally borrowed this or the other definite thought.[35]

Ruskin certainly inherited Carlyle's belief that the differences between men were eternal and irreconcilable; hence Ruskin's rejection of democratic government. Indeed, it is probably fair to say that he derived most of his condemnation of industrial society from Carlyle,[36] but

Ruskin pushed his thoughts to greater depths especially in his critique of political economy, and he expressed a much greater concern for moral ugliness. This latter factor was almost certainly the legacy of that early aesthetic training which led Ruskin to contemplate the social and economic significance of the production of art and architecture. This is what distinguishes him from his contemporaries. It was the very fact that Ruskin was not only exposed to, but also receptive to, such a wide range of disparate influences which gave him that lateral flexibility of thought and interpretation which people call visionary, qualities which when allied to his analytic mind and aggressively radical integrity were bound to seek an outlet, and also to gain him as many detractors as disciples.

The Seeds of Social Criticism and Ruskin's Early Reception
A subtle change in the reception of Ruskin's thought became apparent when he made that indefinable shift of emphasis from art to society in the 1850s. Until then no one had suspected the ferocity of the onslaught he was about to release on the mid-Victorian capitalist ethos, nor could others appreciate the connection he located between art, morality and socio-economic practice. Ruskin himself, however, was unshakeable in his convictions and, far from being at the mercy of artistic whim and personal misfortune, was intent on a conscious and deliberate mission of moral revaluation. In a letter published in *Fors Clavigera* written in Venice on 9 May 1877, he made the following retrospective statement on the synthesis of his social criticism:

> The *Stones of Venice* taught the laws of constructive Art, and the dependence of all human work or edifice, for its beauty, on the happy life of the workman. *Unto This Last* taught the laws of that life itself, and its dependence on the Sun of Justice.[37]

This extract highlights the linkage which Ruskin established between his aesthetic and social philosophy, and also confirms the basis of all his subsequent social and economic criticism. There was a positive and logical sequence in his later writing. As he continued in the same letter, 'the Inaugural Oxford lectures' taught that 'the gracious laws of beauty and labour' should be 'recognized, by the upper, no less than the lower, classes of England; and lastly *Fors Clavigera* has declared the relation of these to each other.'[38] *Fors Clavigera* was not of course Ruskin's last literary output; it predated many other important works, including *Praeterita* written between 1885 and 1889. Neither was *The Stones of Venice* his first foray into social criticism.

There is evidence of the way in which Ruskin's philanthropic nature was tugging at his conscience as early as 1843. In volume one of *Modern Painters*, published in that year, when Ruskin was only twenty-four, he considered the nature and relationship of perception, morality and truth. 'A man of deadened moral sensation is always dull in his perception of truth.'[39] But observations such as these, which may seem to purists like digressions, informed his work with such increasing frequency that they could no longer be considered separately from his theories of art. *Modern Painters* was hailed both as a great work of art criticism, and for its literary excellence, yet something in Ruskin's restless personality would not allow him to be content with this role.

Six years later he published *The Seven Lamps of Architecture* (1849). Written in the shadow of revolutions in Europe and Chartist unrest at home, it secured Ruskin's reputation as a serious moralist. His passion for truth stood revealed as a force which was unlikely to be dissipated through art alone:

> But it is the glistening and softly spoken lie; the amiable fallacy; the patriotic lie of the historian, the provident lie of the politician, the zealous lie of the partisan, the merciful lie of the friend, and the careless lie of each man to himself, that cast that black mastery over humanity, through which we thank any man who pierces, as we would thank one who dug a well in the desert.[40]

The thrust behind Ruskin's emergent social criticism is explained in the above passage. He was already on course to 'pierce' the 'damned lie' of the nineteenth-century interpretation of classical economy, but it took some tortured years and a lot of negative publicity before the plausibility of his message percolated through. Both he and Carlyle could see exactly where the new industrial economy was leading, and no one called more clearly than Ruskin for a re-assessment of the values it incorporated. But he followed a solitary and tortuous route before his social writing received the attention it deserved. The reasons for this early rejection, far from being a straightforward indictment of Ruskin's inadequacy as a social commentator, only served to further vindicate his argument against the lack of moral awareness on the part of the mid-nineteenth century economists.

A country on the crest of a wave of optimism and expansion did not welcome prophets of doom and despondency. Ruskin began writing *The Stones of Venice* in 1851, the year of the Great Exhibition, an event consciously designed to mark a highpoint of Victorian confidence in industrial progress.[41] But if the Great Exhibition did indeed mark a celebration of the success of material progress, it was also the beginning of a new era of intellectual opposition to the dehumanising effects of industrial processes on the urban working classes. Working long hours on joyless tasks in appalling conditions was endorsed by the utilitarian ethic of expedience in the sole interest of financial gain.

The exhibition itself was a visual manifestation of this moral and cultural ambivalence, as heavily ornate examples of Gothic revivalism were displayed incongruously in the Crystal Palace, a construction which certainly owed nothing to medieval craftsmanship. Ruskin was appalled at both the process and the end product. 'We suppose ourselves,' he wrote, 'to have invented a new style of architecture, when we have magnified a conservatory!'[42] His views on art were famously inconsistent, but he never wavered in his contempt for the values of industrial capitalism.

Ruskin's writing was saturated with a loathing of the whole ideological baggage attendant on the processes of capitalist expansion, and it was not insignificant that he began his second volume of *The Stones of Venice* containing his famous passage 'The Nature of Gothic', as the Great Exhibition opened. For him, synthetic ugliness was synonymous with moral ugliness. Hence the depressing red-brick factories, the over-ornate pseudo-Gothic municipal buildings, and the intrusion into the home of machine-made artefacts were all a part of what he perceived to be a process of moral degradation. He commented in 1854:

> Let it not be thought that I would depreciate (were it possible to depreciate) the mechanical ingenuity which has been displayed in the erection of the Crystal Palace, or that I underrate the effect which its vastness may continue to produce on the popular imagination. But mechanical ingenuity is not the essence either of painting or architecture: and largeness of dimension does not necessarily involve nobleness of design.[43]

Ruskin was writing this at a time when the supremacy of the capitalist ideology seemed invincible. The threat from Chartism had been overcome, and there was as yet no serious overseas rival to British industrial success. In Britain itself, however, the squalor of the new factory towns was at its height, still as yet virtually unrelieved by practical improvements in housing, working conditions and sanitation.[44] Large numbers of the labouring population were both physically and spiritually impoverished. There was certainly a requirement for some extensive pragmatic intervention underpinned by a reassessment of values. Ruskin diagnosed the situation, and considered he had found the cure in the form and construction of authentic Gothic architecture. He was not creating any precedents in using the Middle Ages as a paradigm of social organisation. His great mentor, Carlyle, had already done this in *Past and Present,* and indeed, a historicism which slid easily into sentimentalism was endemic throughout the nineteenth century. In fact, the Gothic Revival,[45] with which Ruskin was so strongly identified, reached such absurd extremes that he was later very keen to disassociate himself from it. In a letter to the *Pall Mall Gazette* in March 1872, he noted:

> There is scarcely a public-house near the Crystal Palace but sells its gin and bitters under pseudo-Venetian capitals copied from the Church of the Madonna of Health or of Miracles. And one of my principal notions for leaving my present house is that it is surrounded everywhere by the accursed Frankenstein monsters of, *in*directly, my own making.[46]

Superficial imitation was not to Ruskin's taste. His concern was to emphasise the *values* intrinsic to the organisation and construction of thirteenth-century Gothic craftsmanship and to place them in direct contradistinction to the spiritually impoverished nature of contemporary society. He was not politically motivated; he was more interested in accommodation than in revolution, but in the atmosphere of increasing religious doubt and uncertainty which characterised the second half of the nineteenth century, his ideas found an attentive, if not always a sympathetic, audience.

Some had no enthusiasm for Ruskin's choice of Venice as the exemplar of noble deeds and national pride. Writing in the *North British Review,* H.H. Lancaster remarked:

Mr Ruskin's historical and political opinions are not less singular. Venice is, beyond all others, the country of his love. The plain fact is, that from the first foundation of the state down to her later days, when she deserted the allies whose succour she had implored, and made a shameful peace with the Turks – the history of Venice is the unvarying record of a policy of ungenerous self-seeking.[47]

That was a reasonable observation, which did not, however, allow for Ruskin's penchant for the moral metaphor. Ruskin argued that Venice had used its financial resources responsibly by adding significantly to world culture and by leaving behind a legacy of elegant buildings. He did not propose a return to medievalism. But then Mr Lancaster was writing at the time of Ruskin's publication of *Unto This Last* (1862), an exercise which he considered ludicrous from a man who had previously reserved his literary talent for the appreciation of art and nature. 'Formerly,' complained Lancaster, '[Ruskin's] eloquence was called forth only by the wonders of art, or the stupendous effects of nature; now it is poured forth profusely and indiscriminately on all things.'[48] It is significant that earlier reviews of *The Stones of Venice*, being less aware of Ruskin's covert social criticism, were more generous in their appraisal. An article in the *Westminster Review*, in April 1854, began with a glowing appreciation:

> The literature of Art has been enriched within the last three months by another volume from Mr Ruskin, a man who now has greater influence upon English artists, and also we believe directly and indirectly upon the English public, than any writer upon Art ever held before. We believe him to hold this power in consequence of the truths which he utters.[49]

Thus far, the anonymous critic was full of approval for Ruskin. His books were considered to be of 'practical use to young artists' and, the critic added, the 'effect of his mind upon England is deep and we hope it will be lasting'. The next paragraph, however, indicated that this was not a view shared by everyone:

> 'But' we hear every day, 'Ruskin is so absurd; he is so insufferably dogmatic'. Now we doubt whether he is more dogmatic than any

vehement preacher of any time against corruption, cowardice and falsehood, for he really is one of the greatest 'reformers' of our times; he may deny this, but we assert it dogmatically.[50]

Even at this comparatively early stage in his career, Ruskin was beginning to establish his authority as a serious commentator on social issues, but he was not yet, however, considered to be in any way subversive. Even the critics in the *Westminster Review* were prepared to be generous as long as Ruskin continued to conceal his aspirations for reform under the mantle of aesthetics:

He may perhaps be innocent himself of the tendency of his writings, and would never perhaps applaud the deeds his principles would provoke. He is a straightforward lover of nature, and also a churchman, and therefore inconsistent. As the former he sees heaven written in the earth and sky; as the latter he sees evidences of an eternal hell in external nature. We do not think his studies of nature and theology mix well together.[51]

Although aware of Ruskin's inconsistencies and contradictions, this particular critic was conscious of the value of his contribution to the significance and understanding of the linkage between art and morality. Thus far there was no cause for alarm:

Though vehement, he is candid, and in time may perhaps be less sweeping in his anathemas and less intense in his admiration; but if this change should never take place, we shall always have the satisfaction of feeling that we possess in him a great writer on the morality and spirit of art.[52]

Ruskin had as yet said nothing that could seriously disturb the moral complacency of his readers, but the seeds sown in *The Stones of Venice* were those which were later to blossom with alarming consequences. His insistence on the supremacy of Gothic architecture contained a festering, implicit indictment of contemporary labour processes, which at times threatened in its vehemence to eclipse his central argument. This was misinterpreted initially by some of his readers as pure aesthetic dogmatism, which made claims for Gothic architecture based on wild romanticism rather than upon fact. An article in *Blackwood's Magazine,* which referred to *The Stones of Venice,* gave the following verdict on Ruskin's theory:

> In the light of this strict historic inquiry, by the test of this plain philosophy, built out of simple secular facts, let us judge of the sublime theories of Mr Ruskin. Such theories read so romantic, they have about them the odour of such sanctity, that they should labour under the slight disadvantage of being wholly untrue.[53]

Ruskin did indeed make some rather wild claims for the pointed Gothic arch as being the only true symbol of eternal Christian values. 'The theorem of *The Stones of Venice* is thus stated,' commented the article in *Blackwood's Magazine,* 'Gothic at any cost or sacrifice, under all circumstances, and to the total annihilation of Greek, Roman, Italian, and other styles.'[54] But this response ignored the moral centre of Ruskin's argument, an abstract born of a vision which was both intellectual and emotional. Ruskin was above all, didactic, never a mere commentator, and *The Stones of Venice* which began as an exercise in architectural analysis, became in essence, an appropriate vehicle for his emergent and provocative critique of the processes and values of industrial capitalism.

Gothic architecture, for Ruskin, was far more than an exemplar of good ecclesiastical style; it was the embodiment and expression of a system of values, based on Christianity, but with significance for the whole of mankind. Its secular message was one of cooperation and humanity, and this, claimed Ruskin, was not to be found in its classical counterpart, which denoted only arrogance and exploitation. Another article referring to Ruskin in the *Westminster Review* took up the theme:

> The influence of classical literature gave the tendency to struggle for Roman forms of perfection. One man must plan the whole perfectly, and the work may then be done as well by slaves as freemen. The Gothic architecture which our author loves so much, allowed every workman to use his head and heart as well as his hands.[55]

The writer of this particular article was basically in agreement with Ruskin, although the anonymous critic paraphrased Ruskin with just enough levity to suggest that *The Stones of Venice* was not taken to be seriously contentious. Ruskin 'very rightly insists that what we want now is heart work, not hand work, or head work,' and the critic quoted Ruskin's insistence that art is 'the work of the whole living creature, body and soul, and chiefly of the soul.' It was also a reciprocal arrangement: 'That in which the perfect being speaks, must also have the perfect being to listen.'

This insistence on an equal reciprocity of awareness and responsibility between producer and recipient was to have profound implications for Ruskin's later analysis of wealth in *Unto This Last*, but for the moment his views, outwardly at least, were confined to art and architecture, a factor which the commentator in the *Westminster Review* ultimately found confusing. He complained that Ruskin 'ends by recommending us to adopt the English and French thirteenth-century surface Gothic' as Britain's architecture, because it is 'demonstrably the best architecture that *can* exist; perfect in construction and decoration, and fit for the practice of all time'.[56] Ruskin's vision for the future, growing out of an ethic from the past, was interpreted by this critic as an apparent contradiction, which he was generously prepared to excuse in the interests of religious toleration. He concluded:

> Mr Ruskin's belief in progress and this positive paragraph are intensely inconsistent, but we must pardon all inconsistencies which spring from theological faith. Is the architecture of 500 years back especially adapted to us as we are now, or will our new materials of glass, iron, and slate, and our new mechanical powers, and our different time and character, produce a new architecture? Let us but follow the spirit of Mr Ruskin's teaching, and it will lead us to results which we cannot yet discern.[57]

This latter sentence has certainly proved prophetic, but there are parts of *The Stones of Venice* which made it clear where Ruskin wanted to lead his readers. His studies of the construction of Gothic architecture led him to question not only the values inherent in its contemporary equivalent, but also the effects of modern methods of construction on the labour force. His views on the division of labour, set out quite clearly in 'The Nature of Gothic', invite comparison with the writings of Karl Marx,[58] whose great work *Capital,* designed to expose capitalist exploitation, was in fact ultimately less influential in the policy-making of the newly formed Labour Party at the beginning of the twentieth century.

With characteristic scriptural resonance, Ruskin had this to say concerning the increasingly dehumanising effects of contemporary methods of production:

> It is verily this degradation of the operative into a machine, which more than any other evil of the times, is leading the mass of nations everywhere into vain, incoherent, destructive struggling for a freedom of which they cannot explain the nature to themselves.[59]

The eloquence of this passage, and many others like it, should not be allowed to mask the seriousness of Ruskin's intent. It indicated the beginnings of a positive attempt by Ruskin to attack the amoral nature of current social and economic organisation. It was however, such visionary exhortations which led many of his contemporaries to take a pejorative view of his work.

Ruskin was very concerned with freedom. But it was not political freedom he envisaged; he was convinced that democracy would never work because people were basically unequal. The kind of freedom he advocated was to operate within a hierarchy, but with each individual making his own particular, self-fulfilling contribution to society as, he claimed, the Gothic craftsmen did when building their cathedrals. This ethic, he felt, was being ruthlessly destroyed by the crude interpretation of Adam Smith's division of labour and the replacement of craftsmanship with machine-operated mass-production methods:

> It is not that men are ill-fed, but that they have no pleasure in the work by which they make their bread, and therefore look to wealth as their only means of pleasure. It is not that men are pained by the scorn of the upper classes, but that they cannot endure their own; for they feel that the kind of labour to which they are condemned is verily a degrading one, and makes them less than men.[60]

Adam Smith's much acclaimed division of labour, Ruskin wrote, was in fact a division of men, 'So that all the little piece of intelligence that is left in a man is not enough to make a pin, or a nail, but exhausts itself in making the point of a pin or the head of a nail.'[61] Ruskin was, by the 1850s, well on the way to becoming a serious – and for many capitalists – a dangerous opponent of existing economic practice and its effects on people and the environment. A critic in the *Westminster Review* commented on Ruskin's work:

> It is impossible, in a state of society in which the division of labour has been carried to the extent it must be to make it as productive as possible, that every labourer should feel an artistic interest in the performance of his infinitesimal task which in the majority of instances has no suggestiveness of its own to connect it with the purposes it is ultimately to serve. A man works for independence and moral freedom – for the means of living to his own best insight.[62]

Ruskin was by then well used to being taken too literally. He was realistic enough to accept the inevitability of machine-made goods and was not, in theory, opposed to progress, but he was opposed to mindless exploitation of the labour force and a total disregard for the quality of the end-product. This was why he drew parallels with the medieval mode of construction. For him, the Gothic architect supplied a vision of what all human labour *should* involve in an *ideal* society. He thus used the example of the Gothic craftsman as a vehicle with a serious social purpose: to highlight the gross inadequacies of current capitalist production methods, to generate an awareness of the symbiotic relationship between work, culture and capitalism, and in so doing, to raise the social consciousness of contemporary manufacturers and employers.

In the mid-nineteenth century however, pragmatism, rather than idealism, was seen by most would-be reformers to be the central requirement. 'Mr Ruskin's works,' claimed the above critic, 'are full of vague purposes, illuminated by the golden exhalations of imagination and sentiment, but of practical ends and immediately attainable means to them, no word.'[63] In truth, Ruskin's practical proposals for reform were less clearly articulated than his idealistic exhortations in the early stages of his social criticism. Like Marx, he was very preoccupied with the kind of labour men should do, but whereas Marx was more interested in the social and economic significance of work, Ruskin's emphasis was on its moral centre. His response to current 'evil' practices was un-equivocal:

> It can only be met by a right understanding, on the part of all classes, of what kinds of labour are good for men, raising them, and making them happy; by a determined sacrifice of such conven-ience, or beauty, or cheapness as is to be got only by the degrad-ation of the workman; and by equally determined demand for the products and results of healthy and ennobling labour.[64]

One of Ruskin's greatest achievements was undoubtedly his capacity to change the focus of socio-economic discussion from production and profit to the actual methods of production, the intrinsic value of the end product, and its effects on the quality of life. Moreover, the enabling mechanism for Ruskin was undoubtedly his artistic perceptiveness, and his main point of reference, the morality of the Bible.

The Stones of Venice, with its contentious comments in the chapter entitled 'The Nature of Gothic', confirmed the beginnings of an incur-sion into social, political and economic criticism which was to occupy Ruskin for the rest of his life. It was published in 1853, and a year later used as the introductory pamphlet by the founders of the first Working Men's College,[65] an institution established by the Christian Socialist movement. But despite becoming a lecturer there the same year and directing some fairly strong criticism at current industrial practice, Ruskin was still considered to be primarily a harmless, if slightly eccen-tric, aesthete by most of his readers, and certainly by all the principal proponents of classical economic science. Commenting on his 'Lectures on Architecture and Painting' delivered at Edinburgh in November 1853, an anonymous critic observed:

> In spite of a frequent inclination to argue the point with him, we have no hesitation in classing ourselves with the applauding part of his audience. We may count his inconsistencies, his dogmatisms, and other sins by the hundred, and yet not be able to help preferring him to the ninety and nine just men who have never gone astray.[66]

This affectionate tolerance was soon to dissipate, however, as Ruskin's many 'inconsistencies' appeared suddenly much more threatening.

A Conscious Social Moralist

In his writings and lectures in the 1850s, Ruskin continued to exhibit his accepted primary function in his role as an art critic, but as his intolerance of economic inequality and exploitation increased, he became a deliberate and conscious social moralist. In 1857 he produced some papers entitled 'The Political Economy of Art', first delivered as two lectures in Manchester and later reprinted as *A Joy Forever* and he had this to say in the Preface:

> Political economy means, in plain English, nothing more than 'citizen's economy'; and its first principles ought, therefore, to be understood by all who mean to take the responsibility of citizens, as those of household economy by all who take the responsibility of householders. I might, with more appearance of justice, be blamed for thinking it necessary to enforce what everybody is supposed to know. But this fault will hardly be found with me, while the commercial events recorded daily in our journals, and still more the explanations attempted to be given of them, show that a large number of our so-called merchants are as ignorant of the nature of money as they are reckless, unjust, and unfortunate in its employment.[67]

The closer Ruskin looked at the commercial world the less he liked it and the more compelled he felt to do something about it. His metamorphosis from aesthete to social critic was never total, however. 'The Nature of Gothic', which contains his first direct attack on contemporary production methods, was still heavy with symbolism and biblical allusion. This led to later accusations of utopianism and romantic idealism which were partially, but not wholly, justified. He acknowledged in 1859 the impossibility of the 'renovation of the Republic of Pisa, at Bradford, in the nineteenth century',[68] knowing that England would never emulate Venice in the use of its resources. So although he can certainly be called a Romantic in his vision for a better society, Ruskin was also a pragmatist, determined to apply his analytical skills, born of an architectural principle, to the 'so-called' science of political economy. That he came to society through art in no way lessened the significance of his conclusions.

He was prepared to concede in 1857 that he had not studied economic science in any great detail, but did not consider this a disadvantage.[69] On the contrary, he maintained, it allowed him greater clarity of perception:

> The statements of economical principles given in the text, though I
> know that most, if not all, of them are accepted by existing authorities
> on the science, are not supported by references, because I have never
> read any author on political economy, except Adam Smith, twenty
> years ago. Whenever I have taken up any modern book upon this
> subject, I have usually found it encumbered with inquiries into
> accidental or minor commercial results, for the pursuit of which an
> ordinary reader could have no leisure, and by the complication of
> which, it seemed to me, the authors themselves had been not
> infrequently prevented from seeing to the root of the business.[70]

It was the very fact that the doctrine of economic science was
disorientating, rather than enlightening, which Ruskin found morally
unacceptable. For him, the ethic he had located in the construction of
true Gothic architecture exposed current economic practice for what it
really was – a mask for hypocrisy and exploitation. In Ruskin's economic
theory, getting 'to the root of the business' was paramount and it turned
on his analysis of the nature of wealth and power. And again, he looked
to the past, not simply for inspiration, but for a method of refining his
moral vision and making it accessible to a society increasingly disorientated by the growing marginalisation of Christian belief. Darwin's
publication of *Origin of Species* in 1859 only served to exacerbate an
already burgeoning movement toward agnosticism and dissent. The
choice was not, therefore, as some of Ruskin's contemporaries tried to
imply, simply between Mammon and God; it was more a matter of
materialism or what? There was a moral vacuum which needed to be
filled. In an increasingly secular society, the values attendant on
industrial capitalism needed to be addressed and Ruskin saw this very
clearly. Moral regeneration was not to come as he had hoped through art,
but art, and particularly the example of the Gothic mode of construction,
gave him his access to social criticism and also inevitably led to a great
deal of misunderstanding among his contemporaries. To quote H.H.
Lancaster in the *North British Review* of 1862:

> Eloquent and ingenious [Ruskin] always is; but take him away
> from art, and he seems to us ignorant and delusive. To do him

anything like justice, we must first look at him exclusively as the subtle critic of art, and the eloquent exponent of nature. It will be a less pleasing, but yet a necessary task, to see into what errors he runs himself, and would lead his readers, when he announces his opinions on metaphysics, literature, history, and society.[71]

This commentary showed how difficult it was for many educated thinkers of the time to accommodate what they considered to be Ruskin's ill-advised deviation from art to society. They found no logical development in his thinking. He had, on the contrary, 'been led astray by his own self-confidence'.[72] It was an accusation made by many intelligent men, who not only misunderstood Ruskin's moral vision, but also underestimated, to quote E.T. Cook, 'his love of irony and para-dox'.[73] There is, wrote Cook, 'an inscrutable law by which the influence of men of genius is in nearly every case obscured by some strain of perversity.' Ruskin himself had claimed that 'the highest truths and usefullest laws must be hunted for through whole picture-galleries of dreams, which to the vulgar seem dreams only.' This was one cause of misunderstanding, noted Cook, but in Ruskin's case:

When we add to his habit of speaking in riddling words his habit of speaking on every conceivable subject it is easy to detect another source of confusion. 'The vulgar' may turn away from the whole thing as futile; but others may mistake the dreams for realities, the ironical paradox for practical injunctions. The fact is that some sense of humour and faculty of discrimination are indispensable for the right reading of Mr Ruskin.[74]

There was certainly a danger in interpreting Ruskin's social thought too literally. He was exasperated by many aspects of contemporary society but he was by no means a recluse, nor did he have an ascetic lifestyle surrounded by Gothic artefacts. His emphasis on a reassessment of values led him to make some rather startling attacks on modernity, often disguised by metaphor and illusion, and all designed to disturb the moral complacency of his audience.

Like any visionary thinker intent on reform, Ruskin had the difficult task of making his ideas immediately accessible to a disparate audience, which increased his own sense of frustration and alienation. This was further exacerbated by his distaste for party politics, which precluded him from securing the support of like-minded reformers with political muscle. In his solitary pursuit of exposing the moral poverty of society he therefore continued to express his thoughts and feelings in the terms he knew best, drawing from the example of past cultures with his habitual eclecticism.

In a lecture delivered in Manchester in 1857, he sustained his analogy with the Middle Ages:

> . . . the possessions of a rich man are not represented, as they used to be, by wedges of gold or coffers of jewels, but by masses of men variously employed, over whose bodies and minds the wealth, according to its direction, exercises harmful or helpful influence . . .[75]

This was not so very different from Marx's theories of the corrupting power of wealth, although his forecast that history would replace competition with communism was far from Ruskin's thinking. Despite his own insistence on cooperation, Ruskin clearly did not see himself as a socialist. His emphasis was moral, not political, and, although organicism or cooperation was also at the root of socialist/collectivist thinking, Ruskin sought his organic ideal in a hierarchical form of medievalism. Like Marx, he saw socialism as the inevitable outcome of capitalism but, unlike Marx, he did not welcome it. Yet the apparent ineffectiveness of Ruskin's argument for the redemption of society through a transformation of values led Ruskin to flirt with radical political action. This, P.D. Anthony notes, was a 'fiasco' but, as he points out:

> Ruskin was trapped in the same dilemma as Robert Owen and every other grand reformer of human behaviour. Political change was irrelevant if men did not first change their values; but without something remarkably like political activity the change would either not take place, or in much the same way, would be too gradual to be apparent.[76]

Ruskin developed his thought further in *The Two Paths*, published in 1859, the year of the publication of Darwin's *Origin of Species*. Ruskin was well acquainted with Darwin and, despite frequent indications to the contrary, a keen admirer of his empiricist methodology which relied on a thoroughness and intensity of analysis.[77] In a footnote in *Queen of the Air,* Ruskin commented that he was in 'nowise antagonistic to the theories which Mr Darwin's unwearied and unerring investigations are every day rendering more probable.'[78] Ruskin was also fully aware of the hierarchical implications of Darwin's theories of natural selection and the analogy which could be drawn between the battle for individual survival and *laissez-faire* economics; but that is not to say that Ruskin drew the same conclusions. The apparent contradiction of an approval of the waywardness of nature, which characterises the form and ethos of Gothic architecture, and a disapproval of the self-regulatory nature of *laissez-faire*, can easily be accommodated, if it is accepted that Ruskin made no Spencerian analogy between 'natural selection and social competition'.[79] Ruskin's emphasis was on a form of organicism, which embraced social interdependence and mutual responsibility. The very structure of true Gothic architecture enacted, for him, an almost tangible sense of interdependence and cooperation, which he was soon to translate into his vision for a new society.

'Organic Form' was, for Ruskin, 'at the root of all that I have ever tried to teach.' 'It is also the law most generally disallowed.'[80] It was, Ruskin insisted, a law which was not being observed in the contemporary interpretation of Gothic architecture. He wrote in the preface to *The Two Paths* that:

> So-called Gothic or Romanesque buildings are now rising every day around us, which might be supposed by the public more or less to embody the principle of those styles, but which embody not one of them, nor any shadow or fragment of them; but merely serve to caricature the noble building of past ages, and to bring their form into dishonour by leaving out their soul.[81]

This was the key to Ruskin's interpretation of organicism and it owed nothing to Social Darwinism. It was very firmly entrenched in the romantic tradition,[82] which is characterised by a desire for wholeness or unity. Whether in nature, art or society, for Ruskin, all things must be seen in relation to one another, given life by a unifying spirit; nothing can survive in isolation. Hence his distaste for Smith's 'division of labour', which Ruskin expressed so forcibly in *The Stones of Venice,* and his insistence upon the symbiotic relationship between the artisan and his work:

> . . . all great art is the work of the whole living creature, body and soul, and chiefly of the soul. But it is not only *the work* of the whole creature, it likewise *addresses* the whole creature. That in which the perfect being speaks must also have the perfect being to listen. Senses, fancy, feeling, reason, the whole of the beholding spirit, must be stilled in attention or stirred with delight; else the labouring spirit has not done its work well.[83]

Organic unity made manifest in great works of art, whether it be Turner's paintings or Gothic cathedrals, thus provided the original metaphor for Ruskin's social criticism. Far from being a deviation from his original path, his incursion into the field of socio-economics was a moral obligation in which his studies of art, nature, the classics and the scriptures reconfigured as a complexity of mutually sustaining ideas. It was, wrote Cook in 1894, 'the payment, as it were, of "ransom". He wanted to go and come back – bringing the millennium with him; and when the millennium tarried, terrible was the vexation of his soul.'[84]

Whatever value is given to Ruskin's thinking, his emergence as a social critic was gradual, passionate, and thematically consistent. His lectures on art to the manufacturers of Manchester and Bradford contained an injunction to moral responsibility, based on an aesthetically conceived analysis of value. 'Remember always,' he said in Manchester in 1857, 'that the price of a picture by a living artist never represents, never *can* represent, the quantity of labour or value in it.' What its price really represents is 'the degree of desire which the rich people of the country have to possess it'. In buying a work of art simply because the artist was fashionable the purchaser was not getting value for money, 'but merely disputing for victory in a contest of ostentation,' and in so doing, not only 'buying vanity' but 'stimulating the vanity of others; paying literally, for the cultivation of pride.'[85] To the businessmen of Bradford, he added encouragingly:

> . . . if you resolve from the first that, so far as you can ascertain or discern what is best, you will produce what is best, on an intelligent consideration of the probable tendencies and possible

tastes of the people whom you supply, you may literally become
more influential for all kinds of good than many lecturers on art,
or many treatise-writers on morality.[86]

Shifting his emphasis from art to society was thus, for Ruskin, a natural
progression in that constant push for moral regeneration which
underpinned every aspect of his work. Up to 1859 he had continued to
hope that such regeneration could be achieved through art, and his
conscious moralising was contained within the esoteric but recognisable
framework of art and architecture. By 1860, at the age of forty-one, he
had accepted that society was not going to be saved by art, and that he
needed to direct his all-pervading sense of justice at political economy
and a system of values which, he considered, were little more than respect
for convention. What he proposed was an alternative set of values,
derived from Christian principles, but devoid of evangelical hypocrisy,
which were to be the salvation of a sick capitalist society. The lectures he
gave in the industrial midlands in the late 1850s – *The Political Economy
of Art* (1857), and *The Two Paths* (1859) – did not indicate a thematic
digression. On the contrary, the ethics they located had developed out of
The Stones of Venice and anticipated *Unto This Last*. As such, the lectures
were a positive statement of Ruskin's continuity of purpose and conviction. But, if the underlying theme remained constant, the reception
of his work was to undergo a radical change.

3

ETHICS AND ECONOMICS:
THE RECEPTION OF
UNTO THIS LAST AND
MUNERA PULVERIS

And now [Ruskin] seems disposed to rest a while, or at least to stray into devious tracks, whither we will not follow. Political economy is not his forte. The series of papers in the *Cornhill Magazine*, throughout which he laboured hard to destroy his reputation, were to our minds almost painful. It is no pleasure to see genius mistaking its powers, and rendering itself ridiculous.[1]

H.H. Lancaster (1862)

This chapter explores the contemporary reception of Ruskin's first serious attack on political economy. The intention is not so much to analyse the merits of *Unto This Last* as an economic treatise (that will be left to Hobson as discussed below),[2] as to understand *why* Ruskin met with such hostility, through a close examination of the comments of some of his critics.

Unto This Last
Ruskin's first major entry into the world of political economy came in 1860 when he published some critical papers in the *Cornhill Magazine*, which precipitated an explosion of wrath.[3] Ruskin himself gave an interesting retrospective account of events in the preface to *Munera Pulveris*, dated 1871.

Eleven years ago, in the summer 1860, perceiving then fully, (as Carlyle had done long before), what distress was about to come on the said populace of Europe through those errors of their teachers,

I began to do the best I might, to combat them, in the series of papers for the *Cornhill Magazine*, since published under the title of *Unto This Last.* The editor of the *Magazine* was my friend, and ventured the insertion of the first three essays; but the outcry against them became then too strong for any editor to endure, and he wrote to me, with great discomfort to himself, and many apologies to me, that the *Magazine* must only admit one Economical Essay more. I made, with his permission, the last one longer than the rest, and gave it blunt conclusion as well as I could – and so the book now stands; but as I had taken not a little pains with the Essays, and knew that they contained better work than most of my former writings, and more important truths than all of them put together, this violent reprobation of them by the *Cornhill* public set me still gravely thinking; and after turning the matter hither and thither in my mind for two years more, I resolved to make it the central work of my life to write an exhaustive Treatise on Political Economy.[4]

The *Cornhill* papers were published in book form under the title *Unto This Last*, and in the preface Ruskin underlined his seriousness of intent in presenting his readers with a close analytical indictment of current economic practice, underpinned by a reassuring reminder of the significance of classical precedent:

> The real gist of these papers, their central meaning and aim, is to give as I believe for the first time in plain English – it has often been incidentally given in good Greek by Plato and Xenophon, and good Latin by Cicero and Horace – a logical definition of WEALTH: such definition being absolutely needed for a basis of economical science.[5]

In publishing this economic critique at the highpoint of Victorian confidence, Ruskin was swimming against the tide, not only of economic orthodoxy, but of an accepted set of values. In *Unto This Last* he pushed a biblical metaphor of communal welfare into the philosophy of *laissez-faire* individualism, with startling results. He seriously questioned the nineteenth-century liberal interpretation of economics by substituting a human ethic for a monetary goal. The true meaning of political economy, he said, should be defined by the Greek term 'polis' as a social, not an individualistic, science. Following the teaching of Plato, Xenophon and Aristotle, Ruskin challenged the autonomy of the current system and pressed home the message that the economy and society were both interactive and interdependent.

In Ruskin's economic utopia, the emphasis was on a form of post-capitalist organicism, which rejected both profit and interest. He had no time for Malthusian notions of a scarcity of resources. In *Unto This Last,* he emphasised their abundance and the need for fair distribution. Competition should be replaced with cooperation and a consumer ethic, summed up in the maxim 'THERE IS NO WEALTH BUT LIFE.'

Labour was to be organised in terms of a well – run household with all individuals performing the tasks to which they were most suited, under the guidance of caring employers, thus maximising their talents. For this service, they would be paid a fixed wage similar to that paid to professionals. There would be no variation in wages with demand: the worker who was inadequate in some way would simply not be employed, but instead, would be either given assistance or retrained in a government school at public expense.

The object of *Unto This Last* was to infuse morality into current economic practice. Ruskin feared individuality and incentive were being destroyed by the division of labour – as he had observed as early as 1853: 'We manufacture everything there except men. To brighten, to strengthen, to refine or to form a single living spirit, never enters into our estimate of advantages.'[6] Goods, he maintained, should be produced primarily for their craftsmanship or utility, not merely for financial gain. Otherwise man would become a mere 'covetous machine', dedicated solely to the over-production of shoddy merchandise. This profiteering, which injured the individual, also harmed the state and was thus the enemy of civic and social welfare.

His proposals for practical reform, although not innovative, had never been voiced so passionately and, in the context of the mid-nineteenth century, were particularly alarming to orthodox economists and redolent of early socialist thought. Although Ruskin never acknowledged Owenite tendencies, his emphasis on cooperation and the exchange of equivalents of labour reflected Owen's thinking and also the more immediate tenets of the Christian Socialist Movement. Gregory Claeys has commented on early working class aspirations for reform:

This vision of gradual but nonetheless complete social revolution received considerable reinforcement from the later political economy of John Ruskin, who also accepted in principle the need for products to exchange on an equal labour basis and strongly criticised the results of the competitive system.[7]

In *Unto This Last* Ruskin, in effect, contravened all the central tenets of the non-interventionist British economic system. Fixed wages, government subsidised industries, state care for the poor, elderly and infirm, quality control of goods, and state education were all recommendations which went against dogmatic utilitarian presumptions and earned him both derision and allegations of socialism.

Socialism may indeed have been a label that could be attached to Ruskin, but in fact there were no socialistic ideals of equality in Ruskin's utopia. He thought equality not only undesirable but unobtainable, because even a system based on mutual interdependence required leaders to initiate democratic programmes of action. Neither did he advocate the nationalisation of land, insisting instead that landlords should retain ownership but should be induced to use their land wisely toward a better quality of communal welfare. Why then, in the light of these anti-democratic trends, did Ruskin's book provoke such hostility?

The initial adverse reaction to the articles which comprised *Unto This Last* cannot be dismissed as simply reactionary responses to what was considered an attack on a successful and well-established economic system. There were other factors involved. Was it simply fear of socialism, allied with an understandable nervousness among middle-class entrepreneurs? Was it indignation from the Church at Ruskin's interpretation of Christ's teaching? Or could his critics truly see no logic in his arguments for economic reform? Ruskin's essays were described in the *Literary Gazette* as 'one of the most melancholy spectacles, intellectually speaking, that we have ever witnessed',[8] and many thought that Ruskin had foolishly strayed way beyond familiar territory into a moral wilderness.

But Ruskin was after all very familiar with the mercantile world, being the son of a successful city merchant, and his economic theory, far from being a deviation from his aesthetic study, was actually, in Ruskin's eyes, a derivative of it. Sucessful capitalists feared that Ruskin had opened a 'moral floodgate'.[9] His book took its title from a gospel parable, and was, ironically, considered virtually blasphemous. Ruskin, however, remained implacable. The opening lines of the preface, dated 10 May 1862, were a testimony to his unwavering conviction:

> The four following essays were published eighteen months ago in the *Cornhill Magazine*, and were reprobated in a violent manner, as far as I could hear, by most of the readers they met with. Not a whit the less, I believe them to be the best, that is to say the truest, rightest-worded, and most serviceable things I have ever written; and the last of them having had especial pains spent on it, is probably the best I shall ever write.[10]

Ruskin's father feared his son would be branded a socialist but Ruskin persisted with his attack on the economic system, not as a political statement, but because he truly believed it was the cause of all social ills. He maintained that the orthodox political economists were misguided in their belief that the sole concern of the market place was financial gain, and he sought to shatter the seeming impregnability of classical economic theory with the humanising doctrine which is the whole thrust of *Unto This Last*: 'THERE IS NO WEALTH BUT LIFE.'

The ammunition which was used by most of Ruskin's detractors was gleaned from this very powerful and emotive ethic and translated as an indictment of his 'unscientific' approach. 'His dogmatism,' snorted H.H. Lancaster, in the *North British Review*, 'is now the dogmatism of ignorance.'

> Mr Ruskin is never impatient of the minutest point in art or nature; in all other things accuracy is held of no account. Thus, he writes on political economy, and lectures on the economy of art; and yet he tells us that he never read any work on economical science save Adam Smith, and for this reason, that all the rest go too deeply into details.[11]

In fact, Ruskin had read many other writers on economic theory from Xenophon to De Quincey, whose writings on antithetic forms of value obviously had some effect. But Ruskin's reading, like his writing, was not systematic, and when faced with the 'nervous' economy of the 1860s, he had an uphill struggle to convince the capitalist economists that there could be anything amiss in their policies. The very theoretical, visionary and quasi-religious nature of *Unto This Last* laid it wide open to derisory comments, yet it is as a theoretical document that it should be interpreted. It was an attempt to redefine the economy in moral terms, a morality based on Christianity, which despite Ruskin's denial of any political affiliation, was very similar in orientation to that of Christian Socialism.[12]

One disadvantage of being a visionary, however, was the inevitable lack of an empathic audience. Ruskin was fighting a lonely battle, and rendered helpless under the weight of middle-class opinion. A thousand copies of *Unto This Last* were published in 1862, and ten years later some still remained unsold. When a growing number of economists finally acknowledged the increasing plausibility of Ruskin's social thought, he was half-crazed with frustration and disenchantment.

There was still, in 1860, an unshakeable confidence among economists in the impregnability of the classical maxims of economic analysis.[13] Yet by opposing competition with cooperation and the need for state intervention, Ruskin attacked the system at its most vulnerable point. The nineteenth-century interpretation of the laws established by Smith and developed by Ricardo left little room for social or ethical considerations. Political economy, according to David Ricardo, was purely concerned with the production of material wealth. He considered that the rigorous pursuit of a labour theory of value would provide all the answers to the successful economic development of capitalism.[14] Political economy was thus considered an exact science, based on hypotheses, with moral concerns given a peripheral status.

The Roots of Honour

In essay one of *Unto this Last*, entitled 'The Roots of Honour', Ruskin attacked this very premise – that political economy was correctly based on a system of preconceived notions. In so doing, he was reiterating Auguste Comte's argument that a separate economic science was impossible, because it was part of a complex, dynamic, interactive organism which involved considerations of individual welfare.[15] Ruskin made this very clear at the outset:

> Among the delusions which at different periods have possessed themselves of the minds of large masses of the human race, perhaps the most curious – certainly the least creditable – is the modern

soi-disant science of political economy, based on the idea that an advantageous code of social action may be determined irrespectively of the influence of social affection.[16]

Ruskin was writing not only at the high point of *laissez-faire* idealism but also at a time when people were beginning to question the autonomy of political economy. He was not concerned with attacking classical economics *per se,* nor did he want to abolish capitalism, but he did most fervently want to press home the message that the economy and society were both interactive and interdependent. Hence the capitalist manufacturer, he claimed, was also directly responsible to society, not only for introducing and maintaining satisfactory industrial processes, but also for the quality of the end-product. It is, he said to the businessmen of Bradford in 1859, 'Your business, as manufacturers, to form the market, as much as to supply it.'[17] Guidance and government of society was paramount in Ruskin's philosophy, but it was some thirty years before government intervention was again accepted as an economic obligation.[18] His plea for greater state intervention was seen as an attack on both economics and politics and was another powerful factor in his early rejection:

> Mr Ruskin informs society, or government, what it must do and do quickly on pain of universal anarchy. It must contrive *to fix the rate of wages so as not to vary with the demand for labour,* and it must manage also, under the same awful responsibilities, to maintain workmen 'in constant and regular employment', and enable them to live comfortably, *whatever be the state of trade.'* How society, or government, is to contrive to do any of these things, Mr Ruskin has not yet explained.[19]

But this holistic approach was an essential part of Ruskin's organicist ethic. It sprang from his most earnest desire to expand his own private aesthetic ideals into a collective scale. He moved easily from the particular to the general and the dogma of *laissez-faire,* which in the mid-nineteenth century was all-embracing, gave him many avenues of attack.

One of these was the way in which classical economy at this time was deeply ingrained with the Protestant values of frugality, thrift and duty. This was a bone of personal contention with Ruskin, who had shed much of his evangelical heritage in the later 1850s.[20] The temporary synthesis of attitudes shared by evangelicals and utilitarians concerning individual responsibility was almost palpable in its intransigence and provided the essence of much of the literature of social criticism.[21] The work ethic was equated with religious fervour by many evangelical businessmen, who confused work with faith and the accumulation of capital as a form of personal insurance against hellfire and damnation. When Ruskin became aware of this situation, he showed no equivocation in continuing this analogy. In volume five of *Modern Painters*, which was published in 1860, he wrote:

> I had no conception of the absolute darkness which has come over the national mind in this respect, until I began to come into collision with persons engaged in the study of economical and political questions. The absolute imbecility with which I found them declare that the laws of God were merely a form of poetical language, passed all that I had ever before heard or read of mortal infidelity.[22]

Despite his break with evangelicalism, Ruskin's own morality was still based on Christianity, at a time when religious belief was being challenged by scientific development and new intellectual enquiries. Darwin's theories not only contributed to the undermining of an already vulnerable faith,[23] but also assisted in the creation of a more secular cultural vocabulary. This made Ruskin's writing less acceptable to those sceptics who seized on his idiosyncratic style as evidence of his unsuitability for the role of economic critic. One article, published in *Fraser's Magazine* in November 1860, had a distinctly sardonic edge:

> When Mr Ruskin, however, labels his essays, the label is as great a riddle as the essay itself. What reader, seeing the words 'Unto this Last,' at the head of a volume, would ever divine that the matter in hand was political economy? It might, of course, just as well be any other branch of human knowledge; and when we add that this fantastical title is a scrap of a text from the Bible, the perplexity is only increased, political economy having no more to do with divinity than it has with botany, chemistry, or the differential calculus – Mr Ruskin has not only reconstructed the whole science

of *The Wealth of Nations*, but discovered that it is all contained in
three words from the following verse in St Matthew's gospel, 'I will
give *unto this last* even as unto thee!'[24]

What, in fact, Ruskin was doing in *Unto This Last* was creating a
complex metaphor to highlight the defects of an existing socio-economic
situation. And, as he considered the defects were largely moral and social,
and he had an intimate knowledge of the Bible, it would be natural for
him to choose a religious context. It was certainly not an unprecedented
medium. But there may have been other reasons for disapproval of his
choice of metaphor. The 'Sermon on the Mount' from which Ruskin drew
his terminology was bound to cause alarm, as its message is ultimately
one of communalism. As Keir Hardie was to comment much later: 'The
Sermon on the Mount, whilst it perhaps lends but small countenance to
State Socialism, is full of the spirit of pure communism.' In fact, claimed
Hardie, in 'its contempt for thrift and forethought' it far exceeds 'the
aspirations of any communist ancient or modern'; 'Christ's denunciations
of wealth are only equalled by the fierceness of the diatribes which he
levelled against the Pharisees.'[25]

The anonymous writer in *Fraser's Magazine*, however, became even more
incredulous as he concentrated on the details of Ruskin's text: Mr Ruskin,
drew his 'grand doctrine' from the parable of the 'labourers in the vineyard',
which states that '*labour ought to be paid without any reference to the value of the
labourer's work, or the demand for the article produced*'; this, he continued, is 'a
position of such incredible absurdity that we might well be excused for
wasting a drop of ink in reply to it.'[26] Ruskin's argument was almost certainly inspired by the parable of the vineyard, as it presumed a very fluid
supply of labour which was not forced to compete with itself, and capital
which provided a living wage both for those who worked and for those forced
into unemployment. And although this led to shouts of derision from
contemporary economists, who doubtless felt they understood the economy
better than did Ruskin, it is of course the whole point of Ruskin's book: the
welfare of all.

The Veins of Wealth

In his second essay, 'The Veins of Wealth', Ruskin concentrated on the
subject of wealth, which he argued, implied power over others. He made
a distinction between political and mercantile economy, the former being

'the economy of a State, or of citizens',[27] which is the true economy, and the latter, the acquisition of individual wealth which Ruskin considered as a form of exploitation. Mercantile economy:

> signifies the accumulation, in the hands of individuals, of legal or moral claims upon, or power over, the labour of others; every such claim implying precisely as much poverty or debt on one side, as it implies riches or right on the other.[28]

The overriding *laissez-faire* attitude to resources, which Ruskin defined as the 'mercantile economy', meant that all goods were given a false price and used as a means of exploitation. In the process, capitalists used their wealth as a further means of exploitation by exerting power over their labourers, thus establishing 'maximum inequality'.[29] It is hardly surprising that *Unto This Last* had such a poor reception among those who were most likely to have read it upon its first publication.

In opposition to the 'mercantile economy', Ruskin proposed a new set of values which could not be measured in existing economic terms. These values, which were central to his 'natural economy', were all-embracing and concentrated on human rather than on economic requirements. They emphasised conservation rather than expediency, and quality of life rather than financial gain. Like a number of other Victorian sages, Ruskin was aware of the dangers of estrangement between the classes caused by a commitment to the supremacy of commercial over ethical concerns. His call for moral reconstruction within existing society was central to his doctrine of economic reform.

The art of 'becoming rich', Ruskin maintained, was not simply a matter of how much money people could acquire for themselves, but involved 'contriving that our neighbours shall have less'.[30] This would lead to an imbalance of power and the distortion of true values. Inequality of wealth is only acceptable when 'justly established' in terms of 'reward or authority according to its class and service'.[31]

Despite this apparent concern for inequality, Ruskin was not himself an egalitarian. Yet he was determined to attack an orthodox economy, which regarded wealth as a fixed and inflexible concept rather than one open to discussion. This inflexibility he regarded as being responsible for current exploitation, where the individual was made to fit the system rather than the other way round. His disregard for making a distinction between national and individual wealth was also part of his moral emphasis:

> And therefore, the idea that directions can be given for the gaining of wealth, irrespectively of the consideration of its moral sources, or that any general and technical law of purchase and gain can be set down for national practice, is perhaps the most insolently futile of all that ever beguiled men through their vices.[32]

This is another area where Ruskin attracted disapproval. His critic in *Fraser's Magazine* considered that Ruskin was totally wrong to mix morality with science:

> Questions of right and wrong, just and unjust, are questions of morals or religion, no more to be mixed up with the science of wealth than with the art of painting.[33]

But Ruskin felt the need to redefine wealth in terms of abstract justice, that is, the wealth of all, again drawing the wrath of his critic:

> . . . political economy is not jurisprudence, nor is jurisprudence political economy. Even the study of municipal law would be impossible, were it perplexed with discussions on abstract justice, so that we may guess how it must fare with the laws of political economy jumbled up with the same utterly foreign and heterogeneous element.[34]

This failure on the part of economists to recognise a symbiotic relationship between society and the economy formed the thrust of Ruskin's argument and his ability to see the whole picture, with all its webs and nuances, rather than to view the economy as a discrete segment, was what made his critique significant. His critic, however, was not sympathetic:

> But one science at a time will not content a philosopher of Mr Ruskin's comprehensive views. All the arts and sciences have, no doubt, their connections and affinities, but nevertheless it has generally been found a highly convenient practice to treat them apart – morality in one treatise, astronomy in another, physic in a

third, and so forth. The subject of wealth has its relationships with morality and politics, but it has its own set of principles, and there is just the same advantage in discussing them separately as there is in confining a law-book to law.[35]

But Ruskin's concern with moral issues led him to question all the received notions of economic orthodoxy. Modern society, he felt, was failing the larger part of humanity by an over-emphasis on 'money-power', which is always 'imperfect and doubtful'.[36] Similarly, he criticised the classical exchange theory for confusing 'profit' and 'advantage'. Exchange, he considered, with a strong echo of Robert Owen, should be mutually beneficial. This again emphasised Ruskin's insistence upon socio-economic interaction. As P.D. Anthony points out, 'Ruskin is contrasting the relationships involved in economic life with the reciprocal exchanges which bind members of a community together.'[37] As an extension of the classical theories of man's place in society posed by Hume and Smith in the eighteenth century, this argument is not in itself evidence of Ruskin's seminality, but his romantic/organicist interpretation identified a quality which he felt had been totally eradicated by industrial capitalism.

Qui Judicatus Terram

Ruskin's third essay, 'Qui Judicatus Terram,' examines the problem of applying justice to wages. The current economic system was, he considered, perpetuating injustice by taking advantage of a man's necessities in order to obtain his labour or property at a reduced price, which, Ruskin maintained, was tantamount to 'robbing the poor because he is poor'.[38] But, again, this concern for the plight of the poor did not make Ruskin an egalitarian. His opposition to *laissez-faire* economics was a part of his organic vision, which took its point of reference from the past, but was, paradoxically, in no way regressive in its aspirations. This is a connection which his critics in the 1860s did not appreciate:

> . . . and just where we had some right to look for his practical suggestions to save us from impending ruin, we find their room provokingly occupied with torrents of 'fine writing', which would have as least as much propriety and be as much in their place, in his *Stones of Venice* or his *Modern Painters*.[39]

This demand for a more positive, practical response from Ruskin was echoed by many whose accusations of idealism and utopianism stemmed from their failure to appreciate that Ruskin always operated through an aesthetic ideal. But the lack of meeting of minds was also a question of timing. Why should a nation at its most confident and optimistic be undermined by the rantings of an art critic? What did Ruskin want them to do?

> Tell us distinctly what is wrong, Mr Carlyle or Mr Ruskin, and we will try to mend it. But when you abuse us as hastening to perdition, and as throwing away the bounty of God, and can specify no deeper ground of offence than building bridges over waterfalls, then we reject you as false teachers and false censors alike, and return to our commonplace but satisfactory belief in the general happiness and advancement of the present generation.[40]

There was also a strong suspicion of Owenite socialism attached to Ruskin's subversive questioning of the economy; and Ruskin concluded this particular essay, after a detailed discussion of the pricing of labour, with a reinforcement of his apolitical stance. 'Lest the reader should be alarmed' that his investigations 'had something in common with socialism':

> . . . that if there be any one point insisted on throughout my works more frequently than another, that one point is the impossibility of Equality. My continual aim has been to show the eternal superiority of some men to others, sometimes even of one man to all others; and to show also the advisability of appointing such persons or person to guide, to lead, or on occasion even to compel and subdue, their inferiors according to their own better knowledge and wiser will. My principles of Political Economy were all involved in a single phrase spoken three years ago at Manchester: 'Soldiers of the Ploughshare as well as Soldiers of the Sword': and they were all summed up in a single sentence in the last volume of 'Modern Painters' – 'Government and cooperation are in all things the Laws of Life; Anarchy and competition the Laws of Death.'[41]

What 'commendable brevity', sniffed the writer in *Fraser's Magazine*, referring to Ruskin's 'soldiers' as 'another miraculous cabinet', and his style of writing as 'conceited effusions'. The best scientific writing, the critic continued, should be 'lucid' and 'dispassionate' – 'Here we have nothing but obscurity, intemperance, and bombast.'[42] Mr Ruskin should confine his 'pretensions to teach, within the sphere of those subjects with which his intimate acquaintance is unquestionable, and which he has every right to address the public.' When he remained within this sphere, his critic agreed, then Ruskin's passionate style was in some measure 'germane to his matter'; but in general the critic considered that Ruskin's emotive writing was totally unsuitable for a subject as scientific and serious as economics. Indeed, so violently opposed was this particular critic that his own rhetoric threatened to eclipse that of his subject. But he was not alone in using this particular angle of attack. In the *Home and Foreign Review* of 1862, an unnamed critic commented on *Unto This Last*:

> Mr Ruskin is more of a poet than a philosopher, and more of a preacher than either. His book is only tolerable when read as an appeal to individual conscience. But when he strives to give a scientific value to his rhetorical figures, his generalisations become ridiculous . . . This fundamental fault reflects itself in the style of the book: with all its affected precision and logic, it is a cloudy picturesque jumble of arbitrary analogies and illustrations grotesquely employed in arguments. The style also fails to impress us with any idea of the writer's good faith. It makes us suspect that he would not attempt to found political science on the individual conscience and a kind of ascetic morality, unless he wished to revolutionise both morals and politics – making the one Judaic rather than Christian, and the other bureaucratic and socialistic rather than constitutional.[43]

Ruskin's homiletic style has always aroused comment, both adverse and laudatory, not least from Ruskin himself, who agonised for some time over the diction of *Unto This Last*. In the end he pronounced it, to quote his biographer, E.T. Cook, 'good in expression because earnest in temper and right in thought.'[44] Ruskin certainly did nothing to modify his expression as the book progressed; his mastery of the moral metaphor was sustained to the end.

Ad Valorem

The final chapter of *Unto This Last*, 'Ad Valorem', concentrates on the keyword 'life' as being central to the concept of value. The practice of English capitalism, Ruskin claimed, was corrupt and destructive. The opposite of wealth, which he called 'illth', was the inevitable result of a labour process which produced only life-destroying products. While the English capitalist celebrated 'progress', people were dying of starvation. This was, said Ruskin, a form of 'nasty play', an 'all-absorbing game' where 'we knock each other down oftener than at football.'[45]

In opposition to this destructive pastime, Ruskin makes his famous declaration '*There is no Wealth but Life*' and advised a concentration on the fruitful production of life-enhancing goods. This concept, which turned on the analysis of value, was central to his philosophy, and transformed what he considered to be the 'bastard science' of political economics into an ethic. The usefulness of any commodity, he said, lay in its capacity to make people into better human beings. He thus wanted to infuse the whole system of capitalist economics with a life-enhancing stimulus, which would not tolerate mass poverty or Malthusian notions of population control. Ruskin's practical proposals for the reorganisation of the economy and his motivation for this moral critique remain clearly humanitarian and significant.

The immediate contemporary response to Ruskin's ethical analysis of value and consumption, however, was one of incredulity tinged with contempt. One unsigned article in the *Westminster Review*, written in response to the first publication of *Unto This Last* in 1862, was scathing:

The attack made by Mr Ruskin on the principles of political economy at once displays not only the weaknesses of his intellect and the utterly unscientific turn of his mind, but also a want of power in seizing upon the real questions at issue between him and his opponents, that is something marvellous in itself. A rigorously inductive body of doctrine is not to be destroyed and scattered to the four winds of heaven by the most energetic disclaimer, even though he patch his motley with apocalyptic spangles . . . When he defines wealth as life, and political economy as the science of consumption, he at once shows that he has no concern with those he chooses to call his adversaries, and that no true issue can be joined where such misconceptions are paraded as discoveries shamefully neglected by economists. Political economy and common sense alike agree to call commodities wealth, and economists profess only to investigate the laws which have regulated and do regulate their production. Economists have no direct concern with what ought to regulate either consumption or production.[46]

The central concern of the classical economist was exchange value; Ruskin wanted to give prominence to use-value, which gave economics that all-important humanising factor. In this final essay, he gave a detailed analysis of his interpretation of the meaning of value. A truly valuable thing, he said, was 'that which leads to life with its whole strength'. It was a fixed concept, independent of market fluctuations and individual opinions:

> Think what you will of it, gain how much you may of it, the value of the thing itself is neither greater nor less. For ever it avails, or avails not; no estimate can raise, no disdain repress, the power which it holds from the Maker of things and of men.[47]

This was a contentious notion, which put Ruskin in direct opposition to existing economic theory, but he later qualified his definition in terms reminiscent of Thomas De Quincey's theory of two 'antithetic forms' of value.[48] Ruskin identifies both 'intrinsic' and 'effectual' value, which led him to another aphorism: wealth is 'the Possession of the Valuable by the Valiant'. This placed an important emphasis both on the manufacturers who produced the goods and on the individual who must learn to appreciate true value. Hence Ruskin's admonition to the manufacturers of Bradford to 'form the market' in addition to supplying it. This considerably annoyed Walter Bagehot who, in an article in the *Economist* in 1860, wrote that Ruskin was making the assumption that the merchant alone of all the professions was motivated solely by greed and 'self-aggrandisement'.[49] Bagehot argued that 'each man chooses his profession as a means of livelihood' but the merchant did not have a fixed salary and was thus 'compelled to consider the remunerative issue of each transaction'.[50] Such procedures, in Ruskin's eyes, occurred at the expense of the workforce and the quality of the goods produced. Money should never be the sole motivation, as it distorted values and diminished the quality of life. Again, Ruskin's aesthetic and economic theories converged, as he pursued his economic ethic:

> You may, by accident, snatch the market; or, by energy, command it; you may obtain the confidence of the public, and cause the ruin of opponent houses; or you may, with equal justice of fortune, be ruined by them. But whatever happens to you, this, at least, is certain, that the whole of your life will have been spent in corrupting public taste and encouraging public extravagance.[51]

Ruskin's ideal economy envisaged a dynamic relationship between the producer and the consumer, where the vital value of goods would not be destroyed by a competitive market. Production, he considered, does not 'consist in things laboriously made, but in things serviceably consumable',[52] and that, of course, demanded certain qualities of the consumer, and a society based on cooperation and interdependence. As James Sherburne notes:

> Production, product, and consumption in Ruskin's vital economics form a triangle of interdependent elements. Man is the center, and the whole structure is potentially infused with utility or value, the life-giving power.[53]

All Ruskin's ideas for economic reform had this essential moral basis, which was readily dismissed by those liberal economists who rationalised their ethical neutrality in terms of science and tradition. To quote a writer in the *Westminster Review*:

> Ethical enquiries form no part of their science, except in that important sense in which economists show the only ground on which ethical progress can be hoped for. It is quite useless and beside the mark to indulge in rhetorical descriptions of the high majesty of man's moral nature, or to expatiate on his lofty prerogatives and spiritual possibilities; these things are only attainable when lower requisitions have been complied with. Our animal wants must be supplied before our peculiarly human ones can make themselves regarded; the stomach must always take precedence of the head and heart; our material existence must be first

secured before our spiritual needs can be felt, much less attended to.[54]

This response took little account of Ruskin's proposals for practical reform which, in their insistence on state intervention, did nothing to calm the nerves of liberal entrepreneurs. Practical social improvements were not even considered to be the concern of the economist. As the critic in the *Westminster Review* continued:

> Political economy is the science of the laws of the production of the material bases alone of our existence; whenever these laws involve any determinate relation between man and man, they cease to be purely economical ones, and are determined by conditions with which political economy, as such, has no concern, and to which its conclusions are as subject as men themselves . . . It may be questioned whether Mr Ruskin's extension of the sphere of political economy to include politics, education, and police, be the result of ignorance or wilful misrepresentation . . . The whole argument of his book rests upon the fallacy that the State should constitute itself into a temporal Providence watching over and controlling all its members. However Mr Ruskin may disclaim socialist tendencies, this assumption is the very essence of those theories on which he verbally turns his back, only to reproduce them in a dress of his own.[55]

Ruskin always denied that he was a socialist but his radical critique of industrial society and political economy indicated a strong sympathy for the socialist cause. Apart from the Christian Socialists who perpetuated some Owenite thought, there was no political movement with which he could be firmly identified in the 1860s. But it was his linkage with Owenism which made him the inspiration of much socialist thought in the revival years of the late nineteenth century. Ruskin's condemnation of *laissez-faire* economics in *Unto This Last* was not a covert incitement to social revolution, but a call for individual moral regeneration and cooperation. Yet even his call for cooperation was moral rather than political and could not, he felt, be achieved in a corrupt climate. In a letter in 1879, addressed to George Jacob Holyoake on receipt of his book *History of Cooperation: Its Literature and its Advocates,* Ruskin indicated his wariness:

It utterly silences me that you should waste your time and energy in writing 'Histories of Cooperation' anywhere as yet. My dear sir, you might as well write the history of the yellow spot in an egg – in two volumes. Cooperation is as yet in any true sense – as impossible as the crystallisation of Thames mud.[56]

Ruskin operated from a principle of organicism and supported the concept of cooperative workshops; but he did not see them as the sole answer to existing social evils. The problem went much deeper and required a complete revision of values. His accusers were not convinced, however. 'The principle of competition,' commented the *Westminster Review*, 'is the *bête noir* of all enthusiastic reformers'; yet it is 'simply the salt of the earth; by it only are men educated to the height of their powers, and their wants supplied by a delicacy of adjustment unattainable by any human intellect without its aid.'[57] Many, also, did not share Ruskin's optimistic view of human nature in an economic context. A writer in the *Home and Foreign Review* declared that:

The great laws of human interest and social goodwill will never of themselves work out the true principles of this science; for selfishness preponderates in society, and social, as distinct from political, economy, is sure to acquire a mercantile bias, which will tend to establish a social system such as we see in India, with plethoric usurers at one end of the scale, and beggared workmen and peasants, out of whom the usurers screw their gains, at the other, and no middle class in between. Mr Ruskin appears to imagine that all persons who pursue wealth are agreed that greater gains can be extorted from paupers than can be made by the profits of a brisk trade and a much-devouring yeomanry.[58]

Faced with such colossal intransigence, and with no specific political affiliation, Ruskin had nowhere to turn for significant support or any hope of an immediate practical implementation of his proposals. Only the passage of time, the changing consciousness of the nation, and the dedication of his disciples eventually served to heighten an awareness of the increasing relevance of his writings. His lack of sympathy with the effects of industrial capitalism was not tolerated initially, because it was not generally shared. With the exception of small groups of socialist sympathisers and a circle of fellow romantics who expressed their fears through the medium of their art, he stood alone among a very hostile group of economists. Dickensian gloom and prophetic Turneresque skies had failed to shake their complacency or shatter their faith in the orthodox economy. And if Darwin's scientific theories had challenged an already wavering belief in Christianity and pre-ordained notions of a natural hierarchy, then that too could easily be accommodated. 'Survival of the fittest' was, after all, a doctrine which could sit very comfortably with the economic system of '*laissez-faire*' and Malthusian notions of population control.

Ruskin thought that existing capitalist ideology was totally antithetic to Christian morality, and that his higher convictions would only be achieved through a radical revision of the values of the current economic system. Under no circumstances was there any justification for continuing to see society and political economy as separate, unrelated concepts. No assessment of Ruskin's influence would be accurate without a repeated emphasis of his insistence on this principle. It was born of a determination to temper enlightenment rationalism with the hindsight of the experience of industrialisation. In this sense, and indeed in the very nature of his education, Ruskin was both a classicist and a romantic simultaneously. In *Unto This Last,* a burning romanticism, energised by a genuine concern for the moral and physical welfare of the working man, was contained within his commitment to a scientific analysis of wealth, operating within a just but hierarchical society.

Thus, with the same apparent contradiction of ideologies, Ruskin's secular message for society was contained within a religious metaphor. This factor was neither understood nor appreciated. An entry in his father's diary, dated 31 May 1862, recorded that Ruskin senior found 'people bewildered' by his son's recent publications and on 3 August in the same year, the father again expressed his personal concern and confusion: 'I am changed in political economy – nervous – His health is my main thought, don't care how long he is getting to the end of P.E. [Political Economy].'[59] This is further proof of the extent to which Ruskin was intellectually isolated at this time; people simply could not see the validity of his argument, any more than many could understand his admiration for the artist, J.M.W. Turner, whose paintings had ceased to have conventional definition of form. The editor of *Fraser's Magazine* was quick to draw an analogy:

That work of Turner's seems to us a happy illustration of Mr
Ruskin's style with the pen; the majority of his writings having
exactly the same perfections or the same defects, according as we
consider intelligibility a fault or a virtue in artist or author. But
Turner did not always paint fiery fogs . . . he did not always paint
enigmas; nor is a label always necessary to tell us the subject of his
work . . . When Mr Ruskin, however, labels his essays, the label is
as great a riddle as the essay itself.[60]

Ruskin's perception of society was indeed analogous to the work of his
friend; Ruskin feared that, in the grip of industrialisation, society was
losing its familiar shape and cohesion and leaping forward at an alarming
pace. His use of the New Testament parable was not only to emphasise the
moral centrality of his message, but also to provide a suitable and
recognisable medium for the depiction of the lot of the contemporary
labouring man. It was not a sentiment endorsed by theologians, however.
At the time of the publication of *Unto This Last,* many clergymen, with a
few notable exceptions, were facing difficulties in appealing to their
working-class congregations. Ruskin attributed that to their collective
inability to address their faith to existing social evils. He had long despised
this moral inflexibility and he suffered the consequences of ecclesiastical
disapproval accordingly. J.H. Whitehouse was to comment years later:

It is worthwhile considering in connexion with the outcry which
greeted Ruskin's social theories, whether he was not really the victim
of the infidelity of the formal Church to the principles of Christianity.
Those preaching religion, as Ruskin has so often pointed out, never
attempted to apply the meaning of the faith they professed as a
solution of the social evils around them. Religion was a thing of creeds,
of intellectual belief, of formal observances which made one day duller
than all other days, but which had no connexion with what were
regarded as economic laws and the working of our industrial system.
Ruskin in his teaching denounced the methods of the Church, and
applied Christianity as he understood it to the problems of those six
days so long neglected by the custodians of the faith.[61]

A footnote in *Fraser's Magazine* explained the position of some of these
custodians with regard to Ruskin's work:

'Of the many interpreters,' says the Dean of Westminster, 'of the parable of the Labourers in the Vineyard, there are first those who see in the equal penny to all the key to the whole matter, and for whom its first lesson is this – the equality of rewards in the kingdom of God.' Mr Ruskin was the first to maintain that this equality is as much the economy of earth as of heaven. But even as respects 'the kingdom of God', the Ruskinian interpretation is not considered by theologians to be tenable. 'However,' continues the Dean, 'this view may appear to agree with the parable, it evidently agrees not at all with the saying which sums it up and contains its moral, "*Many who are first shall be last*," etc., for such an equality would be, not a reversing of the order of first and last, but a setting of all upon a level.' Mr Ruskin, however, has confidence enough to set up for a leveller in the next world as well as in this. Having reformed the Political Economy, perhaps he may be induced to undertake the reformation of Divinity.[62]

The Dean had obviously not read Ruskin's work very closely, for apart from the fact that, at this stage in his life, Ruskin no longer believed in personal salvation, his opposition to equality comes through fairly strongly in *Unto This Last,* where he advocated a hierarchical system of government. But, within this hierarchy, there was to be justice, not exploitation:

And with respect to the mode in which these general principles affect the secure possession of property, so far am I from invalidating such security, that the whole gist of these papers will be found ultimately to aim at an extension in its range; and whereas it has long been known and declared that the poor have no right to the property of the rich, I wish it also to be known and declared that the rich have no right to the property of the poor.[63]

As an entry in Ruskin's diary stressed: 'It is not enjoyment of, but power over wealth which most men covet.' It was therefore necessary to 'consider more in detail the manner in which wealth may be used, misused, or consumed: and also the way in which the true wealth is sifted from the false.'[64] The nature and definition of wealth was always a key concern for Ruskin and it formed the greater part of his critique. It was patently obvious to him that the existing language of economics was obscuring the truth, perpetuating injustice and ensuring that many of the 'meek' had little chance of survival, let alone of 'inheriting the earth'. Both Church and State were culpable. As Whitehouse observed: 'The responsibility for the reception which Ruskin's attempts in applied Christianity met with rests in part upon the whole social spirit fostered by long generations of formal ecclesiasticism.'[65]

Munera Pulveris

In 1862 Ruskin followed up his writings on political economy with four further essays, which were published in *Fraser's Magazine*. The first was published in June 1862, and the other three in September and December 1862, and April 1863, respectively. They were later published in book form under the title *Munera Pulveris*, but not until 1872. The reason for this delay was that Ruskin experienced a very similar response to the one he had received when he published his essays in the *Cornhill Magazine*. He explained the situation in the preface to this work:

> I resolved to make it the central work of my life to write an exhaustive treatise on Political Economy. It would not have been begun, at this time, however, had not the editor of *Fraser's Magazine* written to me, saying that he believed there was something in my theories, and would risk the admission of what I chose to write on this dangerous subject; whereupon, cautiously, and at intervals, during the winter of 1862–3, I sent him, and he ventured to print, the preface of the intended work, divided into four chapters. Then, though the Editor had not wholly lost courage, the publisher indignantly interfered; and the readers of *Fraser*, as those of the *Cornhill*, were protected, for that time, from further disturbance on my part.[66]

Ruskin's chief purpose in *Munera Pulveris* was to attack the contemporary concept of wealth, and was in effect an elaboration of the ideas first mooted in *Unto This Last*. Many of Ruskin's book titles caused speculation, if not exasperation, among scholars and *Munera Pulveris* was no exception. The approximate literal translation was explained by E.T. Cook as 'Gifts, or Functions of the Dust'.[67] The title was meant to express Ruskin's increasing distaste for the current misplacement of values. He wrote in the preface that 'to the date [1863] when these Essays were published, not only the chief conditions of the production of wealth had remained unstated, but the nature of wealth itself had never been defined.' In the preface, dated November 1871, and dedicated significantly to Carlyle, Ruskin insisted:

> There is not one person in ten thousand who has a notion sufficiently correct, even for the commonest purposes, of 'what is meant' by wealth; still less of what wealth everlastingly *is*, whether we mean it or not; which it is the business of every student of economy to ascertain.[68]

He accused Mill of having 'no clue to the principles of essential value' and for relying on public opinion as 'the ground for his science'.[69] In fact, Ruskin commented, modern political economists had proved themselves incapable of understanding intrinsic value at all or its opposite, 'Intrinsic Contrary – of – Value.'[70] The aim of *Munera Pulveris* was thus:

> to examine the moral results and possible rectifications of the laws of distribution of wealth, which have prevailed hitherto without debate among men. Laws which ordinary economists assume to be inviolable, and which ordinary socialists imagine to be on the eve of total abrogation.[71]

Both socialists and economists, Ruskin claimed, were deceived as 'the laws which at present regulate the possession of wealth are unjust, because the motives which provoke to its attainment are impure':

> But no socialism can effect their abrogation, unless it can abrogate also covetousness and pride, which it is by no means yet in the way of doing. Nor can the change be, in any case, to the extent that has been imagined. Extremes of luxury may be forbidden, and agony of penury relieved; but nature intends, and the utmost efforts of socialism will not hinder the fulfilment of her intention, that a provident person shall always be richer than a spendthrift . . . the adjustment of the possession of the products of industry depends more on their nature than their quantity, and on wise determination therefore of the aims of industry.[72]

So Ruskin persisted with his moral attack on the political economists but, again, publication was curtailed and Ruskin did not take it well. Cook commented:

> This second veto was a bitter vexation to Ruskin. Mr Allen well remembered the day on which Ruskin heard the news; he paced his terrace-walk for hours like a caged lion, and deep gloom gathered upon him. Froude had clearly not lost faith in his contributor; for, a few months later, when Ruskin's views had called forth a reply in *Macmillan's Magazine* [by Professor Cairnes], Froude invited Ruskin to write a rejoinder. This supplementary paper – in the form of a dialogue on Gold – was sent to Froude, but it was not printed at the time. Probably it was Ruskin's father who stopped it; he was particularly sensitive, as a City merchant, to his son's heresies on questions of currency; and Ruskin had promised his father 'to publish no more letters without letting you see them'.[73]

Cook further related how *Munera Pulveris*, in its original essay form in 1862, was inevitably doomed before it was published, coming so closely in the wake of the violent hostility aroused by the publication of *Unto This Last* the same year. The outcry was 'at its height', wrote Cook; and 'the contemptuous tone of the writers in the press, and the remonstrances of private friends, hurt Ruskin's father not a little, and a strain of vexation in the son's letters at this time was caused by alternate entreaties for alterations or suppressions.'[74] Ruskin had little support at this stage, with the notable exception of Carlyle who wrote to him, on 30 June 1862, that he 'approved in every particular; calm, definite, clear; rising into the sphere of *Plato* (our almost best), which in exchange for the sphere of MacCulloch, Mill and Co. is a mighty improvement!'[75]

Like Carlyle, Ruskin was certainly influenced by Plato's writings, referring to him frequently throughout his own work, which resonated with a platonic mistrust of total democracy and an insistence on the integration of economics with politics. It was also most likely that Ruskin's utopian vision of a new moral order came more from Plato and Thomas More than it did from Owen, although the Christian Socialists with whom Ruskin had associated in the mid-1850s were certainly influenced by Owenite assumptions. But the eclecticism of both Ruskin and the Christian Socialists has been noted. Sherburne comments:

Ruskin's concept of a social whole in economic behaviour owes much to the Romantic tradition of organicism. Coleridge, Southey, and Carlyle warn of the dangers of a mechanical approach. They refuse to isolate the economic aspect of social processes. Ruskin is chary of recognising his immediate forebears. Instead, he claims that his task in economics is simply to call attention to the wisdom of the ancient Greeks. Ruskin's vision of the scope of economics does bear a remarkable similarity to that of the Greeks . . . They never contemplate writing separate treatises on economic phenomena.[76]

The people about whom Ruskin was most concerned were, of course, at this stage, not the greatest readers of his work. Like the early romantics, he wrote for the poor but was read by the relatively rich.[77] In espousing the cause of the working man, he had an uphill task, not only in terms of opposition from the economic and political establishment, but also in making his work accessible. The limitations of literacy among the labouring classes, the logistics of publishing, and the cost of printed matter did nothing to enhance the circulation of Ruskin's writing. These were factors, however, of which he was not totally unaware. Eventually, he took some steps to amend the situation by moving the publication rights of his books from Smith & Elder of London to George Allen at Sunnyside, Orpington, Kent in 1873.

His biographer, E.T. Cook, recorded the commercial progress of *Unto This Last* in 1911: 'The edition of 1862 consisted of 1,000 copies, and ten years later it was still not exhausted.'[78] In 1873 Ruskin transferred the publication of his books to George Allen, leaving Smith & Elder with unsold copies: 'Of *Unto This Last*, 102 copies remained, and the publishers estimated that two years would be required to dispose of them. A few years later, Ruskin re-issued the book on his own account, and the rate of sale during the following thirty years was 2,000 per annum.'[79] Ruskin had applied his own economic principles to the world of publishing, and by establishing a successful cottage industry and partially eliminating the middleman, was able to secure a substantial profit for himself and later to produce more widely accessible pocket editions of his works.[80] On being told of a working man who could not afford to buy the book and had copied it out word for word, Ruskin had a selection of extracts printed and circulated widely among the working classes for a penny each. Once again, he had proved his critics to be wrong. Cook commented:

> 'His system for publishing 'in the wilds of Kent' has – like most other schemes of his devising – been derided as unpractical, visionary, and mad. On closer inspection does there not seem to be some method in Mr Ruskin's mad work?'[81]

The success of this venture was of course only a minor factor in the increased sales of Ruskin's work. The opposition to *Unto This Last* in 1860/2 was, as already noted, largely a hysterical reaction to innovative theories. In *Unto This Last*, dismissed by many as an unworkable economic utopia, Ruskin had opposed the 'scientific' with the 'moral'. And he had challenged the whole complacent middle-class ethos which, he maintained, had turned its back on poverty and secured its wealth at the expense of others. The aim of political economy should rather be 'the multiplication of human life at the highest standard'.[82] Ruskin's writings had, in effect, provided a much-needed move toward the more humanitarian concerns of collectivism. It is this factor which secured the allegiance of men like Harrison and Hobson, and also, the later Christian Socialists. To quote from Edward Norman:

> . . . the originality and value of [Ruskin's] critique ought not to be in doubt. The hostility which he encountered at the time was able to exploit his lack of practical knowledge; he was only too easily made to look like 'a man of genius who has travelled out of his province' . . . Most important of all, however, were not Ruskin's economic redefinitions, but his prophetic denunciations of a materialist society corrupted by avarice.[83]

Despite a period of continued antagonism, Ruskin never lost faith in the 'rightness' of his publication of *Unto This Last*. And while its moral centre remained steadfast, the social and economic background it so passionately condemned moved inexorably toward a state which vindicated his approach and called for a re-evaluation of his thinking.

4

VINDICATION: A CHANGING SOCIETY AND A MORE FAVOURABLE RECEPTION

When Ruskin began to write, *laissez-faire* was as much a political dogma as it was an economic doctrine. His writings undermined the doctrine in both of its applications. He pleaded for an extension of State interference – and the vogue of his writings enabled him, perhaps more than any other writer, to help men to shed the old distrust of the State, and to welcome, as men since 1870 have more and more welcomed, the activity of society on behalf of its members.[1]   E. Barker (1915)

Barker's comments illuminate the political reasons for Ruskin's initial poor reception as a social critic. After 1870 he enjoyed a much more favourable response to his writings. The reasons for this were complex, involving both private and public factors, but essentially they reaffirm the importance of timing in any assessment of Ruskin's status as a social critic.

Munera Pulveris, published in 1863, had reinforced the message of *Unto This Last*, and in 1865, still smarting after his poor reception, Ruskin published *Sesame and Lilies*, a series of lectures covering a variety of topics but always with that same moralising, didactic overtone which was guaranteed to give further ammunition to his enemies. 'Mr Ruskin,' commented the editor of the *Westminster Review* on the publication of *Sesame and Lilies*, 'has lately been stoned by the critics.'

They have flung enough stones at him to build his monument, and enough mud to cement it together. Doubtless, his book is very provoking to some minds. In his logic he draws too large conclusions from too small premises, and in his political economy draws them from none at all. Then he is transcendental, carries himself on his own shoulders, jumps down his own throat, eats the wind, and drinks the clouds.[2]

This is sardonic criticism which in its extravagance pandered to the mid-Victorian tendency to ridicule the unconventional, a tendency which the writer soon covertly acknowledged with the admission that sometimes it was 'The duty of the critic to leave the faults alone, and dwell only on what is valuable and explain what is likely to be misunderstood.' 'Everybody has enjoyed their joke at it,' wrote the editor, 'but nobody brought a grain of sympathy.' And then with a complete climbdown: 'Nonsense there is enough in this book, but Mr Ruskin's nonsense is sometimes more valuable than his critics' sense.' Indeed, so determined was this critic by now to be fair that, at the end of this particular passage, he seemed quite stricken with remorse and forced into an admission of the value of Ruskin's sound, if unpalatable, moralising. For all his gloominess, he declared, 'Mr Ruskin's strictures upon the national hardheartedness and the national lust for money are needed.' And continuing in the same vein:

> Anyone who has lived for the last four years, that is to say, during the space of the American civil war, in one of our large manufacturing towns, and has heard, as we have heard, Southern brutalities, applauded by men and slavery upheld by women, will not say that Mr Ruskin has overcoloured one line or overcharged one sentence. Utopianism is at times good for us, if it be only to lift us out of our usual atmosphere of prudence and pence.[3]

Ruskin was used to the accusation of utopianism but he never allowed it to alter his course. In the preface to the small edition of *Sesame and Lilies*, dated 24 August 1882, he recorded that he wrote the book 'while my energies were still unbroken and my temper unfretted; and that, if read in connection with *Unto This Last*, it contains the chief truths I have endeavoured through all my past life to display.'[4] Although Ruskin was at this stage rather frail, he must have taken comfort from the fact, noted in the same preface, that 'the influence of [his] books was distinctly on the increase.'[5] It was, he said, 'chiefly written for young people' and was 'wholly of the old school' assuming some 'old-fashioned conditions and existences which the philosophy of today imagines to be extinct with the Mammoth and the Dodo.' This was written with hindsight, but certainly with no regrets for the warnings of the first publication of 1865 – far from it in fact. There had been some small improvements in society, Ruskin acknowledged, but many of the changes, although 'extremely clever, irresistibly amusing, and enticingly pathetic', were 'all nevertheless the mere whirr and dust-cloud of a dissolutely reforming and vulgarly manufacturing age.'[6] His convictions had only been endorsed with the passage of time and his earlier critique of industrial values vindicated. The editorial in the *Westminster Review* that has already been quoted added:

> Others, beside Mr Ruskin, have set themselves to bring about the millennium of peace – peace which is so often more chivalrous than war – but they have all paid the penalty of being too far in advance of their day; and Mr Ruskin's eloquent sentences will, equally with the plain words of Cobden, fall upon deaf ears.[7]

This implicit recognition of Ruskin's prophetic role would be impressive were it not for the writer's denial of the same a few paragraphs later. In reviewing a book by Alexander H. Japp, rather grandly entitled *Three Great Teachers of Our Own Time: Being an Attempt to Deduce the Spirit and Purpose animating Carlyle, Tennyson and Ruskin,* also published in 1865, the reviewer commented:

> In no single sense can any one of the three, Carlyle, Tennyson, and Ruskin, be said to be the teachers of the day . . . It would be absurd to deny that all three are not men of genius, and have not exercised a certain influence on the time; but we do deny the permanency of that influence.[8]

And, reverting to his previous acerbity, the same author remarked: 'How far Mr Ruskin understands the day may be seen in the political economy of *Unto This Last*, and his senseless outbursts against commerce.' Perhaps Ruskin understood the day only too well for the taste of the editor of the *Westminster Review*. At any rate, his critic finally conceded that, in praising Ruskin, 'Mr Japp means well', even if, as he added drily, 'the best parts of his book . . . are the quotations.'

That Ruskin was not in harmony with his time is indisputable, and to a great extent this accounts for the initial ridicule to which he was subjected, but he was also a threat to the *status quo*. *Time and Tide*, published in 1867, the same year as the Second Reform Bill, was written by Ruskin in the form of letters to a Mr Thomas Dixon, a working cork-cutter of Sunderland.[9] The purpose of these letters was clearly stated in the preface as an injunction to the working men of England to think less about actual parliamentary power and more about what they wanted to do with this power in the interests of social reform. Mr Dixon's response to these letters displayed enthusiastic support for Ruskin's own proposals for reform and also a strong deference to Carlyle's notions of benevolent despotism, inspired apparently by his reading of Carlyle's *Frederick the Great*. In a letter to Ruskin dated 7 February 1867, Dixon wrote:

> I find you and Carlyle seem to agree quite on the idea of the Masterhood qualification. There again I find you both feel and write as all working men consider just. I can assure you there is not an honest, noble working man that would not by far serve under such *master*-hood, than be the employee or workman of a cooper-ative store. Working men do not as a rule make good masters; neither do they treat each other with that courtesy as a noble master treats his working man.[10]

Mr Dixon was, however, pleased to note that one such 'noble master', a Mr Morley, described rather ambiguously as 'a large manufacturer at Nottingham', has 'been giving pensions to all his old workmen', very much a part of what Mr Dixon referred to as Ruskin's 'noble plans' He therefore concluded optimistically:

> I hail with pleasure and delight the shadowing forth by you of these noble plans for the future: I feel glad and uplifted to think of the good that such teaching will do for us all.[11]

The tide was indeed beginning to turn for Ruskin. He had survived long enough for his gloomy prognostications to materialise and, unlike Carlyle, he had managed to establish some measure of rapport with the working man. But any consideration of a change in the reception and influence of his thinking has to be viewed in conjunction with an awareness of the shifting social and intellectual background which came increasingly to form a more acceptable medium for Ruskin's critical works.

Social and Economic Background

This was due, historically, to a number of factors. Firstly, by the time of the second publication of *Unto This Last* in 1877, Britain was entering a trough of economic depression, which emphasised the need for new strategies to ease the problems of indigence.[12] At the same time, Benthamite individualism, sanctioned by the economic doctrine of *laissez-faire,* was being gradually superseded by a movement toward greater sympathy with collectivism. Despite a period of comparative inertia in the promotion of working-class political representation after the collapse of Chartism in 1848, there was still a steady stream of protest, not least from Carlyle and Ruskin, against individualism and *laissez-faire* which continued into the 1880s. This opposition was at first cultural rather than political; Christian Socialism in its early stages of the 1850s made but a brief impact under the auspices of Maurice and Kingsley, and Marx was not to become a significant force for change until the 1880s.

The political and economic atmosphere which formed the backdrop to the republication of *Unto This Last* was therefore one of transition and contradiction. Bentham had presented two rather conflicting proposals: the right of man to pursue his own interests, and the duty of the state to provide 'the greatest happiness of the greatest number'. The state, under the influence of reformers like Lord Shaftesbury, gradually began to acknowledge the rightness of the latter and to give it precedence over the former in practical terms – such as the implementation of a cluster of Factory Acts.[13] J.S. Mill, himself subject to many contradictions and a fierce defender of the concept of freedom, also later reinterpreted Utilitarianism in terms of a shift away from the supremacy of individual liberty and self-interest toward a more social doctrine which helped to pave the way to collectivism.[14] There was definitely a growing dis-enchantment in all quarters with the values attendant on undiluted industrial capitalism and to quote Martin Weiner, late Victorian England was 'ripe for reevaluation.'[15] He continues:

The reevaluation was begun by Arnold Toynbee, an Oxford don and a disciple of Ruskin. Toynbee saw the previous hundred years as blighted by a false philosophy of life that centred on the set of 'intellectual suppositions' known as 'Political Economy'. . . . Now, however, he argued, it was time to turn from obsession with production to concentration on distribution and, even more crucial, the quality of life.[16]

Even among those who needed to reduce everything to empirical reality, the second publication of *Unto This Last* in the 1870s received a more sympathetic appraisal. It seemed more plausible to a wide variety of people and proved especially attractive to the newly emergent English radical socialists, for, if not socialist in doctrine, *Unto This Last* nevertheless contained many of the ingredients of collectivist thinking which they wished to promote. Moreover, for those previously disorientated by Ruskin's metaphors and contradictions, his new emphasis on the significance of society as a living, mutating organism began to make his insistence on the interconnections of social, political and economic relationships more readily acceptable. Some of his contemporaries were even sympathetic to his spiritual and intellectual dilemma. Writing an article to accompany a cartoon of Ruskin published in *Vanity Fair* on 17 February 1872, a contributor under the name of 'Jehu Junior' made the following observation:

There is, perhaps, no harder fate in store for a man than to be irredeemably at variance with the spirit of the country and the times in which he lives; and it is Mr Ruskin's great misfortune to be an incurable poet and artist in a materialistic and money-grubbing generation. He is so entirely out of harmony with all of modern life that surrounds him that he is by many regarded as an anachronism rather than as a man, and that his views are looked upon rather as vain protests than as serious opinions.

Like so many of Ruskin's critics, Junior first represented the popular viewpoint of those who were not quite sure what to make of him, and then moved closer to what he perceives to be the unacceptable truth.

It is, however, [Ruskin's] greatest merit that he is utterly careless of the current habits of thought, and that he has been enabled fearlessly to supply to them precisely those elements in which they are most wanting. The English people have become meanly practical, and he is grandly unpractical; they have become essentially commonplace, and he is gloriously poetical; they believe in nothing more than cash, he believes in nothing less; they are thoroughly positive, he is thoroughly ideal. It has been reserved for him, in spite of all such disadvantages, to produce works which from the mere power of their language have captivated even the most indifferent, and which have set many thinking in quite a new direction.[17]

The process of acceptance of Ruskin as a serious critic of society had begun – too late to afford him any real sense of moral vindication, but significant, ironically, in shaping the future development of socialist doctrine. Ruskin's oft-repeated denial of political partisanship did not preclude his disciples from annexing him for their cause; and that is what they promptly did. Christian Socialism, which experienced a resurgence toward the latter part of the nineteenth century, had moved from its initial programme of self-educational and moral reform toward a greater awareness of political inequality.[18] Ruskin's complex intellectual relationship with the movement and his influence on the founding members of the Labour Party will be dealt with in detail below, but for the present it is essential simply to establish the connection. Despite many areas of disagreement, Ruskin did have a strong affinity with Christian Socialism, and indeed, with other newly emergent left-wing movements, and, if one accepts as Gareth Stedman Jones does, that 'religiosity was not extrinsic but inherent in the structure of early socialist thought',[19] it is easy to see why the second publication of *Unto This Last,* pursuing its social doctrine under the guise of religious metaphor, found a more sympathetic audience.

Fors Clavigera

This phenomenon did not happen overnight, however, and neither did it occur without some very conscious and deliberate self-advertisement by its author. In 1871 Ruskin began to publish monthly open letters, addressed rather optimistically 'To the Workmen and Labourers of Great Britain' and collectively entitled *Fors Clavigera*. These letters, which Ruskin continued until his mental breakdown in 1878, were a testimony to both his moral outrage and his strong sense of personal failure. As he commented in his first letter:

I have listened to many ingenious persons, who say we are better off now than we were before. I do not know how well off we were before; but I know positively that many very deserving persons of my acquaintance have great difficulty in living under these improved circumstances: also that my desk is full of begging letters, eloquently written either by distressed or dishonest people; and that we cannot be called, as a nation, well off, while so many of us are either living in honest or in villainous beggary.[20]

He was by no means alone in this somewhat gloomy assessment and sense of foreboding at the possible outcome of social deprivation at this time. This first publication coincided chronologically with the rise and fall of the Paris Commune, and Ruskin was among a group convinced that similar events would occur in England if something was not done to remedy the problems of poverty and crime. He declared his commitment to this end, saying 'I will endure it no longer quietly; but henceforward, with any few or many who will help, do my poor best to abate this misery.'[21]

An article by Leslie Stephen, which was published in *Fraser's Magazine* in 1874, endorsed the gloom generally felt at this time and then commented on Ruskin's recent contribution to social improvement expressed in *Fors CLavigera*. 'The world is out of joint,' wrote Stephen. 'It is difficult even to take up a newspaper without coming upon painful forebodings of the future. Peace has not come down upon the world, and there is more demand for swords than for ploughshares.'[22] It was, he stated, a situation which was causing untold misery in England:

Everywhere the division between classes is widening instead of narrowing; and the most important phenomenon in recent English politics is that the old social bonds have snapped asunder amongst the classes least accessible to revolutionary impulses. Absorbed in such contests, we fail to attend to matters of the most vital importance. The health of the population is lowered as greater masses are daily collected in huge cities, where all the laws of sanitary science are studiously disregarded. Everywhere we see a generation growing up sordid, degraded, and devoid of self-respect. The old beauty of life has departed. A labourer is no longer a man who takes a pride in his work and obeys a code of manners appropriate to his station in life. He restlessly aims at aping his superiors, and loses his own solid merits without acquiring their refinement. If the workman has no sense of duty to his employer, the employer forgets in his turn that he has any duty except to grow rich.[23]

Ruskin's response to this dismal scenario, was, for Stephen, entirely consistent with Ruskin's 'unusual if not morbid sensibility'. Referring to *Fors Clavigera,* Stephen explained 'One seems almost to be listening to the cries of a man of genius, placed in a pillory to be pelted by a thick-skinned mob, and urged by a sense of his helplessness to utter the bitterest taunts that he can invent.' This, Stephen pointed out, was not an inducement to favourable reception: 'Amongst Mr Ruskin's crotchets are certain theories which involve the publication of his works in such a manner as to oppose the greatest obstacles to their circulation.'[24]

Ruskin's biographer, W.G. Collingwood, commented:

> Mr Ruskin's attacks on commercialism – his analysis of its bad influence on all sections of society – were too vigorous and uncompromising for the newspaper editors who received *Fors,* and even for most of his private friends. We don't like agitators.[25]

Ruskin did have some support, however, not least from Carlyle, whose wholehearted approval of *Fors* was expressed in a letter he sent to Ruskin from Cheyne Row, dated 30 April 1871. The text is worth repeating in its entirety:

> This *Fors Clavigera,* Letter 5th, which I have just finished reading, is incomparable; a quasi-sacred consolation to me, which almost brings tears to my eyes! Every word of it is as if spoken, not out of my poor heart only, but out of the eternal skies; words winged with Empyrean wisdom, piercing as lightning, and which I really do not remember to have heard the like of.

> *Continue,* while you have such utterances in you, to give them voice. They will find and force entrance into human hearts, *whatever* the 'angle of incidence' may be; that is to say, whether, for the degraded and *in*human Blockheadism we, so-called 'men', have

mostly now become, you come in upon them at the broadside, at
the top, or even at the bottom. *Euge, Euge!*

> Yours ever,
>
> T. Carlyle.[26]

Despite such eminent and energetic support, Ruskin's relationship with
the press, however, remained very uneasy. The editor of the *Westminster
Review* certainly did not take *Fors Clavigera* too seriously, writing the
same year as Carlyle: 'Mr Ruskin's Letters to the Workmen and Labourers
of Great Britain still continue to pour out a monthly shower of gentle
instruction on political economy, morals, history, and politics, for the
benefit of all who submit themselves . . . to the genial influence.'[27]

> The present letters have much to say about the late War and
> Communistic movement in France. In spite of Mr Ruskin's
> affected abomination of liberty . . . it is only an outburst of his
> cranky dislike to terms which have once been vulgarised and
> abused that is really conveyed. Mr Ruskin is a radical and a
> republican of the deepest dye, though he would be a dangerous
> partisan to any cause.[28]

And the following year: 'Mr Ruskin still continues his oracular vatici-
nations' although he 'always combines some sterling material with his
egotism' and 'says some sharp things of the intensely competitive nature
of modern education'.[29] In the autumn edition: 'Mr Ruskin continues his
prophetic denunciations against things that are, though some of the
objects against which his quaint, half-comical, half-self-conceited, half-
satirical, and half-insane battering-ram is directed have already been too
much bruised by more potent machinery to be worth the expenditure of
Mr Ruskin's precious time.'[30] And early in 1873:

> Mr Ruskin's *Fors Clavigera* still pursues its motley, erratic, and
> nondescript course. It is certainly lively reading, though the reader
> quite as often laughs at the writer as with him. Between truisms,
> puerilities, exaggerated statements of real truths, paradoxes,
> artistic descriptions (though the writer reminds us 'his *forte* is
> really not description, but political economy'), and courageous
> skirmishings with the most complex problems of political

economy, it is difficult to divine the exact result on the brain of the 'workmen and labourers of Great Britain', which a systematic study of this series of publications is likely to have.[31]

This was not untypical of the 'official' response to Ruskin's social commentary throughout his lifetime. He was still, at this stage, unable to reach the people he most wanted to help and nowhere does this come through more strongly than in these letters, where his sense of desperation is almost palpable. To quote Jeffrey Spear: 'His public frustration in *Fors* is that of a man crying, "See, can't you see?" to people who, if they can be made to see the same thing at all, will see it with different eyes.'[32]

A greater part of this general variance with authority lay in Ruskin's continued refusal to identify with any particular political party. As he proclaimed in the first letter of *Fors Clavigera*:

> Men only associate in parties by sacrificing their opinions, or by having none worth sacrificing; and the effect of party government is always to develope hostilities and hypocrisies, and to extinguish ideas.[33]

Leslie Stephen regarded this notion, not unsympathetically, as a personality defect rather than a mark of intellectual integrity. He decided that Ruskin 'suffers from a kind of mental incontinence which weakens the force of his writing. He strikes at evil too fiercely and too rapidly to strike effectually.'[34] This was to his own disadvantage in terms of official acceptance, but nevertheless people must learn to acknowledge the soundness of much of his teaching:

> But we must take Mr Ruskin as he is. He might, perhaps, have been a leader; he is content to be a brilliant partisan in a random guerrilla warfare, and therefore to win partial victories, to disgust many people whom he might have conciliated, and to consort with all manner of superficial and untrained schemers, instead of taking part in more systematic operations. Nobody is more sensible than Mr Ruskin of the value of discipline, order, and subordination. Unfortunately the ideas of every existing party happen to be fundamentally wrong, and he is therefore obliged in spite of himself to fight for his own hand.[35]

As Stephen was keen to stress, Ruskin's problem was not lack of conviction but that he was 'so thin-skinned as to be unable to accept compromise or to submit contentedly to inevitable evils'. He always looked at the world from an artistic viewpoint, which, said Stephen, gave Ruskin 'an exaggerated tone of feeling', which 'bursts all restraints of logic and common sense'. It was however, undeniable to Stephen that the world *had* become uglier and that any superiority over earlier generations was 'not a superiority of faculty, but simply of inherited results'. Ruskin was therefore right to deplore the existing moral vacuum, where 'our eyes have grown dim, and our hands have lost their cunning' and to call for a greater awareness of decay; but, of course, such romantic notions inevitably led to accusations of utopianism, as has been noted on many occasions in response to Ruskin.

Stephen referred to an article in the *Spectator,* which had claimed that:

Mr Ruskin wished the country to become poor in order that it might thrive in an artistic sense. 'If,' it said, 'we must choose between a Titian and a Lancashire cotton-mill, then in the name of manhood and of morality give us the cotton-mill;' . . . [Mr Ruskin] would summarily sweep away all that makes men comfortable to give them the chance of recovering the lost power. Let us burn our mills, close our coalmines, and tear up our railways, and perhaps we may learn in time to paint a few decently good pictures.[36]

This presumably deliberate oversimplification of Ruskin's argument caused Stephen to elaborate on Ruskin's insistence upon the 'essential connection between good art and sound morality', a conviction which he never shed. 'If a nation is content with shams in art,' wrote Stephen, it 'will put up with shams in its religious or political or industrial life'. It was because of this basic and enduring premise that 'In works professedly dealing with social questions [Ruskin] is apt to regard the artistic test as final.'

An indefinite facility in the multiplication of shoddy is not a matter for exulting self-congratulation . . . Cruelty and covetousness are the dominant vices of modern society; and if they have ruined our powers of expression, it is only because they have first corrupted the sentiments which should be expressed in noble art.[37]

In *Fors Clavigera,* Ruskin set out to criticise the condition of England with much the same passion Carlyle had shown in *Past and Present*, and also to illustrate the possibility of an alternative society in which the production of great art would be possible. The practical result of this vision was the creation of the St George's Guild, a scheme to which Ruskin gave a great deal in terms of both energy and finance between 1871 and 1884. It was to have Ruskin as its master, presiding over a small community which, in return for spiritually rewarding labour, would enjoy fixed rents and good working conditions. It was, in the words of Frederic Harrison, 'characteristic in its conception and in its form, and throws much light on Ruskin's real nature and inmost ideas'.[38] It was also a scheme which, like most of Ruskin's practical experiments, was doomed to failure. Leslie Stephen offered an explanation:

> Utopia is not to be gained at a bound; and there will be some trouble in finding appropriate colonists, to say nothing of competent leaders. The ambition is honourable, but one who takes so melancholy a view of modern society as Mr Ruskin must fear lest the sons of Belial should be too strong for him.[39]

Ruskin's real problem lay in still being ill at ease with his time and out of touch with his audience. *Fors Clavigera*, like the St George's Guild, was to some extent an expression of guilt that he could not do more to ease the problems of indigence:

> I begin to question very strictly with myself, how it is that St George's work does not prosper better in my hands ... Here is the half-decade of years past, since I began the writing of *Fors*, as a byework to quiet my conscience, that I might be happy in what I supposed to be my own proper life of Art-teaching – and through my own happiness, rightly help others.[40]

But, despite his persistence in trying to make his social writings accessible to a wider audience through his lectures and letters to the press, Ruskin was still a lone voice at this time. This situation was set to improve, however, and this was due to a number of factors, one of the most significant being the use he made of his position as Slade Professor at Oxford, to which he was appointed in 1869.

Ruskin, Oxford and Mill

Ruskin's newly acquired professorship at Oxford gave him a platform for self-advertisement, a situation which he used to full advantage. A review in 1871 of his printed lectures made the following observations:

> Mr Ruskin's powerful and fascinating individuality never leaves him; and in reading these pages as they are printed one can realise well enough, in that remote degree, the working of the spell which filled the theatre, in the Hilary Term of 1870, with such throngs from far and near as hardly any Professor had ever drawn around him before . . . The truest and most instructive strokes of these lectures are more often to be found in their episodes and digressions than in their main thesis.[41]

Ruskin certainly did not confine his subject matter to art. One of his students was Herbert Warren,[42] who years later had this to say:

> Ruskin wanted to talk of Political Economy, we wanted to hear him discourse on art. Brought up on Mill and Ricardo, we thought we knew all about 'the Dull Science', and we wished to hear of Mantegna, and Raphael, and, above all, to see his Turners. We did see his Turners, a revelation. Above all we saw him. Gradually it dawned on us that he might be right, that John Stuart Mill, as Disraeli said of his father, was not infallible because he was dull. But it was only later and gradually that I learned the full import of these hours.[43]

Ruskin's response to anyone who objected to the tone and content of his lectures was unequivocal:

> There are three volumes published of my Oxford lectures,[44] in which every sentence is set down as carefully as may be. If people want to learn from me, let them read them or my monthly letter *Fors Clavigera*. If they don't care for these, I don't care to talk to them.[45]

The fact is, some people did object. Ruskin, however, had no qualms about using his lectures in the furtherance of practical social and economic reform. E.T. Cook commented:

> Mr Ruskin was fond of preaching what has been called the 'slum crusade' in his lectures at Oxford, and the movement for University and College 'Settlements' owes not a little to his exhortations. 'My University friends came to me,' he said, 'at the end of my Inaugural Lectures, with grave faces, to remonstrate against irrelevant and Utopian topics being introduced.' They may have been irrelevant; they certainly were not Utopian.[46]

His professorship gave him exactly the forum he needed to spread his social and economic critique among thinking people. And the timing was right. The country was beginning in the 1870s to move away from the political and economic 'creed' of *laissez-faire* toward a greater demand for state intervention in social matters.[47] This, to a certain extent, was based on a false view of classical economics. As W.H. Greenleaf argues:

> However misleadingly, conventional economics was associated with a *laissez-faire* emphasis, so the new, supposedly more concrete, understanding of economic life was explicitly associated with the idea of an active role for the state in dealing with the problems revealed.[48]

Greenleaf points out that the indictment against the classical school was not 'the inadequacy of its (supposed) view of the extent of legitimate state intervention but rather the abstractness and unreality of the method of analysis employed'.[49] This led to misleading generalisations. However, the call was definitely for a more paternalistic form of government:

> The association between such a collectivist tendency and the new style of economic analysis derived from a number of the intellectual influences that assisted in its establishment. Among these were the German historical school with its stress on the role of corporate authority, the diatribes of critics such as Ruskin, and the paternalist emphasis associated with much of the new economic history of the day.[50]

Like Ruskin, John Stuart Mill had expressed a firm conviction of the need for social change, but his commitment to reconciling his belief in individual liberty with collectivist principles made him reluctant to abandon the practice of *laissez-faire,* to which Ruskin was so vehemently opposed. As Ruskin saw it, Mill's attempts to temper the classical economics of Smith and Ricardo with radical sympathies had precluded any suggestion of a significant role for the state.[51] He would never have endorsed Ruskin's proposals for a paternalistic style of government, especially when it was underpinned with Christian ethics. The political struggle was between collectivism and competition and Mill was too wedded to the latter wholeheartedly to embrace the former.

Ruskin's ideas for social and economic reform, therefore, enunciated so eloquently in *Unto This Last,* repeated in his lectures and in the passionate letters which comprised *Fors Clavigera,* were far closer to the kind of socialism which could operate within the existing society than were the ideas of Mill, who saw in state socialism a threat to individual liberty. Perhaps it was indeed possible that Mill 'was not infallible'. Ruskin may have despaired of redeeming society through art, but the time was ripe for a more favourable reception of his social and economic thought, and this factor, allied to his decision to hand the publication of his works to George Allen, was instrumental in determining his future influence. Allen himself supplied the details of Ruskin's accelerating book sales, describing it later as:

> . . . a gradually expanding business. It began sixteen years ago with Mr Ruskin employing me to sell *Fors Clavigera* . . . Messrs Smith and Elder printed *Fors* at first, and I sold them . . . After 1873 Mr Ruskin's connection with his old publishers ceased, and he gradually threw all his publishing on me . . . the business has grown and grown ever since.[52]

The process of Ruskin's acceptance as a social critic was gradual, however, and at this stage even his supporters still had some reservations about his economic theories.

Leslie Stephen commented in 1874:

> Mr Ruskin's polemics against the economists on their own ground appear to me to imply a series of misconceptions. He is, for

example, very fond of attacking a doctrine, fully explained (as I should say, demonstrated) by Mr Mill, that demand for commodities is not demand for labour. I confess that I am unable to understand the reasons of his indignation against this unfortunate theorem.[53]

Stephen's interpretation of Ruskin's economics implied an emotional response to a scientific problem: 'The technical language of the economists' affected Ruskin, he stated, 'like the proverbial red rag. His indignation seems to blind him, and is the source of a series of questionable statements.'[54] What Stephen and many other of his contemporaries chose to ignore was that the emphasis Ruskin placed on a form of post-capitalist organicism which would reject both profit and interest was, in his eyes, both scientific *and* systematic. The maxim 'There is No Wealth but Life' was not mere sentiment. It was a basic premise from which conclusions could be drawn empirically. Ruskin had no time for Malthusian notions of a scarcity of resources. In *Unto This Last,* he emphasised the abundance of resources and the need for fair distribution.[55] His insistence on the inextricability of the moral and the material elements of economics was part of his plea for the restoration of lost values. In an appendix to *Unto This Last,* he stressed:

It is highly singular that political economists should not have yet perceived, if not the moral, at least the passionate element, to be an inextricable quantity in every calculation. I cannot conceive, for instance, how it was possible that Mr Mill should have followed the true clue so far as to write, 'No limit can be set to the importance – even in a purely productive and material point of view – of mere thought,' without seeing it was logically necessary to add also, 'and of mere feeling'. And this the more, because in his first definition of labour he includes in the idea of it 'all feelings of a disagreeable kind?' It can hardly be supposed that the feelings which retard labour are more essentially a part of the labour than those which accelerate it. The first are paid for pain, the second as power. The workman is merely indemnified for the first: but the second both produce a part of the exchangeable value of the work, and materially increase its actual quantity.[56]

For Stephen, Ruskin's insistence on replacing competition with cooperation was the root cause of his unpopularity. But, added Stephen, had Ruskin approached his argument with less vehemence he might have had a more favourable reception:

> To regard the existing order of things as final, and as imposed by irresistible and unalterable conditions, is foolish as well as wrong. The shrewder the blows which Mr Ruskin can aim at the doctrines that life is to be always a selfish struggle, that adulteration is only 'a form of competition', that the only remedy for dishonesty is to let people cheat each other till they are tired of it, the better; and I only regret the exaggeration which enables his antagonist to charge him with unfairness.[57]

Ruskin had used the Platonic analogy of domestic cooperation to emphasise his distrust of the existing individualistic political economy, and, by the end of the nineteenth century he had helped thousands of others to question it too. The economist's notions of an abstract 'economic man' devoid of human affections had no place in a healthy, interdependent society. As Ruskin declared:

> Political economy is neither an art nor a science; but a system of conduct and legislature, founded on the sciences, directing the arts, and impossible, except under certain conditions of moral culture.[58]

Ruskin's emphasis was on the whole person, exercising his or her own particular skills and using wealth wisely with a greater respect for the quality of life. And Ruskin's message was beginning to find sympathetic ears. By the end of the 1870s, many thinkers were querying the status of economics as an exact science; the possibility that Ruskin, this increasingly eccentric aesthete, may have had a valid argument in *Unto This Last,* was fast becoming a certainty.

Support came from hitherto hostile areas. In 1879 the *Westminster Review*, considering the writings of Professor Bonamy Price, had this to say:

> ... the task of political economy is, we agree with Mr Price, in the main practical, and not speculative, and it has been the error of political economists, from Ricardo onwards, to treat it as in the main

a speculative science . . . With Mr McCulloch and Professor Bonamy Price may, in this respect, be associated Mr Ruskin, a writer whose great command of first principles is hidden from the mass of men by reason of his arbitrariness and impatience of temper.[59]

This was praise indeed from a publication which seventeen years earlier had claimed that Ruskin was guilty of 'shallow presumption' in accusing 'men like Ricardo and Mill of having misunderstood the scope and tendency of their doctrines'.[60] Time and the course of events had, however, ultimately provided its own vindication of Ruskin's moral economics. Ruskin, Bonamy Price and McCulloch, claims the *Review* of 1879, share a 'fundamental likeness' in the accounts they give of 'the office of political economy'. And the article continued:

> . . . it will be felt how widely different [their accounts] are from that mere investigation of laws, which, according to the Ricardian school, is the object of political economy. And with the Ricardian view of the subject, which even yet is certainly the dominant view in England, but which we hold to be essentially inadequate, we propose immediately to deal.[61]

Ruskin's reputation as a social critic rested heavily on this growing rejection of current economic practice. In this same article one Dr Ingram, President of the Economic section of the British Association,[62] was quoted as also 'being at issue with the school of Ricardo'. 'No one,' the article claimed, 'has written better on the faults of the ordinary economic definitions.' Dr Ingram was reported as criticising the economists' abandonment of 'the use of the most necessary terms, such as *value, utility, production*', and expressing these ideas instead with 'circuitous phrases'. These 'endless fluctuations of economists in the use of words' indicated a 'general failure to apprehend and keep steadily in view the corresponding realities.' The Ruskinian ethic of human affection in economic matters was endorsed by Ingram as a long overdue correction to existing malpractice:

> A vicious abstraction meets us on the very threshold of political economy. The entire body of its doctrines, as usually taught, rests on the hypothesis, that the sole human passion or motive which

has economic effects is the desire of wealth . . . The consumption,
or more correctly the use, of wealth, until lately neglected by
economists, and declared by Mill to have no place in their science,
must, as Professor Jevons[63] and others now see, be systematically
studied in its relations to production and to the general material
well-being of communities.[64]

This was excellent advice from Dr Ingram, claimed the *Review*, but it
neglected one very important aspect, namely that political economy is a
practical rather than a theoretical discipline. Dr Ingram's idea of
constructing a theory and then acting upon it was unsatisfactory. A child
learns to walk by walking, not by learning the theory first. 'We have to
act before we know the extremity of the phenomena on which we act.'
The theory and the practice improve concomitantly.

The political economist must not learn the theory of wealth first,
and then advise the world on the grounds of that theory: he must
advise as best he can, on grounds which, though real, will often be
too imperfect for the construction of a faultless theory.[65]

Dr Ingram's insistence that political economy is essentially a science
because it contains scientific elements was tantamount to saying that
architecture and navigation are both sciences because they embrace the
same qualifying criteria:

In short, we affirm that political economy is not merely capable of
being utilized for practical ends, but that practice is interwoven
into the very fibre and substance of it, and cannot be separated
from it. This is the sum of our contention against the scientific
economists, to whom Dr Ingram, though largely differing from
them, yet essentially belongs.[66]

Political economy, claimed the *Review*, should thus be 'removed from the
list of true sciences' and be acknowledged as the study of disparate, yet
inextricably related, components, a factor already recognised by an
enlightened minority:

We are clear then, that anyone who fairly considers, not some special part of political economy, but its entire scope, will conclude with Mr McCulloch, Mr Bonamy Price, and Mr Ruskin, that this is practical and not theoretical. The office of it is to direct, not to discover: 'Do this,' not 'Know this,' is its keynote.[67]

Ruskin had been saying this for some twenty years: 'At a severe crisis, when lives in multitudes and wealth in masses are at stake, the political economists are helpless – practically mute.'[68] Indeed, so much had Ruskin now become economically credible that the *Review* pursued this particular argument by holding the two eminent economists Ricardo and John Stuart Mill as being culpable by being in opposition:

> But we must now treat of those writers who have aided or advocated the opposite view, namely that Political Economy is a true science . . . principally valuable for its theoretical results. The two powerful writers, by whose influence it is that this view has chiefly prevailed, Ricardo and John Stuart Mill were far from being wholly dominated by it [but] it was definitely professed by Mr Mill.[69]

Ruskin was pre-eminent among the critics of classical economics. His eloquence and popularity had convinced his readers in the 1870s to question the abstract motivation of the economists and to recognise the need for a consideration of social affections in economic concerns. He had used his Oxford professorship to advantage, but only to impress his own long-held convictions on the '*soi-disant* science' of political economy. Society was catching up with him, not the other way round. And it was this coalescence of factors which led many ultimately to reconsider the nature of the orthodox economy and the status of its principal exponents, Ricardo and Mill.

Mill's reputation suffered a sharp decline after his death in 1873 and this can only be considered another factor in Ruskin's favour, although it would be shallow to confuse cause and effect.[70] An article in *Fraser's Magazine* of that year commented:

> It would be difficult to specify a more rapid change in the public mind, or a more startling collapse of reputation, than took place within a few weeks of the death of John Stuart Mill.[71]

The immediate response of the press, claimed the article, was sycophantic and ill-considered. The 'working men were told that they had lost the best friend they ever had, although he did call them habitual liars'; the women 'whom he had encouraged to shake off the iron yoke of the male sex were in tears'; and in general 'the chorus was swelled by all who hoped to make political capital or gain credit for intellectual pursuits by applauding him.' Yet how many of the noblemen and statesmen who eulogised at his death actually agreed with his convictions? Very few, claimed one anonymous writer:

> When we are dealing with a teacher of morality, intellectual eminence cannot be accepted as a title to public honours apart from its employment and its tendencies.[72]

Apart from a strong tendency to inconsistency [only excusable when it is unconscious], 'He supported ballot when it was making little way even under the able advocacy of Mr Grote: he turned against it when, with the assent of most thinking politicians, it passed into law.'[73] Mill also, continued the same writer, deliberately courted publicity and support from those least qualified to judge by 'flattering or humouring the larger public'. His truly well-earned reputation was only 'enjoyed in a select and limited circle'.[74] And to add to his popularity in 1859, 'in a wish frequently expressed to him by working men' (or so, allegedly, Mill maintained), he had then published cheap editions of 'those of his writings which seemed most likely to find readers among the working classes.'

> The Grecian orator, when vehemently applauded by the multitude, turned round and asked, 'Have I said anything foolish?' Mill might well have asked a similar question when he found his writings most popular with the least qualified class of readers, and himself the idol of meeting after meeting assembled to assert rights or promote movements at utter variance with his own well-understood doctrine of utility.[75]

While being aware of Mill's many fine qualities, this writer concluded that one of the best ways of doing honour to his memory would be 'to endow a Mill Professorship for the delivery of an annual course of lectures against the noxious doctrines he has diffused'.

This was harsh criticism indeed. Others were more generous but still began to see Mill as a transitional figure, part of an outmoded and immoral system.[76] As the argument against the status of political economy as an exact science continued, Mill's posthumous reputation was to suffer further attacks. *Fraser's Magazine* in January 1879 carried the following indictment:

> At any moment we may be confronted with a glib speaker or writer on wages who will tell us as a clearly established scientific truth, that it is absurd to expect of an employer any other wages than those which 'the unalterable laws of supply and demand' compel him to pay – that the market rate of wages, even if it be but starvation wages, is all that it is incumbent upon him to give his men . . . And these glorifications of selfishness are preached in the name of political economy . . . What says Mr Mill on this point? Does he countenance such teachings? I fear it must be admitted that he does.[77]

It was considered by many that Mill's teaching, for all its humanitarian gloss, did not allow for the removal of competition. 'Every restriction of it is an evil, and every extension of it – is always an ultimate good.'[78] This is where, for later liberals, Mill's philosophy broke down; it professed a moral but could not tolerate the practical outcome. As a moralist, claimed *Fraser's Magazine*, 'Mr Mill may deem it 'most desirable' that sentiments of liberality should operate on the minds of employers. The results, however, to which such liberality would lead are 'results which he deplores'.[79] The 'logic' of Mill's teaching was summed up thus:

> . . . the influence of competition is represented as not merely beneficial in the main, but *so* beneficial that the more unbridled its operation the better for society. If competition drives poor needlewomen to make shirts at twopence-halfpenny each, it is better, it seems, that they should receive such a wretched pittance than that they should owe a better scale of payment to any 'custom' of generosity or of justice. To reign is worth ambition, though in hell; and to enjoy the glorious consciousness that you are receiving no favours, in other words, not a farthing which your employer can avoid paying, is a benefit worth purchasing, even though the price be starvation.[80]

In 1869 Ruskin had accused Mill of being 'the root of nearly all immediate evil among us in England'.[81] Mill's philosophy, however, rested less on a lack of generosity than on a totally different concept of society from that of Ruskin. Mill was not immoral. Even Ruskin admitted this, writing to Charles Norton: 'I do not (in my books) dispute Mill's morality; but I do deny his *Economical science*, his, and all others of his school.'[82] Ruskin could never subscribe to Mill's mechanistic view of society. Ruskin insisted that economics cannot be considered separately from ethics because it deals with the use of wealth by the members of society to promote a better quality of life, and not wealth as an end in itself. And, unlike Mill, Ruskin was prepared to risk enormous unpopularity among the orthodox economists by insisting that his Platonic principles could and should be realised in the nineteenth century, through the adoption of the measures of social and economic reform he so carefully spelled out in *Unto This Last*. He wrote to Charles Norton:

> . . . do not confuse my spiritual Platonism with my Economical abstractions. It is not Platonism, but a mathematical axiom, that a Line is length without breadth. Nor is it Platonism, but an economical axiom, that wealth means that which conduces to life . . . Also remember this great distinction – All common political economy is bound on the axiom, 'Man is a beast of prey.' (It was so stated in those words by Mr Mill at a social science meeting.) My political economy is based on the axiom, 'Man is an animal whose physical power depends on its social faiths and affections.'[83]

'Which of these principles,' Ruskin asked, 'do you reckon as a theory, and which as a fact?' And he ended his letter: 'Ever your 'affectionate (theoretically and platonically) J. Ruskin.' The lectures Ruskin delivered in Manchester in 1857, later printed as *A Joy Forever*, had already professed these principles, reinforcing the Platonic analogy of the household, to urge cooperation instead of competition and the replacement of *laissez-faire* policies with the guidance of wise paternalism in the hands of responsible businessmen. In this final precept, however, Ruskin was, of course, being as elitist as some of the people for whom he reserved his fiercest criticism.

Mill's position was perceived to be more in the eighteenth-century liberal tradition. His insistence that paternalism was illicit because it inhibited personal freedom led him to propose a meritocratic form of democracy, where the franchise was extended to all literate adults but weighted in favour of an educated elite. It also made him and many other liberals reluctant to abandon the economic doctrine of *laissez-faire*, a situation which was beginning to change in the 1870s.

After 1880, many liberals had begun to realise that new measures were necessary to cope with the anomalies engendered by a belief in the natural harmony of a free-market economy in an industrial society. They came to recognise the need for greater state involvement to rectify the shortfalls of market capitalism and for the replacement of *laissez-faire* philosophy with a mixed economy, bolstered by some plans for social welfare. And it is at this point that their thinking largely converged with Ruskin's, for if Ruskin is to be applauded for his attack on economic science, he is also to be hailed as a formidable proponent of the extension of state intervention in the interests of a healthier and happier society.[84] As such, he was certainly, despite his protestations to the contrary, a profound influence not only on new liberals, but also on many would-be English socialists. In the *National Review* of 1894, E.T. Cook referred to the 'historic phrase' of Sir William Harcourt: 'We are all Socialists now.' Cook's response was that 'He might have said, with at least as much truth, "We are all Ruskinians now."'[85]

It was stated at the beginning of this book that its purpose was to try to give as true a picture as possible of Ruskin's reception and influence, with an awareness not only of the symbiotic nature of these two factors, but also their own dependence on the character of the nineteenth century social, political and economic background. Reception is easier to assess than influence, but out of a complex cluster of determinants it is possible to isolate several indisputable factors. Firstly, it is undeniable that Ruskin's social ideals were initially not well received. Secondly, it is also undeniable that by the 1870s this situation was changing dramatically, although Ruskin had in no way modified his argument. Thirdly, many of Ruskin's recommendations for practical reform have gradually been adopted. Fourthly, and this is perhaps the most significant, Ruskin's greatest response came ultimately from the working classes.

In his address on the centenary of Ruskin's birth in 1919, J.H. Whitehouse deliberated:

No teacher before Ruskin had been so successful in the ultimate appeal which he made to unlettered people . . . Ruskin's strength,

after all, came from the fact that he appealed to the conscience of
the entire nation. The widest response to his appeal came from the
working classes. They have always been the greatest readers of his
books . . . When once the poorer classes began to read Ruskin they
understood him. His magic eloquence in its influence was to them
like the discovery of a new Holy Scripture. Their material demands
for better conditions of life were now given spiritual significance.
The demand for reform became part of the eternal conflict between
right and wrong.[86]

By the end of the century, sales of Ruskin's books escalated in the
industrial cities and *Unto This Last* was no longer cast aside. Malcolm
Hardman comments that, at the Bradford Subscription Library, the first
edition acquired in 1862 caused little interest, but the third edition
purchased in 1882 'became very well worn all through'. The first edition
was later 'rebound in black like a Nonconformist hymn-book' and so
remained in good condition but 'the edge of almost every page had to be
reinforced, very many of them twice'. This, as Hardman points out,
'could hardly indicate anything other than attentive reading by a great
many people during the remaining effective years of the library.'[87]

And should there remain any doubt as to Ruskin's increasing
popularity at the end of the nineteenth century, and indeed, spilling
posthumously into the twentieth century, the following publication
figures should suffice to dispel it. They are taken from the back of the
1907 popular and affordable edition of his works.

SESAME AND LILIES. Two Lectures. With Preface. 140th
  Thousand, in Original Form.

UNTO THIS LAST. Four Essays on Political Economy. With
  Preface. 104th Thousand.

FRONDES AGRESTES. Readings in 'Modern Painters.' 59th
  Thousand.

TIME AND TIDE. On Laws of Work. 41st Thousand.

THE CROWN OF WILD OLIVE. Essays on Work, Traffic, War,
  etc. 80th Thousand.

A JOY FOREVER. On the Political Economy of Art. 50th Thousand.

THE TWO PATHS. On Decoration and Manufacture. 46th
  Thousand.

THE QUEEN OF THE AIR. A Study of Greek Myths. 37th Thousand.

THE ETHICS OF THE DUST. On the Elements of Crystallisation. 44th Thousand.

THE RUSKIN READER. 14th Thousand.

Ruskin's work also sold well overseas. *Unto this Last* was translated into French, German and Italian, and later into Gujarati by his disciple, Gandhi, and Russian through the influence of another great admirer, Tolstoy. Ruskin was also widely read in America. E.T. Cook noted in 1890 that 'his American readers numbered tens of thousands'. Although much of this was 'pirate trade', Cook explained that 'Mr Ruskin's profits are steadily growing every year, and exceed, I imagine, those made by any other serious author of the time.'[88]

No great claims can be made for the originality of Ruskin's economic theory. He admitted himself that his ideas reached back to ancient Greece. His true seminality lies in his own particular organicist approach, which initially undercut many of the basic premises of the 'bastard science' and eventually found its true audience in the readership of the newly enfranchised working classes. James Sherburne writes:

Ruskin's significance [is] as a barometer of some of the deeper implications of the change in value theory which occurred after 1870. The chaotic, unprofessional, even mixed-media character of Ruskin's economic writings reveals underlying assumptions in a way which no professional economic treatise could.[89]

On this count, alone, Ruskin was important. Just *how* important can be investigated further through the work of some of his prominent disciples. Their work showed that Ruskin was not just a phenomenon of his own time, but had launched a fruitful avenue of fresh theoretical enquiry that was open to extension, development, and advocacy by other original thinkers.

5

FREDERIC HARRISON:
POSITIVE THINKING

The brutal, ignorant, and inhuman language which was current about capital and labour, workmen, and trades-unions is heard no longer. The old plutocracy is a thing of the past. And no man has done more to expose it than the author of *Unto This Last*.[1]

F. Harrison (1899)

Frederic Harrison (1831–1923) was one of Ruskin's keenest supporters.[2] A prolific writer and philosopher, he was influential in many areas of reform and was from an early age committed to the thinking of Auguste Comte, the French positivist. Harrison later found many similarities with Comte in Ruskin's social criticism. This link was never acknowledged by Ruskin; but as Martha Vogeler has argued,[3] there is very little difference in Ruskin and Comte's basic criticism of the economy except for the fact that Ruskin was far more passionate and analytical. Ruskin and Comte also, despite religious differences between Christianity and positivism, shared a belief in the need for moral and spiritual guidance in a hierarchically structured society. Because of these similarities, and because English positivism was very influential between 1860 and 1880,[4] Harrison never lost his determination to establish an intellectual synthesis between Ruskin and Comte, and to heighten a consciousness of their significance.[5] In this chapter, the use of little-known correspondence between Ruskin and Harrison highlights these issues and further confirms the nature and extent of Ruskin's influence on contemporary intellectuals.

Conversion to Positivism
Born into a middle-class family in Muswell Hill, North London, Frederic Harrison was able to reflect in later life on an almost idyllic childhood –

'the easy gliding life of a well-to-do family of many children'.[6] After an early education at home, a day school at King's College in London gave him a certain social awareness, and sowed the seeds of radicalism. He was thankful, he commented later, to have avoided 'the evils of the public boarding-school'. Public schools were the training ground for the 'rigid caste-system' on which British society was based. He himself, however, 'cannot attribute either divine origin or celestial inspiration to that society, [and therefore does] not regard the public school system as an infallible nursery of morals or an indispensable academy of enlightenment.'[7] Oxford in 1849 was to confirm these irreverent opinions. He went up with 'an incurable distaste for any of its honours and its prizes: and its dominant authorities did not inspire [him] with awe or attract [his] allegiance.'[8] He entered Oxford with 'the remnants of boyish Toryism and orthodoxy still holding on' and left six years later 'a Republican, a democrat, and a Free-thinker'.[9] From being a Puseyite High Churchman, he underwent a conversion to the positivism of Auguste Comte between the years 1850–61, and remained its most prominent defender throughout his ensuing career as a lawyer and a writer.

Harrison's disenchantment with religious doctrine and dogma was fuelled by the diversity of opinion he encountered at Oxford. He recalled how 'Sunday after Sunday, year after year, the official pulpit rang with some different point of view, from the extreme Ritualist to the ultra Calvinist.'[10] He commented that 'No method could be devised more certain to breed a confused chaos of religious thought than University sermons.' The effect of this diversity of doctrine was gradual but profound.

After extensive reading and meetings with the major contributors to the *Westminster Review,* Harrison wrote to Auguste Comte craving a personal audience in Paris. This he achieved, and was so influenced by Comte that it confirmed his growing belief that it was 'inconsistent and illogical to hold firmly the positivist scheme of philosophy and of sociology, and yet formally to hold a vague and arid theism.' He came to condemn all forms of orthodoxy as no more than a 'Magnificent allegory'.

It was this conviction which had prompted Harrison to write an article in the *Westminster Review* criticising the defenders of orthodoxy.[11] On its publication he received much the same response as Ruskin did, when he published *Unto This Last.* Harrison was amazed at 'the hubbub which ensued in the Clerical world', and 'disgusted at the intolerance with which Mr Jowett[12] and his friends were assailed.' All he had done, Harrison recorded, was 'to put a match to an explosive train of thought which had been long and laboriously prepared by far wiser and abler men.' But the violence of this opposition induced him to write 'A Confession of Faith' as a diary entry in January 1861. In this intensely spiritual document, he explained his final conversion to the positivist philosophy. The 'ancient legends' and 'old fictions of innate knowledge', he wrote, had been 'cast aside'. 'Scripture and miracles' were things of the past. Auguste Comte had laid out the foundations of a new humane form of creed which would better serve the needs of modern society and which from that moment Harrison took as his 'sole-abiding religion'.[13]

These central tenets of Comtean philosophy held the key to Harrison's later support for Ruskin. Comte argued that, in the nineteenth-century post-revolutionary industrial society, people needed guidance rather than government, direction rather than coercion. There was to be a partnership, but not one of equals. Authority was to lie in scientifically observable facts underpinned by a secular morality, which would ensure that power did not reside in the hands of the rich. A doctrine of community would further counteract the socially and economically divisive nature of division of labour. Moral restraint and spiritually empowered government intervention were essential ingredients of this doctrine, which would ultimately produce economic and political harmony.[14]

The attraction of this systematic and authoritarian positivism in a society already beginning to redefine its faith is an indication of the severity of the mid-Victorian spiritual crisis. In an atmosphere of growing religious doubt and controversy there was a reassertion of conservative orthodoxy which was deeply resistant to science. Religion in the 1850s was still being justified in terms of Paley's 'grand design',[15] which had survived eighteenth-century rationalism and seemed set to survive the utilitarian rationalism of Bentham and Mill. It was seemingly a foolproof *riposte* to all external challenges and yet, paradoxically, it also encapsulated the polarisation of the mid-Victorian state of mind. The evangelical theology was unsystematic and insensitive. It survived for a time by dismissing doubt as sinful, but the inherent conflict between the harsher doctrines of evangelicalism, which made individuals unaccountably responsible for their own misery, allied with an emphasis on humanitarian ethics, was bound to generate revulsion.

Science, therefore, fuelled the challenge to an already faltering belief in the doctrine and dogma of Christianity. Intellectual freethinkers such as Frederic Harrison could no longer tolerate the unsatisfactory climate of dissent and the failure of the Church to address the needs of society. Every day, he explained in a letter to his mother, he 'saw the Church gathering more mediocrity within its pale – day-by-day growing more hostile to learning and intellect'. When men such as Maurice and Kingsley tried to 'meet their duties', they were 'silenced – driven out – maligned.'[16] Harrison thus came to the positivist epistemology as much through his concern for social deprivation as from any lack of religious conviction. Indeed, his account of his conversion was deeply spiritual in nature and emphasised his search for a more meaningful way to live.

The timing of this explanation of his conversion in 1861 coincided with the furore over the publication of *Unto This Last*, a book also designed to shatter sacred hypotheses. On reading Ruskin's first publication of economic criticism in 1860, Harrison recorded, he was filled 'with a sense of a new gospel on this earth, and with a keen desire to be in personal touch with the daring spirit who had defied the Rabbis of the current economics.'[17] Toward the end of 1860 he was introduced to Ruskin by a letter from Dr Furnivall, a man whom Harrison refers to as 'the most active spirit in the Working Men's College',[18] and was then invited to Ruskin's home at Denmark Hill. Harrison described their first meeting glowingly:

John was the ideal of an airy, generous, fantastic, lovable man of genius, whose fancies bubbled forth clear and inexhaustible like a mountain spring. He was everything that one could imagine of friendly welcome, of simple nature, of incalculable epigram and paradox. Of course I wanted to induce him to study Comte not on any matter relating to religion or philosophy but solely as to the social and economic principles laid down in the Positive Polity. The basis of the economics of Comte and of Ruskin were, if not identical, distinctly parallel. Both saw that organic society rested on property – but property as created by the social cooperation of Labour and intellect, and also as being rightly devoted to the good of society as a whole, and not to the enjoyment of individuals. I never dreamed of Ruskin reading Comte himself, but of his taking

the ideas from me. Little did I know then that John would take no
ideas from the Angel Gabriel himself.[19]

Harrison and Ruskin had more in common, however, than shared
principles. Neither would consider themselves as lapsed Christians, but
both had experienced a moral crisis in the late 1850s, which had called
for a rejection of static traditional belief in favour of a new dynamic and
interactive social order. Harrison found in Comte a way of redefining his
beliefs in terms of a more humanitarian doctrine:

> The Positivist ought to have all the Christian virtues and none of the
> Christian vices – must be really, not falsely, charitable, ready to join
> with all working men in spirit – accepting any practical good –
> enjoying all forms of happiness that are harmless, and in sympathy
> with all that is frank, happy, beautiful, and sound in human life.[20]

In Ruskin's case his spiritual crisis had led him to attack the classical
political economy, which he undertook with no great reference to earlier
theorists. As Harrison remarked drily: 'The father[21] asked me to direct
John to some standard authorities on Political Economy. I might as well
have asked John to study Hints on Deerstalking, or The Art of
Dancing.'[22] Despite this 'waywardness' of Ruskin, however, Harrison
came away feeling delighted with his charm and brilliance:

> I felt profound admiration for the genius by which John Ruskin,
> alone, untaught, erratic as he was, had pierced to the bone the
> Giant Despair of Plutonomy in its decrepitude. And I was proud
> to have been admitted so generously to the intimate circle of one
> who, in magical gifts of expression, and in irrepressible eloquence,
> had certainly no living rival.'[23]

In fact, Ruskin never acknowledged any influence from Comte, although
Harrison repeatedly tried to establish the link. In 1868 he wrote to
Ruskin 'to show how largely the doctrines of Positivism formed a
scientific ground for his own economic theories'. But, noted Harrison,
'he did not care to discuss the question.'[24]

Ruskin's reply demonstrated a considerable degree of impatience with
Harrison.[25] Ruskin wrote that he would be 'most happy' to hear of 'the

principles' Harrison had stated 'being promulgated under *any* man's name' but that his own work was 'already done'. And as for acknowledging any influence or affinity with Comte, Ruskin was very scathing, saying that he was too much preoccupied with his natural history work to read through 'a severe philosophical treatise, merely to ascertain that its author is, or was before [him], of one mind with [him] as to twos usually making four.' What is more, he continued: 'Nor do I care at present to ascertain wherein Comte differs from me, which he certainly does (I hear) in some views respecting the spiritual powers affecting animal ones.' As for political economy, Ruskin declared that all 'men who can think and who will think honestly,' including Harrison and Ludlow, 'have long seen, quite clearly how matters stand.' And in Harrison's 'practical and earnest work, any independent determination of the same laws which Comte has made the basis of his system,' should, wrote Ruskin, be of much greater use to him than 'any mere coherence to an aggregate of disciples'.

Ruskin felt, moreover, that he himself had gone further in his definition of 'welfare', in that he had 'separated distinctly the productive occupations which maintain life, from those which refine it: and shown how the common political economy fails in enunciation even of the first.' He was annoyed with Harrison and Ludlow for not helping him long ago to beat into people's heads 'that very different consequences were likely to result from making a common ball – or a pudding.' It was now up to Harrison, Ruskin urged, to find as many people as possible who had 'agreed in what is right and to use their testimony collectively.' Ruskin concluded with a declaration of 'great interest' in Harrison's work and declared that, if he would care to make the journey to Denmark Hill to tell him 'more about Positivism', he would 'delightedly listen'.[26] But Ruskin, in fact, never listened 'delightedly' to anything Harrison, or indeed anyone else, had to say on the subject of positivism.

Harrison, Comte and Political Economy

In 1865, Harrison published an unorthodox article in the *Fortnightly Review,* entitled 'The Limits of Political Economy', in which he considered the nature of economic science in the mid-nineteenth century. Following Comte, Harrison emphasised the inextricability of social and economic problems and condemned the intractability of modern economists in refusing to recognise this fact:

Few opinions are more rooted in the mind of our industrial nation than this: that there is a science of production, definite, distinct, and exact – the axioms of which are as universal and demonstrable as those of astronomy; the practical rules of which are as simple and familiar as those of arithmetic. Economists, it is believed, have worked out a system of general truths, which any shrewd man of business can practically apply.[27]

But the economists were not in fact in agreement among themselves, even on 'first principles' such as 'the true theory of rent', 'the remuneration of labour', and 'the economical results of direct and indirect taxation, of strict entails, of trade unions, of poor laws, and so on'. 'Let us suppose,' wrote Harrison, 'these questions asked from a body of economists, and we should have them all at cross purposes in a moment. McCulloch would expose "the erroneous views of Smith", Ricardo and Malthus would confute each other, and scarcely one would admit the philosophical basis of Mr Mill.'

This would hardly prove satisfactory, Harrison indicated: 'Indeed, we find ourselves not in a science properly so called at all, but a collection of warm controversies on social questions.'[28] This raised serious questions as to the status of any of the present economists as true scientists. Harrison himself praised Mill, but decided that 'he is, in truth, not an economist at all', but a 'social philosopher – who in his great work deals with economic laws as part of and subordinate to social laws.' Mill therefore belongs with the classical economists of the eighteenth century, who recognised the importance of moral concerns in economic matters.

In 1861, Harrison made a close study of Adam Smith's *Wealth of Nations* and also, he commented acidly, 'of the economical system which pretended to be based on this'.[29] Smith's approach, he reported, 'formed the essence' of his social views throughout his life. But 'How utterly different,' he continued, 'is Adam Smith from all the herd of economists who call him their Father!' Smith was not an economist but a social philosopher whose main concern was 'the general good of the community, and especially the condition of the poor'. 'The so-called 'Political Economy' – the Abracadabra of McCulloch and Ricardo – is a delusion to which Adam Smith gave no countenance.'[30] *The Wealth of Nations*, Harrison claimed, concentrated on 'the prosperity of the community', not 'the accumulation of capital'. The process by which the 'narrower minds' of the present-day economists had 'distorted his theories' was 'very obvious'.

In the nineteenth century, Harrison considered, the moral dimension had become submerged in the pursuit of gain, at a time when morality was most needed. Harrison's insistence on a return to a more holistic approach to economic problems was paramount and was more an endorsement of Ruskin than of Comte, who never spelt out his organicist approach to the economy in Ruskin's both passionate and analytical terms.[31] Harrison's voice echoed Ruskin's frustration:

> All human acts being voluntary, economic acts depend on the whole of human motives. These are determined by the sum of all the human instincts acting together. No rules of human activity of any value can be constructed unless based on a complete consideration of man as a whole and his surroundings as a whole, that is, on a systematic social philosophy.[32]

Mill, whose emphasis on individuality and competition was at odds with his enlightened insistence on social reform, was seen by Harrison as an unwitting exemplar of Comte's teaching on the interrelationship between the industrial, the intellectual and the moral phenomena of society. Harrison commented on Mill:

> Neither in theory nor in practice has this powerful thinker, much less have his profound predecessors, Hume, Turgot, and Adam Smith, ever countenanced the notion that the laws of production, as a whole, can be studied or discovered apart from all the other laws of society, without any reference to the great social problems, by men who have no fixed notions upon them, or none but a few unverified hypotheses; who are without a system of politics, or a theory of human nature, or a philosophy of history, or a code of social duty.[33]

It was unfortunate, mourned Harrison, that 'This truth has not generally been grasped, and [that] the name of economist has been claimed by men whose qualifications are limited to some acquaintance with statistics and a talent for tabular statements.'[34] They believed economic questions to be 'fixed and defined' unlike other social problems. The result of this

form of 'spurious economics' was, in Harrison's view, 'a tissue of pretended laws of industry by which selfishness glosses over to itself the
frightful consequences of its own passions.'[35] The similarities with
Ruskin's thinking here were very obvious; and, although Harrison was
unable to extract any admission of an affinity with Comte from Ruskin,
Harrison's article did at least provoke a response. In a letter to Harrison,
dated 12 December 1865, Ruskin wrote praising its 'excellence'. He
added that he was 'heartily glad' that Harrison was working on the
subject. Yet Ruskin was not sure it was necessary to prove the 'limits' of
economic science. 'What I want to see insisted upon,' he explained, 'is
the fact that there can be no such science as long as wealth is an
undefined term.' He added that he would very much like to see 'a list of
the articles which a Utilitarian calls useful', and that, 'as soon as the
substance of wealth was so defined', a limited science would become
possible, but at present there was 'no science'.[36]

It seems that this rejoinder was not without its impact on Harrison, for
while later acknowledging Mill's obvious moral concerns for society,
Harrison, like Ruskin, began to challenge Mill's claims for a purely
economic science:

> About two thirds of Mr Mill's work on Political Economy is really a
> treatise on Social Philosophy. Professor Cairnes himself is, at least,
> as well known as a political and social thinker, as he is an
> Economist.[37] Both he and Mr Mill have lately written most valuable
> essays in this *Review* on the question of the Land. But the instructive
> lessons in Economy there given are given us from a political and
> social and not an exclusively economic point of view. Both of them
> write inspired by deep social purposes. They are not inspired by the
> Science of Wealth. Their aim is to show, not how the greatest
> amount of wealth can be produced, but the best state of society.[38]

Harrison defined economics as an organic phenomenon within the higher
organism of society, in refutation of a paper published two months earlier
by Professor Cairnes. This had acknowledged Comte's contribution to
the founding of social philosophy, but criticised his accusations that
political economy was 'not properly a science'.[39] Professor Cairnes, said
Harrison, was a man of 'high philosophic power', but he had
misunderstood the nature of Comte's definition of science. Comte

maintained that in the study of organic matter 'Science, throughout the whole range of its special analyses, must keep that idea of composite life steadily before it.' Even when science required the investigation of a single thread for a time, it must always be remembered that it was only one part of a vast complex system – 'The organic means something which has a complex function over and above that of any of its elements.'[40] This, maintained Harrison, was the 'golden rule' which was 'infringed by those Economists who propose to make a separate science of the Facts of Wealth' when the facts of wealth are indisputably an integral part of the facts of human action. Political economy was not a separate science but 'a branch of social science'.[41] Comte's position, Harrison concluded, was therefore incontestable as his views on political economy were not addressed in a few isolated pages on a fictitious science, but were contained within the entirety of his social system.

Having decided that there was no justification for considering the existing economy as an exact science, and having rejected the nineteenth-century interpretation of Smith's *Wealth of Nations* as spurious, Harrison next determined to turn his thoughts, after Ruskin, to the more urgent problem of 'the depressed state of the labouring masses'. The cause of this depression, he claimed, was the 'Devil's Gospel in Political Economy', which had been formed 'in order to justify and give system and force to all the other influences which crush the workmen'.[42] During the 1860s, Harrison therefore set about examining the conditions of working men and women through frequent visits to a wide variety of factories, going down coal-mines and attending Trades Union Congresses and meetings of Cooperative and Industrial Associations. From 1867–9 he was an active member of the Royal Commission on Trades Unions and, as he recorded, 'collected and tabulated an enormous amount of evidence on both sides'.[43] This work, which he considered as the practical and social dimension of the positivist moral creed, was a major occupation throughout his life. He sought thus to justify the claims of positivism and, although he was less utopian than either Ruskin or Comte, his approach displayed an ethical synthesis of Ruskin's humane form of Christianity with Comtean scientism.

Harrison, Ruskin and *Unto This Last*

Harrison's support for Ruskin's economic criticism was not without reservations, but Harrison clearly continued to identify Ruskin with the

positivist cause. In his biography of Ruskin, Harrison observed that
Ruskin's assault on the economy was not original. It followed the moral
outrage of Carlyle, Dickens, Kingsley, Maurice and the Christian Socialists,
as well as the later disaffection of Mill. Ruskin, however, attacked the same
target as did the positivists, albeit using different ammunition:

> He was saturated with the thought of Carlyle, and he was in close
> touch with Maurice and his friends, and both these men were in
> touch with the revolutionists and socialists whom the European
> events between 1848 and 1860 made familiar to thoughtful
> Englishmen. Ruskin was thus not by any means the first to throw
> doubts over the gospel of Ricardo and McCulloch. But he was no
> doubt the first to open fire on the very creed and decalogue of that
> gospel, and he certainly was the first to put those doubts and
> criticisms into trenchant literary form such as long stirred the
> general public as with a trumpet note.[44]

Harrison was of course referring to *Unto This Last,* which, whatever its
failings as pure economic doctrine, certainly provided a strong moral
corrective to economic orthodoxy. English positivism remained a fairly
esoteric philosophy more concerned with humanity than politics, but its
central tenets of socio-economic interaction and wise guidance were also
those of Ruskin. Comte's social goals, which he drew from Saint-Simon,
prefigured Ruskin's argument that 'There is no Wealth but Life.' Comte
had also used the medieval model as a paradigm of social and moral
organisation long before Ruskin, but hardly to the same extent. Ruskin's
strength lay, as Harrison said, less in originality of thought than in his
unique ability eloquently and ruthlessly to expose the abstract
motivation of political economy, and to emphasise the need for greater
state intervention for a better quality of life.

In his biography of Ruskin, Harrison stressed that these two points,
which were also made by Ruskin in *Unto This Last,* caused such a violent
outburst of opposition at the time of publication not because they were
new, but because Ruskin made them with such alarming clarity and
immediacy. Ruskin began *Unto This Last* with a statement of the
tendency of economists to pursue a course of social action irrespectively
of the influence of social affection. Commenting on this particular
passage, Harrison wrote:

This crucial truth, if we understand it as meaning that a science of wealth cannot be carried beyond a few corollary deductions of special application, drawn from a comprehensive system of social economy at large, that is, a true 'philosophy of society', had never before been stated so boldly and so dogmatically except by Auguste Comte.[45]

Harrison had no confusion about the source of Ruskin's inspiration, nor about his ability to make an impact where others had failed, commenting that 'Ruskin rushed at the problem wholly from the medieval, sentimental, and social point of view; but he grasped the root of the matter keenly, and argued it with his glowing style.'[46]

By the 1860s, the nineteenth-century interpretation of classical economy was becoming increasingly unacceptable to many thinkers, and Harrison was happy to stress that it was Ruskin, in *Unto This Last*, who had shattered a system of values which owed more to convention than to logic or ethics. When insisting that the 'conditions producing material wealth are inextricably intermingled with the general conditions of a healthy and happy body politic' Ruskin was not breaking new ground, but this 'central and saving truth' had 'never been illustrated with more incisive eloquence, nor enforced with a more intense conviction.'[47]

Influence is always a difficult thing to evaluate, but it is possible to draw further parallels between Ruskin and Harrison in terms of social and economic thought. One of these was the false view generally held by economists, of the nature of man and society. Harrison declared:

The laws of political economy are essentially abstract and hypothetical. In them man and society is conceived under conditions in which he is never actually found, and which indeed could not be actually realised whilst human nature remains what it is. Political economy professes to exhibit man as a producing animal exclusively, which in fact he never is, actuated. Social institutions generally, moral impulses altogether, by the conditions of the subject, are excluded. Otherwise political economy would be social or moral philosophy. Political economy, therefore, has two postulates – production as the sole end, competition as the sole motive – postulates of which the human race and its history can show no actual example.[48]

In *Unto This Last,* Ruskin had pronounced competition as 'the Laws of Death' and this endorsement by Harrison in 1865 was an indication of growing opposition to the individualistic doctrine of *laissez-faire.* The ordinary economists, wrote Harrison, have a 'very loosely conceived' general theory of society which they would be 'quite unable to prove'. Most of them, he insisted, 'are more or less conscious adherents of that perverse phase of Benthamism which places the roots of morality in the selfish instincts, and the basis of society on absolute non-interference.'

> With the moral doctrine of self-interest and the political doctrine of *laissez-faire* (vaguely understood) the pure statistician thinks himself prepared for investigating production. But the authors of these principles were not specialists. Their theories of self-interest and individualism were not based on systematic education, on thorough moral training, on entire social reconstruction. To leave all these to take care of themselves is to seize on the mischievous side of their doctrines alone.[49]

Ruskin had similarly attacked the classical economists' interpretation which assumed a predominately selfish instinct: 'All political economy founded on self-interest being but the fulfilment of that which once brought schism into the Policy of angels, and ruin into the Economy of Heaven.'[50] Harrison also echoed Ruskin's distaste for a crude interpretation of freedom, which was used as a justification for the pursuit of gain. He commented that 'to Bentham self-interest meant a very cultivated sense of duty', whereas the economist saw it in terms of 'a gross personal appetite'. Bentham had objected to government coercion, saying that men should be 'educated to justice', but the economists protested against state interference so that 'the instinct of gain' remained 'unchecked'.[51]

Reflecting on Ruskin in 1902, Harrison identified him with a form of socialism, also to be found in Comte, which was ridiculed and distrusted when *Unto This Last* was published in 1860:

> And now, as we look back across forty years upon these social Utopias which were met with such a storm of anger and ridicule, it is curious to note how many of them are familiar to our age. 'We are all Socialists now,' said a leading politician. And although Ruskin is not a Socialist – there is in all his social theories that

element of the ascendancy of the State, or of Society, over the
individual, the precedence of moral over material and practical
aims, the necessity for organisation of labour, and a moral and
spiritual control over self-interest, which is the fundamental
essence of Socialism.[52]

Ruskin's vision, decided Harrison, was a 'Sociocracy' in a Comtean sense,
and 'with Comte, [Ruskin] rejected both pure Democracy and abstract
Equality'. As to Ruskin's influence, Harrison was unequivocal:

His idea that the wise use of wealth, the distribution of products,
the health and happiness of the producers, come before the
accumulation of wealth, is a commonplace, not of philanthropists,
but of statesmen and journalists. His appeal for organisation of
industry, the suppression of public nuisances, and restriction of all
anti-social abuses, is a truism to the reformers of today.[53]

Harrison praised Ruskin's *Munera Pulveris* as far 'more constructive and
more comprehensive' than *Unto This Last*. But it similarly argued: 'that
the orthodox economists assumed men to be moved solely by interested
motives.' In fact, Harrison commented, men and their societies were
'exceedingly complex organisms', that can only be fully understood when
regarded as complex organisms.[54]

Ruskin had grasped the root of the matter, 'that there can be no
rational political economy apart from a comprehensive Sociology.' For
this task, wrote Harrison, Ruskin was 'utterly unfitted by his very scanty
learning, by habit, and by the cast of his mind'. 'Nothing less adequate
as a coherent and systematic synthesis of society can be imagined.' Yet
his influence was profound, for as a 'self-taught, desultory, impulsive
student of poetry and the arts', he had rushed in 'to achieve the mighty
task which Plato, Aristotle, Aquinas, Leibnitz undertook – and failed,
and which Locke, Kant, Hume, and Bentham touched only in sections.'[55]
Unto This Last, in its insistence on moral and economic interaction, was,
in Harrison's estimation, the ultimate proof that Ruskin and Comte had
very similar aims.[56]

Harrison on Ruskin's Other Social Writing
On Ruskin's other works of social criticism, Harrison was equally honest

in his assessment. The letters that Ruskin published under the title of *Time and Tide* in 1867, contained, in Harrison's view, a mass of 'startling proposals and sweeping anathemas'.[57] But they contained also many 'noble, wise, and memorable sayings', such as the advantages of wise mastership, and gradual rather than violent social change. These 'social Utopias', as Harrison called them, were 'the passionate sermons of a religious enthusiast'.[58]

Ruskin's practical philanthropy was no less vigorous than his written works of social criticism. Harrison recalled Ruskin's biographer, Cook, saying that 'his [Ruskin's] pensioners were numbered by hundreds; his charities, if somewhat indiscriminate, were as delicate as they were generous.'[59] He gave liberally to schools, colleges, and to individual students. He pioneered the opening of a model tea-shop and organised gangs of street cleaners for the relief of the unemployed. He also gave to Octavia Hill[60] 'the means of managing house property on the principle of helping tenants to help themselves.' His philanthropy was tireless: 'He thought no trouble too great to encourage a pupil or befriend the fallen'[61] and in the distribution of his personal wealth he was equally generous.[62]

Fors Clavigera received a great deal of attention from Harrison, who claimed it to be the most 'human document' of anything Ruskin ever wrote and 'one of the most original, most frank, most tantalising in all modern literature'.[63] He provided further evidence of its very mixed reception upon publication:

> A book so mysterious has been judged with curiously different minds. Nothing 'so notable,' said Carlyle. 'Watery verbiage,' said the *Spectator*. 'Studies in reviling,' said a fine poet. 'Ruskin's "Hamlet" and also his "Apocalypse",' said his biographer in the 'Men of Letters' series; and the editor himself now cites and adopts that judgement. Whatever else it may be, this huge book of 650,000 words written month by month between 1871 and 1884, is the man, John Ruskin's self.[64]

The first number of *Fors Clavigera,* published in 1871, coincided with Ruskin's famous experiment in bookselling in a village in Kent. Harrison noted that: 'It was not advertised, there was no discount, no abatement, the price was sevenpence, afterwards raised to tenpence.'[65] And yet, Harrison recorded, 'in spite of these obstacles', thousands of each number

were sold, which was an 'extraordinary tribute to the author's popularity'.[66] Ruskin came to see that 'to publish his writings only in forms
which no moderate purses could meet was to exclude the very people
whom he most desired to reach.'[67]

Harrison confessed that, despite being one who 'deeply enjoyed *Fors*,
and, perhaps, somewhat excessively rated it as Ruskin's central work', he
did not read the letters as they were published, but read the edition
published in 1896 in four volumes. This version, he considered
preferable to the 'unadulterated torrent' published later, which was
'overlaid with cuttings from the *Daily Telegraph*' and 'stuffed with silly
letters from anonymous correspondents and the gossip of aesthetic old
ladies'.[68] He thought that *Fors* should not be read consecutively as a
whole, which would be like trying to 'read through the *Encyclopedia
Britannica* volume by volume'. It was rather a book to 'dip into' and 'to
take up in a mood as desultory as that of the writer'. If opened in this
'fortuitous way', Harrison wrote, it proved 'stimulating' and 'devotional'
in spirit. He was, however, full of praise for the library edition, and
admired especially Cook's introduction to volume 27 for its insights into
the complex web of interrelated ideas underpinning Ruskin's social
criticism.

In his own biography of Ruskin, Harrison commented on the
'fantastic, wayward, egoistic' nature of *Fors,* which strays at times from
the paths of 'rational discourse'.[69] But, he observed, 'If we look calmly at
these ninety-six Letters taken together, we shall see a very definite
purpose and plan of action running through the whole.' *Fors* remained
Ruskin's 'essential gospel or message to a perverse world'. To understand
this gospel, it was necessary to appreciate the perversities and nuances of
Ruskin's language, where 'The tone is at heart that of Swift in *Lilliput*,
or of Carlyle in *Sartor*, or of Thackeray in the *Book of Snobs*.' In substance,
Fors is 'a satire on our modern vices, ignorances and vulgarities' but
written in the form of 'child's play, badinage, musical raillery, and
courteous irony'.[70]

For Harrison, *Fors* was a 'satire on modern life', with thoughts
apparently 'wildly incongruous' until the 'link of ideas is perceived'. It was
written with a 'definite scheme of ideas and a real working aim', as
Ruskin's 'indignation at the fraudulent character of so much in modern
trade deepened at last into a judgement on modern trade itself as criminal
and degrading.'[71] When he wrote *Fors* Ruskin was, as Harrison noted,

becoming very disillusioned, yet amongst the 'thousand dark allusions'
there were 'fulminating flashes of lurid light'.[72] There was also a great deal
of humanity, which was soon to find its rightful audience among the
labouring classes, and an affinity with later socialist thought. But, as
Harrison noted, Ruskin was 'never a political revolutionist; he was a
spiritual and moral reformer', who, despite many 'follies and blunders' in
Fors, had reached 'curious coincidences with one of whom he knew
nothing'.[73] Because of the importance of *Fors Clavigera* as a social
document, Harrison was keen to draw analogies with Comte. Ruskin, he
wrote, had been called a follower of Carlyle and likened to Tolstoy, Swift
and Rousseau; but 'in a great many judgements of history, and in most of
his schemes of a social Utopia', his views were very similar to those of
Comte, 'of whom he spoke with abhorrence and contempt'. And although
Ruskin was in many ways violently opposed to positivist thinking,
Harrison recalled that he himself 'often had occasion to remind [Ruskin],
in public and in private', that most of his social doctrines had been
anticipated by Auguste Comte.[74]

In fact, much of Ruskin's intolerance of Positivism was based less on
Comte's social doctrines than on his denial of Christianity as a basis for
morality. This was amply illustrated in the correspondence between
Harrison and Ruskin, which was precipitated by Ruskin's curt reference to
Harrison in *Fors Clavigera*. In letter 66, Ruskin had mentioned 'Mr
Frederick Harrison's gushing article on Humanity, in the *Contemporary
Review*',[75] and in letter 69 he added that 'What Mr Harrison calls the
Religion of humanity' – ought to be called "the religion of Manity", (for
the English use of the word "humane" is continually making him confuse
benevolence with religion).'[76]

Harrison's official response to these accusations was published in the
Fortnightly Review in July 1876.[77] Ruskin, Harrison wrote, was rebuking
him for 'believing with Auguste Comte that the human race is worthy
of our regard, that it is growing wiser, stronger, nobler' instead of, as
Ruskin claimed, being 'crazy and utterly vile', an opinion for which he
had no scientific evidence. Harrison continued: if Ruskin would but read
Comte thoroughly, Ruskin would realise the rightness of Comte's
thinking. Indeed, Comte acknowledged the 'spiritual meaning of
medieval art' not only as thoroughly as did Ruskin, but long before him.
As to humanity, Harrison argued that Ruskin did not understand how
the positivists define the term. Ruskin claimed that 'an aggregate of men

is a mob' but this was surely not so, continued Harrison – a family or an army is not a mob. Where 'men work and live together gregariously, in a disciplined and organic way, they are not a mob', any more than Ruskin's St George's company was a mob. It was a question of language.

Harrison also attacked Ruskin's denial of the evolutionary progress of mankind as further evidence of his unwarranted pessimism. Science was evolutionary and progressive, while Christianity, Harrison claimed, was neither. And while Ruskin was right to say that science without religion was immoral, he did not trouble to understand that Comte, although not a Christian, was both scientific and deeply moral in his teaching. Was not Ruskin, in denying the 'goodness and wisdom of man' also denying 'the goodness and wisdom of God'? There was no merit in both rejecting tradition and at the same time resisting the progress of thought. Nor was it acceptable to follow Rousseau's example and to 'build an Utopia with eloquent phrases', manipulating the name of God to whatever convenient argument.

If Harrison never fully agreed with Ruskin, then it is equally true that Ruskin never fully agreed with Harrison, or indeed, made the effort to do so. He warned Harrison in 1875 that he would be featured in *Fors*, writing: 'You will have to answer for your creed or else let it be what you call "reviled" to an extent which – all I can say is – I wouldn't stand if I were you – but then I'm not you.' Ruskin maintained that he did not attack Harrison's beliefs as such but his 'mere impertinence and falsening of language' – not for 'professing Positivism but for not knowing the meaning of the word "Positive."'[78] And in a letter following Harrison's essay in the *Fortnightly Review*, Ruskin wrote that, if Harrison continued to decline a debate about 'words', there was little point in their discussing anything. Harrison was 'talking nonsense without knowing it'. How could he claim that Ruskin was using his 'power against Humanity', when the second article in his creed for the Companions of St George was: 'I believe in the Nobleness of Human Nature'?[79] Not surprisingly, Harrison's relationship with Ruskin was very fragile at this point, as a letter from Ruskin two days later indicated. 'I had no conception,' wrote Ruskin, 'of your depth of feeling'; but Harrison had none of his 'modes of using language' and there was therefore 'extreme difficulty' in their 'conversing at all'! Ruskin continued to wonder how with the 'flattering feelings of regard' Harrison had always shown, he never either wrote to him 'as a friend' or attacked him 'as a foe'. If

Harrison considered some of his sayings in *Fors* as 'so deadly and blasphemous', why had he not either supported him in his 'war with all the iniquity of England' or corrected him? After all, Ruskin concluded, 'We *can't* both be right.'[80]

It was a measure of Harrison's admiration for Ruskin, however, that Harrison was not deterred by these retorts. He saw obvious differences in the characters and ideology of Ruskin and Comte, yet believed that they were 'substantially agreed in many of their views', including their 'disbelief in all that is offered by modern industrialism, by political economy, by the emancipation of women, by democracy, by parliamentarism, by the dogmatism of scientific hypotheses'. There were definite parallels to be drawn between 'the poetic, sentimental, metaphysical' nature of *Fors* and 'the systematic science and the historic religion of the *Positive Polity'*.[81] It could be argued that it would be too easy to prove Harrison's point by careful selection of Comtist philosophy. The parallels with Ruskin were, however, very evident and central, which is why Harrison was so keen to make the analogy. Ruskin should not have objected so strongly. Certainly, many of Harrison's points of comparison with Comte, far from detracting from Ruskin's credibility as a social commentator, actually gave him more weight. Compared with some other contemporary biographers of Ruskin, such as Marshall Mather (1890) and Collingwood (1893), Harrison was more aware of the political significance of Ruskin's intellectual vision and more acutely conscious of his role in the history of social reform. And on the question of economics, only Hobson, who was eminently qualified to do so, gave a closer analysis of the value of Ruskin's insights.

The Comtist Utopia

One factor which confirms an intellectual concordance between Ruskin and Comte was their common opposition to existing industrial values and their advocacy of utopian alternatives. Both also chose utopias which rejected outright democracy in favour of a reliance on a Platonic-style ruling elite for moral and political guidance.

In an article published in 1869 entitled 'The Comtist Utopia',[82] Leslie Stephen observed that the Comtists 'represent certain tendencies in moral and social questions, the importance of which it is difficult to over-estimate.'[83] He outlined some of the central tenets of Comte's Utopia, where unpaid patricians would be required to 'regard themselves as labouring for the good of humanity', where wealth would 'be deprived of its selfish character', and where there would be 'a new chivalry', directed at 'righting the wrongs of the oppressed'.[84] Apart from the unquestionable altruism behind this ideal world, its dominant characteristic, according to Stephen, was that it 'reverses so much of what we have been accustomed to consider as progress'. Like Ruskin's Guild of St George, Comte's ideal society took its inspiration from the past 'in spirit medieval, but purged from the cruelty of Feudalism'.[85] Stephen then touched on a subject very close to Ruskin's heart; the division of labour:

> Some of the most prominent evils of modern society centre round the increasing tendency to minute sub-division of labour. The world is like one of those huge manufactories in which an artisan passes his whole life in performing some one trifling operation. When a human being becomes nothing but a machine for sharpening the points of pins, his intellectual and moral powers are necessarily stunted.[86]

The destructive nature of this process, Stephen wrote, extended into the realm of political economy, for 'the man who is sharpening pins all day finds it difficult to realise the degree to which he is labouring for the good of mankind.' He could not easily identify with the needs of society. He was simply earning a living and 'nothing in his work or in his education tends to raise him to a higher point of view.'[87]

Stephen then mocked the economists, who interpreted this selfish instinct in terms of an involuntary 'vast cooperative society'. And, in a direct reflection of Ruskinian thought, Stephen added that 'cooperation is necessarily imperfect – so long as we are forced to depend upon the purely personal desire of acquiring wealth.'[88] This was also a sentiment endorsed by Harrison. However, Harrison's modern biographer comments that he was 'even-handed about cooperatives – he appreciated their utility, but he pointed also to their failure to reach the poorest, who could no more afford shares in them than unskilled workers could afford union dues'.[89] Ruskin, despite his organic approach to society, never saw this sort of cooperation as the answer to anything. He referred to it as 'cooperation among rascals', which was 'essentially fermentation and putrefaction – not cooperation.'[90] Ruskin's type of organicism was based upon fellowship, and the higher collectivist principles necessary to the improvement of the quality of life.

Writing some ten years later, Stephen reflected those Ruskinian aspirations as also central to the Comtist Utopia:

> When the new regime is introduced the cooperation will be consciously carried out, and the happiness of mankind become the object for which each individual is knowingly labouring, instead of being, as at present, a collateral and incidental result, imperfectly secured at best.[91]

Comte was less dogmatic than Ruskin, but then Ruskin's problem, according to Harrison, was his moral intractability, caused by his isolation in childhood and a 'saturation of the mind by a mystical theology, which taught him to treat all things as *absolutely* good, or *absolutely* evil, or *absolutely false*'. This, wrote Harrison, was unrealistic, 'in a world where humanity can know nothing but *relative* truths, and can hope for nothing but *relative* good'.[92] As he tried to explain in a letter to Ruskin:

> As to the word 'Positive', nothing can be more philosophical and accurate than the meaning assigned to it by Comte. With him it always means that which is laid down by logical methods from the best obtainable evidence. He never uses positive for absolute truth, or absolute knowledge. The distinctive mark of his teaching is that all our ideas are relative. He does not put Positivism for wisdom, or knowledge, or truth. It is never more than what we lay down as practical data to act upon – from scientific reasoning upon our observations.[93]

Ruskin's absolutist moral stance led him to intolerance of men such as Comte and Mill, although all three had some points in common. In a letter to Harrison dated July 1876, Ruskin wrote that he could 'show any man of average intellect who will learn to read accurately, that this entire school of modern rationalists is a mere fungoid growth of semi-education provoked by facility of printing into idle talk.' He quoted 'Stuart Mill especially', who 'measured by any man trained firmly in the laws of either mental or verbal logic, is a mere loathsome cretin.' Indeed, he was 'as disquieting in the impudence of his half-formed jolterhead as any of the goitered idiots of Savoy'.[94] A week later Ruskin was prompted by

Harrison to moderate his language somewhat, writing: 'Had I known Mill was your personal friend, I would never have said what I did.' But Ruskin obviously did not change his opinion, as he repeated at the end of his letter that he could actually prove Mill to be 'cretinous' and that Harrison was in no position either to judge or to condemn any of his words 'having at present no conception of the manner of their weighing'.[95]

Ruskin, in fact, had always been rather harsh in his judgement of Mill who, like himself, had been influenced by Carlyle but interpreted him in different ways.[96] Mill was as concerned as Ruskin for quality of life and the promotion of cooperative patterns of labour, but Mill's nervousness over the loss of personal freedom led him to reject the hierarchical organism favoured by Carlyle and Ruskin, and to a certain extent by Comte.[97] Indeed, in some ways Ruskin was closer to Mill than to Carlyle, for he was wary of Carlyle's 'heroes' and used the medieval model more as a metaphor for interdependence than as an authority. Ruskin also chose, unlike Carlyle, to attack political economy on its own terms.

Where Comtist and Ruskinian thought converged, in opposition to Mill, was on the subject of non-intervention. Mill's attitude was increasingly unacceptable to Harrison, as to many other reformers. Harrison exclaimed in 1869 that 'the utter want of organisation in England' was a 'great evil', yet every attempt to remedy this defect was 'met by an outcry against the dangers of centralisation, over-government, and bureaucracy, and the tyranny of the majority'. Even Mill was so keen to preserve 'individual eccentricities' that he was suspicious of state intervention, and always keen to extol the 'merits of variety as compared with uniformity'. The Comtist school, as Leslie Stephen noted, reacted strongly against this sentiment: 'Individualism' was their 'bugbear', as the oppression of the individual was that of their opponents.[98]

Harrison's solution to these moral and social problems was the adoption of a Comtean-style, practical form of moral philosophy, which would not concentrate on how to produce more, but on how to produce in a more humane manner. In the Comtist Utopia, 'Industry must be moralised.' As Stephen indicated:

> The duty of the Positivist priesthood will be to inculcate a loftier mode of morality, to encourage capitalists to view themselves as public functionaries, and to impress upon all men that the direct

object of their labour should be the good of society at large, and their wages not a remuneration for their labour, but the means of enabling them to do their duty.[99]

Comte's view of society was that it would gradually evolve, in a Spencerian fashion,[100] toward some distant utopian goal. Ruskin had tried to realise this goal in his own way through his practical experiments; but, concluded Harrison, St George was 'an experiment impossible to classify'. It could not be held 'in comparison with any known type of social utopia'.

> It was to be fervently religious, without any consistent religious creed except a Theism, half Biblical, half artistic. It was Socialist, in that it was to divert all production from a personal to a public use; but then it preserved and stimulated the institution of hereditary property and the ascendancy of the orders who owned it.[101]

It was also, Harrison continued, 'wildly anarchic' and yet 'inculcated obedience'. These contradictions would not be encountered in Comte's Utopia, for, although some of the aspirations of positivism might seem doubtful, its attractions were easy to understand. Stephen commented that:

> It [Comte's ideal society] is a protest against two tendencies: against those who would improve society by trying to go backwards and revive obsolete forms of faith: and more emphatically against those who consider the present anarchical condition of the world to be its final and permanent state, and render chaos still more chaotic by preaching individualism and the denial of all authority as the ultimate gospel. Positivists would restore authority, but would found it on reason unreservedly.[102]

Harrison, Ruskin and Authority

The location of authority was a key concern of both Ruskin and Comte and the spiritual power which both thinkers would invest in their leaders was seen by Harrison as a common feature. But although Ruskin's insistence on government by an enlightened bureaucracy and the guidance of the workforce through the voluntary goodwill of captains of industry was very close to Comte, it was much more easily accommodated within the socialist/collectivist philosophy. Ruskin's authoritarianism rested in a belief in fundamental Christian fellowship, tolerance and interdependence, but Comte's advocacy of a form of scientific absolutism, which demanded uncritical loyalty from its followers, was viewed with suspicion. Harrison was eager to make the positivist position more acceptable.

Writing on 'The Revival of Authority' in 1873, he considered the two apparently antithetic principles of 'personal Authority' and 'popular Will'.[103] 'For ages,' he wrote, 'the two have waged eternal war; yet neither can destroy the other, and utterly overcome it.' 'Every party is animated by one or the other of the maxims – the only good government is that of the best men: or else by this other maxim – the only just government is that of the national will.'[104] No party, Harrison claimed, 'equally professes both'. Rather, they spent their time opposing the opposite principle. The positivist however, sought an accommodation of the two principles. Both personal authority and public opinion were valid principles that could work in harmony. They might be rival doctrines but could they not also be 'complementary parts of a single principle'? The true expression of the general will could prove to be systematic government by an educated aristocracy which was the only effective kind of republic. Harrison thus concluded that the present political dilemma was not a question of personal authority versus general will, but the need to establish 'Authority without oppression upon a Public Opinion without democracy.'[105]

This was indeed the kind of socialism to which Ruskin also looked: cooperation for the common welfare, but imposed by a hereditary aristocracy and upheld by the voluntary actions of caring employers and landowners. There was to be no 'mob rule' or nationalisation of land or capital. Reform was to come instead from a moral appeal to the hearts and minds of the ruling classes, who were currently riding on the backs of the labour force. 'The socialist,' Ruskin wrote, 'seeing a strong man oppress a weak one, cries out – "Break the strong man's arms"; but I say "Teach him to use them to better purpose."'[106] Harrison, via Comte, had very similar theories on the need to moralise the 'captains of industry', but Harrison's ethic, unlike that of Ruskin, was not located in Christianity, which, for Harrison, had not proved equal to the task of addressing practical industrial problems. 'What prospect is there,' he wrote, 'of Christianity really dealing with the great industrial problem? It has nothing to say, except that queer bit of affectation called Christian Socialism which merely means a sentimental leaning to Socialism from the point of view of the Sermon on the Mount.'[107] Christian Socialism, claimed Harrison, had done nothing practical. The maxims of Comte were very different: ' Know, in order to foresee, and do that in order to provide.' 'Act through affection, and think in order to act.'[108] But this could only flourish under wise leadership and the re-assertion of moral authority: 'Some brain must guide, some pair of hands must drag, some opinion must overmaster all others, or the mob evaporates and disintegrates.'[109]

But the alliance of Christian orthodoxy with radical politics was not Harrison's only objection to Socialism. Positivism, he wrote, was 'in a large and true sense of the word, itself an organised Socialism – but Socialism with a difference.'[110] Current Socialism, he wrote, was considered by positivists to be 'essentially right in idea', but 'limited and incomplete',[111] in that it left the social organism out of its account of society and placed the blame for all society's ills at the feet of the capitalist. This was short-sighted, Harrison continued, for society, in order to operate effectively, needed men with a 'genius for business' to control capital. If business were the property of the state under the management of a government department, would it function any more liberally than it did at present, or would it simply replace one kind of tyranny with another? 'The humblest workman would feel the despotism of the State quite as much as the great capitalist whom he is to depose.'[112] A new society, if it was to have a fair chance, Harrison stated, required 'an entire reconstruction of our whole social system and all our principles of public life,' and that was its whole point. 'Socialism offers no such fundamental social regeneration. Positivism does.'[113] It addressed the 'subtle and complex unity' of 'human nature and society', which 'can only be radically regenerated by a complete treatment of their needs'. The 'religion of Humanity – will prove equal to the mighty task of regenerating even our corrupt industrial system,' because, unlike Socialism, its methods were 'human, practical, and scientifically true'.[114]

Like Ruskin, Harrison emphasised a form of society as an organic whole and he exhibited much of Ruskin's exasperation in trying to illustrate that even such a system based on mutual interdependence would require leaders to initiate programmes of action. He quoted 'extreme cases' of disciplined societies, such as an army, where the 'organic action' of the whole could not function without a person 'from whom the action radiates'. There was no 'collective brain' to direct operations. Public life with its 'polls, assemblies, committees, and boards', representing so many different wills and opinions had blinded people to the basic inner truth that 'all combined action of many implies a personal organ as its agent'.[115]

Opposition to total democracy was pursued by Harrison in section two of his argument for 'The Revival of Authority', which amply illustrated the influence of Comtean paternalism on his thinking. In 'The Principle of Opinion',[116] Harrison turned to the 'rival doctrine' that 'government must spring from the will of the people' in which, he maintained, we would find the same 'eternal verities mingled with the same dangerous consequences'. He quoted the Paris Commune of 1871 as an example of the failure of the democratic method of government. It was an example of 'the inherent fatuity of mere democracy',[117] but it was not the only example. From 1848 to the present day, wrote Harrison, the same thing has been 'shown in fifty movements and on fifty battlefields', and what the present generation was 'slowly learning' was that the inevitable social revolution will not have democracy as its method.[118]

What then was to be learned from this? Should people, asked Harrison, lose faith in public opinion and succumb to a form of 'benevolent despotism'? In an advanced society, 'force becomes less and less efficient of good'. It is too brutal for complex and intelligent communities, where the way men live and interact is 'everything' and the 'particular acts they are compelled by the magistrate to do, or abstain from' are 'almost nothing'. A healthy state of society was dependent on the good character of its citizens – 'In the infinite complexity of modern life, the intelligent, disciplined cooperation of citizens makes up ninety-nine parts of their social action.'[119] In such a society, the role of the statesman would be solely 'to harmonise' this heightened awareness of cooperation. Public opinion would thus be 'the essence of political life', and any attempt to impose a single will or mind on that opinion will reduce society to a 'discordant mass'.[120]

This was why, in Harrison's view, socialism and communism would not work. Advocates of both imagined that, if they gained control of the machinery of the state, 'they could suppress poverty, annihilate misery, and reward merit'. Their error was in their 'ignorance of the infinitesimal power of Government to supersede the individual wills of the citizens' and also of the 'nullity of any authority that runs counter to the opinions around it'. Great rulers had always been to a great extent 'organs' of the State, as much the 'expression of their collective will as they have been sources of it'. The despotic and the communistic theory of society thus derive from the same fallacy – 'that of attributing to government a function which in modern societies it is utterly powerless to fulfil.'[121] This was an impressive analysis of some of the later problems that faced 'command economics' and 'command politics' in peacetime.

Public opinion was, Harrison insisted, not to be confused with democracy. In democracy, 'each unit is strictly assumed to be the equivalent of every other'; but 'public opinion abhors this fatal mathematical equality.' It was, 'on the contrary eminently elastic' and could tolerate leadership from its most capable citizens. So what appeared to be 'a stumbling rush toward Democracy' was in fact progress 'towards a higher sense of Public Opinion'.[122]

Ultimately, Harrison hoped for 'The Reconciliation', accommodating harmoniously the two apparently antithetic principles of authority and public opinion: both 'real leadership' and 'genuine consent'.[123] 'All is lost if we leave rule to numbers, all is lost if we ignore numbers.' It was a total misconception that the inevitable expansion of public opinion precluded the ascendancy of the individual, leaving no alternative but 'simple democracy'. Great statesmen were needed to be 'the servants of the people' but not 'the instrument of their orders'.[124] The statesman should be 'for ever modifying public opinion' and be 'for ever modified by it'. He should not have to win the vote of an absolute majority, as the strength of public opinion was not measured numerically. Most significant changes of history demonstrated 'a resolute few asserting the ascendancy of conviction'. To avoid the risk of oppression, leaders must never be sustained by military muscle nor entrusted with the power of taxation. Parliament must remain 'an intense modifying force, ready at all times to be the sovereign expression of the national will.'[125]

Harrison concluded his argument with a Ruskinian plea for improved standards of education, to 'raise up' the 'organic conviction of the active citizens', so that a harmony could be achieved between wise moral government and genuine freedom of speech. Once people realised that was possible, he decided, they would shed their distrust of personal authority and realise that wise leadership meant no more than 'the organ and expression of intelligent popular conviction'.[126]

Harrison thus reinforced Comte's paternalism with dismissal of its undemocratic implications. But despite this plea for authority, he did not invest his leaders with as much power as Carlyle would have allowed, and in this Harrison came closer once more to Ruskin, whose opposition to total democracy was underpinned by the same sentiments, but derived from Plato rather than from Comte.[127] Ruskin believed that competition had destroyed Christian morality and his wish to see lost values reinstated rested on a recognition of the need for wise leadership, especially in business matters. The fundamental paradox of *laissez-faire* economics, whereby Adam Smith's 'natural order' was interpreted by industrialists as their right to rig the market in their own favour was not lost on Ruskin. Harrison, moreover, insisted that the principle of *laissez-faire* was an ideological impossibility anyway, because ultimately some one person was making the decisions: 'What is done in the collective name of the body is the work of one, or, at least, each substantive part is the work of one.'[128] Although coming from different directions, both Ruskin and Harrison were essentially in agreement, not only on the rightness but also upon the inevitability of authority. In Harrison's words:

> The convenient sophism that the people are not to govern directly, but through representatives, that they are not to be ministers, but only to choose ministers, that they are not to carry out measures, but merely to dictate them, and to initiate them, does not come to much. They who dictate the Government, govern; and they who are to originate all acts of authority, do not much differ from being its masters.[129]

Harrison clearly identified with Ruskin's concept of an organic society: 'Every collective group, large or small, can only work through personal organs; that is round centres organically, and not atom by atom co-equally.'[130] But Harrison's adherence to Comtean scientific positivism allied him with a small esoteric group, who emphasised social and moral rather than political remedies, thus precluding them from any real political engagement. Indeed, the English positivists, who enjoyed considerable intellectual respect among the Labour movement between 1861 and 1881, largely because of their influence on the firm establishment of Trade Unionism, later lost that influence.[131] By 1880, the positivists became aware that their relationship with Trade Union leaders was fragile and that the positivists' status as champions of the working classes was being increasingly challenged by the Socialists. In fact, as Royden Harrison commented, positivism actually 'contributed to the Socialist revival of the eighties'.[132] Most of the Socialists were influenced by its moralising centrality, an area in which they found Marx to be deficient, but the average working man was deterred by the elitist intellectualism of positivism and its lack of practicality. Positivism could not help the ordinary worker and they looked therefore for someone who could speak to them directly in terms they understood.

Ruskin provided the necessary compromising formula. In the period of economic depression at the end of the nineteenth century, Ruskin's call for a broad form of Christian cooperation, delivered in his inspiring homiletic tones, ultimately found its appeal in a working-class audience. It found in him a form of spiritual guidance to temporal problems, unfettered by doctrine and dogma. Ruskin's obvious paternalism was not a deterrent. It was not treated with the same suspicion as Comtean scientific authority or Carlylean hero-worship and it was accepted by many, who would not normally subscribe to such anti-democratic sentiments, that Ruskin's rejection of pure democracy was based on the sincere belief that it would do nothing to improve the degrading conditions and lifestyle of the working man.

Ruskin's social thought was therefore close to positivism in many ways, but more appealing and accessible to the working classes, who looked for something more than 'cold philosophy'. They looked for something closer to a new religion. Many dissident intellectuals, among whom Harrison can certainly be counted, saw themselves as deeply religious, but free from what they considered to be the egotistic individualism of Christianity with its emphasis on personal salvation. Although they interpreted their faith in various ways, they were all in agreement that the time was ripe for a new form of religion, which would combine fundamental Christian ethics with the intellectualism of modern science.[133] For Harrison, if not for the working man, positivism (despite some of its absurdities) answered this prescription. It emphasised the centrality of evolution and gradual improvement in any programme of social reform, because scientific discovery itself was gradual and progressive. As Vogeler has indicated, Harrison thought that Ruskin, like Comte, offered a new non-religious social faith.[134]

Ruskin, however, remained immune. Again in 1884, he advised Harrison to concentrate on social reform instead of wasting his time with positivism, which as far as Ruskin was concerned should be called 'meology', for what, he wrote, 'is Positivism but the Everlasting me'? It would be far more useful, he said, if Harrison would help him 'finish up usury – or smoke – or poison – or dynamite or some much lowlier nuisance'.[135] Harrison, however, continued in his attempts to draw analogies between Ruskin and Comte. That indicated Harrison's own confusion over the question of influence. He clearly attributed his crisis of faith to a combination of dissatisfaction with the growing erosion and fragmentation of traditional belief and his association with Auguste Comte, but the nature of his subsequent attack on political economy drew closer parallels with Ruskin than with Comte.[136] And, of course, Harrison knew Ruskin personally and was sufficiently inspired by him to write his biography.

Although Ruskin claimed to be opposed to a religion of humanity, Harrison quoted him in *Praeterita* as saying 'The only constant form of pure religion was in useful work, faithful love, and stintless charity.' 'That,' exulted Harrison, 'is the essence of the religion of Humanity.'[137] And it was here, whatever their other differences, that the real synthesis of interest lay between Harrison and Ruskin: in a mutual desire to see much-needed social and economic reform, no longer underpinned by pious platitudes and political cant, but by humane and intelligent moral guidance in a hierarchically structured organism. Writing about him in 1902, Harrison commented that so much of what Ruskin had written forty years previously was now the concern of contemporary reformers:

So is much of what [Ruskin] said about national education long before Mr. Forster, about old-age pensions long years before Mr Chamberlain, about the housing of the working classes long years before the Statutes, Conferences, and Royal Commissions of our own generation. Read all he says as to the necessity of training schools, technical schools, State supervision of practical and physical education, help to the unemployed, provision for the aged, the recovery of waste lands, the qualified ownership of the soil – read all these glancings of a keen and pure soul from heaven

to earth on a multitude of things social and humane, and you will
recognise how truly John Ruskin forty years ago was a pioneer of
the things which today the best spirits of our time so earnestly
yearn to see.[138]

From being a pre-committed disciple of Comte, Harrison ultimately
moved closer to Ruskin's thinking.

6

HOBSON, RUSKIN AND
NEW LIBERALISM

The confusion wrought in the minds of readers by the failure to find in any of his works a full application of his principle has been responsible for an unjust disparagement of the truly scientific service rendered by Ruskin towards the foundation of social-economics.[1]   J.A. Hobson (1914)

John Atkinson Hobson (1858–1940) was, like Harrison, heavily influenced by Ruskin. Although there were some points of departure, Hobson was indebted to Ruskin for two basic principles. Firstly, for the principle of humanism, which underpinned Ruskin's economic critique and from which Hobson came to believe that all scientific principles should be subservient to ethical ones. And secondly, he was also heavily influenced by Ruskin's organicist vision of society, which prompted Hobson to redefine his own concepts away from individualism toward a more collectivist ideal of communal welfare. Michael Freeden comments: 'When Hobson saluted Ruskin, in his later thorough study, it was in order to secure the ultimate seal of authentication for his own qualitative assessment of human life and activity.'[2] And John Allett observes: 'Hobson endorsed Ruskin's call to put commerce on an ethical basis and the attendant claim that economics should be an instrument of that purpose.'[3] As a highly respected intellectual, who sought fundamentally an accommodation of socialism and liberalism, Hobson's reputation is a crucial factor in any assessment of Ruskin's influence. It highlights those areas where Hobson considered Ruskin's thinking was more acceptable than that of Marx, who had (in Hobson's view) underplayed the moral dimension in his critique of capitalism, and more relevant than that of Mill, who was never enthusiastic about abandoning the principle of competition, and who saw in state socialism a threat to individual liberty.

Hobson's Background

Hobson was born in Derby, in 1858, at the high point of Victorian confidence in its industrial supremacy. His family and location were very middle class, and he was, he later wrote, 'favourably situated for a complacent acceptance of the existing social order'.[4] He did not observe any significant social unrest in his youth, commenting that 'There was no serious attempt of the working classes to push their economic or social claims upon the upper classes.'[5] He did however, feel that 'all was not right in this best of all possible worlds', when he saw the poverty-stricken families at 'the bottom of the social-industrial ladder', most of them Irish, and their condition generally attributed to 'their shiftless, thriftless, reckless way of living', rather than to socio-economic inadequacies.[6]

In this 'placid epoch', Hobson wrote of the 1860s and 1870s, politics had 'little social or economic significance'. No serious attempt was made to interfere with 'competitive capitalism' and, although there was a good deal of 'loose philanthropic talk' about the plight of the working classes, there was no movement to improve their condition through governmental action. Thus, although he was brought up in an atmosphere of 'active liberalism', he had no idea 'that politics had anything to do with industry or standards of living'. Liberalism was restricted under Gladstone to issues of 'franchise, education, public economy, and foreign policy', and hardly touched on the more serious economic issues. This '*laisser-faire* attitude of the Liberalism of the sixties and seventies' was the basis of his early unquestioning acceptance of 'the gulf between politics and workaday life'.[7]

Hobson's strict orthodox evangelical upbringing was another formative influence in the moulding of his later views on social issues. Like both Ruskin and Harrison, dissatisfaction with orthodox Christianity turned Hobson away from church ritual, in his case toward a form of humanism brought on, he explained, by 'an intellectual failure to reconcile tenets I was brought up to reverence with the dictates of my personal conscience'.[8] He observed the 'social cleavage' in Derby between Church and Dissent, which on the whole meant between 'rich and poor', and this factor, allied with his own growing distaste for 'the doctrines of atonement and of everlasting punishment for unrepentant sinners',[9] confirmed him, by 1876 when he entered Oxford, as a religious heretic.[10]

He gained an added awareness of socio-economic distinctions, almost by default, during his time at Derby's grammar school, later rebranded as a public school by the headmaster, whom Hobson described as 'a persistent "snob" of the crudest order'.[11] The curriculum was calculated to enhance this social elitism: there was a concentration on dead languages with little regard for the 'tastes or aptitudes of the boys'. History 'stopped dead before modern politics began to emerge', and there was no attempt to 'shed light upon current institutions and events'. Any notions of citizenship, Hobson commented, 'never occurred to any teacher and would have been dismissed as unmeaning'.[12] He did, however, gain a valuable perspective on human nature through his independent reading of Shakespeare, Milton, Pope, Bacon and Boswell.[13]

It was not until the mid-1870s that Hobson came into contact with any social or economic study. He read Mill and Spencer at a course organised by the Cambridge University Extension Movement in Derby in 1875, and encountered the prevalent notion that natural forces guided the distribution of wealth and justified the existing economic system.[14] At first, Hobson accepted those 'principles and laws in the spirit of a true believer'; but then he discovered that a 'seed of doubt' had been sown in his mind, which was 'destined to bear perilous fruit'. Mill's 'dogma' that 'a demand for commodities is not a demand for labour', supported by 'the teaching that all wages were paid from a savings "fund"', was even in those early days repugnant to Hobson: the idea 'stuck in my gizzard'.[15]

It was not until the mid-1880s, however, that Hobson's real economic heresy began. Oxford had liberated him from 'the easy acceptance of the current ideas and feelings of an age rightly designated as materialistic and narrowly utilitarian'.[16] Hobson mentioned Jowett, Mark Pattison and T.H. Green as powerful influences but, rather surprisingly, considering that Ruskin lectured at Oxford at this time and was such a tremendous influence on Hobson in later life, he was not then ready for the full implications of Ruskin's heterodox economic critique.

Hobson left Oxford in 1880, and for a period of seven years he taught classics. When, in 1887, he moved to London to work as a lecturer in literature and economics he was appalled at the poverty he witnessed there, which existed, virtually unnoticed by many, in the midst of wealth.[17] He welcomed the fact that Booth's 'sensational revelations', in his study *In Darkest England* (1890), finally convinced people of the iniquity of regarding poverty and distress as the fault of the individual rather than to 'social disease'.[18] This growing social awareness led to 'a widespread breakdown of mid-Victorian complacency' and it brought with it more active protest from a variety of political perspectives. Hobson listed various socialist groups, including the Social Democrats, the Fabian Society and the Christian Socialists, but commented, 'With the exception of the Fabians,' they seemed to him 'either too inflammatory or too sentimental.'[19] And even the Fabians did not address the weakest points of capitalism.[20] Hobson considered that poverty and the extension of trade unionism were the 'direct stimuli' for socialism. He, however, did not consider himself 'a Socialist, Marxian, Fabian, or Christian'.[21]

Hobson's thinking on socio-economic problems had been heavily influenced by his meeting in Exeter with a businessman called Alfred Frederick Mummery, who had convinced Hobson that excessive saving was responsible for the 'underemployment of capital and labour in periods of bad trade'. In 1889 Hobson published a book with Mummery, elaborating this argument. Hobson noted that this was the 'first open step' in his 'heretical career' and that he did not at that time 'in the least realise its momentous consequences'.[22] The book, entitled *The Physiology of Industry*, brought home to him the degree of opposition still prevalent in response to attacks on orthodox economics.

There was some justification in the level of alarm generated by this work as it was, in effect, a direct attack on the Liberal assertion that a 'natural harmony of interests' justified the *laissez-faire* competitive nature of the economy. It was also a clear statement that excessive saving was the greatest cause of unemployment. As such, it was considered by many Liberals as economic heresy and resulted in Hobson being refused a lectureship in economics by the London Extension Board. The senior economics professor apparently considered Hobson's theories 'equivalent to an attempt to prove the flatness of the earth'.[23] To horrified orthodox economists, Hobson commented, this was 'an argument which sought to check the source of all industrial progress.' And the extent of his heresy was further brought home to him when an invitation from the Charity Organisation Society to lecture in the provinces on economic and working-class issues was suddenly withdrawn. 'I hardly realised,' he wrote, 'that in appearing to question the virtue of unlimited thrift I had committed the unpardonable sin.'[24] Hobson seems to have forgotten that he was at odds with the self-improving teaching of Samuel Smiles in the middle of the nineteenth century, which was still very much a part of the middle-class psyche.[25]

Hobson noted that his views on excessive saving were not without precedent. He quoted Shaftesbury, Berkeley and Malthus, but it still 'remained an offence' to challenge the 'new science', which acted as 'the defence and the glorification of the era of capitalism', whose sole *raison-d'être* was the 'illimitable increase of wealth' for those in charge. Hobson claimed that his so-called 'heresy of over-saving' was considered a 'deadly offence', because it undermined the whole justification for economic orthodoxy:

> It contravened the one claim which political economy had to ethical respectability. For the 'economic man', though consciously moved by intelligent self-interest in the pursuit of personal gain, was led by an 'invisible hand' to a line of conduct conducive to the welfare of the community. He could, therefore, figure as a benevolent or kindly being. For it was his function to keep down the costs of production, including wages, to the lowest level, in order that the profit of industry should be as large as possible.[26]

The 'essential selfishness' of this economic theory, claimed Hobson, was only thinly disguised by flashes of 'liberality and humanity' but the 'cold truth remained that the *laisser-faire* theory of competitive capitalism – rested upon a foundation of intelligent selfishness.' Ethical goodness was, in effect, for Hobson, totally lacking in the modern interpretation of classical economics.

In 1887, Hobson read Marx and was initially unimpressed by Marx's attempt to explain the cost of production in terms of labour-time, which Hobson considered impractical. He also strongly repudiated Marx's adoption of a Hegelian dialectic explanation[27] as simply an attempt 'to impart an air of mysticism into quite intelligible historical processes'. Marx's own interpretation of 'Capitalism', he insisted, 'ignored all theory that did not present itself in the actual processes' that Marx had studied.[28] In fact, Hobson's own critique of political economy crystallised in the last few years of the nineteenth century. During this time he completely turned away from the individualistic old-style liberalism toward a new concept of society, which was both humane and organic. And in this ideological transformation, John Ruskin played a very significant role.

New Liberalism

Classical liberalism underwent a fundamental shift in ideology during the second half of the nineteenth century and it was in the early days of this transitional period between old and new liberalism that Ruskin made his attack on classical views of political economy. It is here, also, that the pre-emptive nature of Ruskin's social critique became even more apparent. His passionate denigration of current commercial practice had its counterpoint in the growing dissatisfaction of many liberals with the limitations of classical economics. After 1880 a group of intellectual radicals, who called themselves New Liberals, wanted increasingly to redefine their concept of society from one of self-interested individualism to an organicist principle of community and equality. Members of this group, which included Hobson and Ramsay Macdonald and later Graham Wallas and Charles Trevelyan, came to realise, as Ruskin had before them, that the iniquities of this complex industrial society could only be remedied with the assistance of greater state activity.

This was a concept firmly embraced by Hobson, and indeed, he became its principal exponent. It involved a movement away from an earlier belief in the benevolence of a free market economy, and from Mill's fears of the threat to individual freedom posed by state intervention, toward a more positive ideal of liberty in which the state would actually be the enabling factor. Hobson's liberalism, writes Michael Freeden, was implicit in all his writing, 'It was indeed a new or left liberalism, one that welcomed the state as an impartial and trustworthy agent of society, and accepted society as a claimant of rights side by side with the individual.'[29] But while there is no doubt that in this aspect Hobson and Ruskin were in agreement, there were some fundamental and irreconcilable factors which precluded Ruskin's inclusion in liberal philosophy.

Hobson certainly refined his view of organicism after reading Ruskin, but he found two of Ruskin's doctrines unacceptable: the first that in a truly organic society there should be no profit in exchange, and the second that interest is usury. Hobson, like Ruskin, had queried his evangelical inheritance with its emphasis on individual responsibility, and he shared with Ruskin a concomitant distaste for the a priori thinking of the classical political economists. This combination was not uncommon in the mid-nineteenth century, when evangelical Christianity and *laissez-faire* economics were seen by many reformers as symbiotic entities, feeding off each other and causing untold misery. For Hobson, however, writing later in the century, there was less reason for outright rejection of classical economics, which was, by then, largely free of its religious endorsement and was already open to scrutiny. Indeed, Hobson was like many other reformers, adding to the momentum of opposition initiated by Ruskin in 1860, yet never emulating his level of antagonism. H.C.G. Matthew writes:

> In working on Ruskin, Hobson thus found himself confronting someone more radical, more daring and more vociferous in his social critique than Hobson was ever to be. Perhaps to his surprise, Hobson found himself, vis-à-vis Ruskin, a conservative rather than the dangerous radical he seemed to his friends to be becoming.[30]

Ruskin's extreme radicalism was complex, however. The ambiguity of his political orientation was to be located in his medieval/organicist metaphor. Freedom, for Ruskin, did not mean democracy and this argued for a flexibility of political interpretation, but it was his central ethos of organicism which underpinned the thinking of new liberals and socialists toward the end of the nineteenth century, and, in effect, confirmed a strong ideological synthesis between the two.

Like so many of Ruskin's followers, Hobson never fully understood the medieval vantage point which gave Ruskin both the impetus and the medium for his social criticism, and Hobson couldn't fully approve. Ruskin's organicism was tempered with classical values; 'The teaching of Plato,' wrote Hobson, 'and a fanatical abhorrence of the "radical" doctrine of natural equality' enforced in Ruskin 'a principle of social stratification'.[31] Cooperation and government, Ruskin insisted, should replace an overriding allegiance to the misguided concept of liberty. Hobson, though upholding the desirability of a degree of personal autonomy, yet agreed that there were specific social goals and followed Ruskin in advocating a largely collectivist solution to social problems. His own theory of organicism was thus refined by Ruskin into a definition of society as 'a moral rational organism' with a 'common psychic life'.[32] Both Ruskin and Hobson embraced a concept of the state which would oppose commercial ambition with an ethical principle and this was easily accommodated within the flexible philosophy of later liberalism, as indeed it was within the various interpretations of socialism.

New liberalism was not antithetical to its traditional counterpart: it developed out of it. Hobson insisted that organic society was a natural phenomenon which simply needed to be raised to new levels of consciousness in order to address the evils of industrialisation:

> Indeed, it is difficult to see how any reasonable person can confront the grave practical problems presented by the industrial societies of today, such as those contained in individual, class, sex, national differentiation of economic functions, without realising that the hypothesis of humanity as itself a collective organism can alone furnish any hope of their rational solution.[33]

For Hobson, an emphasis on an organic, unified society was not only the key to social reform, it was also the main difference between traditional and new liberalism. He did not seek to abandon classical liberalism completely, but to take what was best from it, while seeking to rectify its faults. In a lecture he prepared for the Rainbow Circle on 4 October 1905,[34] Hobson's Ruskinian emphasis on the organic nature of society was very much in evidence. The paper, which was read in Hobson's absence by the Honorary Secretary, was entitled: 'To what type of organisation does Society correspond?'[35] It was summarised under the following headings:

The meaning and limits of Society.
Metaphors, organic and inorganic.
Society regarded as a physical and psychical entity.
The State as an instrument of Society.
Resolution: That the formulation and attainment of the individual end involves the prior formulation and attainment of the social end.

In this lecture Hobson's emphasis on the significance of a transcendent moral or spiritual dimension to society was analogous to Ruskin's insistence on the moral centrality of art and architecture and its significance in the portrayal of national character. Hobson commented that 'the evolution of Society is a psycho-physical process', and that 'there is no reason why the term organism may not be applied in a spiritual as well as a material sense.' This aspect had been largely ignored by politicians, leaving a situation where 'the economic solidarity of human society is better developed than its political solidarity and its moral or conscious solidarity is least developed of all.'

But organicism, if defined as the necessity for collective rather than individual goals, was only one of three significant aspects by which new liberalism could be distinguished from the old. The second related feature was a desire for economic reform, with greater emphasis on the need for equality. Classical liberalism had, to quote John Allett, 'compromised too quickly with the interests of the rising bourgeoisie'. In so doing, it had 'sacrificed equality for liberty . . . and virtually abandoned the lower classes to a life where liberalism was little else than a parade of false promises and unrealisable ideals.'[36] This iniquity was to be rectified by the provision of an equality of opportunity in education and enterprise, and a move to push true social welfare into the realms of industrial economy, thus exposing the inadequacies of the individualistic philosophy of orthodox liberalism.

The third difference between old and new liberal thinking, which was closely related to the two previous points, centred upon the classical liberals' emphasis on the limitations of individual reasoning, which apparently precluded any capacity to cope with central control. It was an argument which, as Allett points out, justified 'the liberals' faith in the necessity of *laissez-faire*'.[37] It was also a further endorsement of the early liberal tendency to view society as a collection of self-seeking individuals, exclusively responsible for their own fate. Hobson, under the banner of new liberalism, sought to change these attitudes and to insist on a more collectivist perspective. Ernest Barker later acknowledged that point:

> Mr Hobson in particular has urged that the individual is not the only unit of economic production; that the community is itself a producer of values; and that the State, which is the organ of the community, may claim a special right to impose special taxation on such values. The old individualistic view of the State thus seems to be definitely shed by modern Liberalism; and Mr Hobson, in restating the liberal case, can even enlist the conception of a social organism under its banner.[38]

Hobson on Ruskin

When Hobson first read Ruskin in the early 1890s, he took from him two essential, related principles, which Hobson termed 'organicism' and 'humanism'. The way in which Hobson then translated this organicism into political terms cannot be overemphasised as it is crucial in understanding Ruskin's influence, not only on Hobson, but on other radical reformers.

Ruskin's organicism, as has already been noted, stemmed from a Romantic tradition which predated Darwinian/Spencerian sociobiological analogy. The New Liberals were pro-Darwinists. Ruskin was not; his organicism, at the risk of labouring the point, rested on a romantic concept of an integrated society which was mutually sustaining but hierarchically structured.[39] There was no question of a competitive 'survival of the fittest' individualism in Ruskin's organic society. Instead, following the example of Robert Owen, he was a profound influence on a later interpretation of social Darwinism, which suggested that cooperation rather than competition was central to the evolutionary process.[40]

By the end of the nineteenth century, social Darwinism was being used to support a wide range of often antithetic analogies and suppositions. Yet, in its very flexibility of interpretation, it failed, in Hobson's view, adequately to address the problem of the relationship between society and economic orthodoxy. Ruskin's organicism, in contrast, had concentrated on unity or wholeness rather than growth and development. Hobson wrote of his mentor:

> This organic conception everywhere illuminates [Ruskin's] theory and his practical constructive policy: it gives order to his conception of the different industrial classes and to the relations of individual members of each class: it releases him from the mechanical atomic notion of equality, and compels him to develop an orderly system of interdependence sustained by authority and obedience.[41]

Ruskin's organicism was thus incompatible with the fragmentary, individualistic teaching of classical liberalism and was at the basis of his social criticism. Hobson followed him in this, considering that old liberalism gave a distorted view of society. 'A social interpretation of industry,' Hobson commented, 'is not possible except by treating society as an organic structure.' Whether it was regarded as an 'organism' or an 'organisation', it must be regarded as 'a vital structure capable of working well or working ill'.[42]

This insistence on the relationship between the parts and the whole came directly from Hobson's reading of Ruskin. Ruskin had given a new depth to the organic metaphor by proposing that individual values promoted corporate values and thus created a sense of community. The fact that Ruskin derived his theory from his medieval studies rather than from the sociological implications of natural selection was irrelevant. It provided, for Hobson, the missing factor in the reinterpretation of liberal thought. John Allett comments:

> Hobson vigorously endorsed Ruskin's criticism of classical liberalism for its failure both politically and economically to comprehend the organic structure of society . . . Furthermore, classical liberal thinking, as a consequence of its non-organic viewpoint, was dogged by the fallacy of composition and this, as Hobson spent a lifetime determining, lay at the root of its failure to understand the causes of economic underconsumption crises in particular, and of its general inability to appreciate the Ruskinian logic (not always adhered to by Ruskin himself) that 'social evils require social remedies'.[43]

The translation of this organic principle into economic theory was central to Ruskin's social critique and further confirmed his profound influence on Hobson. Having come to the view that competition was the enemy, rather than the upholder, of equality, Hobson was only too ready to endorse Ruskin's indignant condemnation of the iniquities of *laissez-faire* economics. Indeed, he quoted Ruskin's analogy of the human body in *Unto This Last* as being a far more apposite organic metaphor than those favoured by Spencerian sociologists, for its 'bearing on the theory of production and of distribution of wealth'.[44] Ruskin's 'organic conception of industry' was, he claimed, 'essential in order to justify the epithet "political"'. And the fact that this organic conception was lacking in 'the inductive science' of those economists who were 'dominated by an individualist philosophy' was a 'fatal defect' in their thinking.[45]

Significantly, this comment, taken from Hobson's biography of Ruskin which was published in 1898, shows that Hobson still considered it necessary to defend Ruskin's reputation as an economic critic. By this time Ruskin had attracted a good deal of respect as a social critic and classical economics was already seen to be defective in those very areas in which he was most censorious. Socialists were rallying to his message but, despite the human cost of poverty, many liberal politicians still remained convinced that state intervention posed a threat to individual liberty.[46] There was, wrote Hobson, 'a curious notion still widely prevalent, that Mr Ruskin abandoned his proper work as an art-teacher in order rashly to embark in Political Economy'. In this area, it was still considered by some that he lacked both 'aptitude' and 'training'.[47] Hobson saw it as his duty to set the record straight and, at the same time, to use Ruskin's thoughts to expedite a liberal-socialist synthesis.

Hobson on Ruskin's Economic Reforms

Hobson began his defence by listing the many ways in which Ruskin was fitted for the role of economic analyst: he was an expert on the subject of work which, both in terms of production and consumption, was central to political economy; he was himself a skilled artist and craftsman and had also spent a great deal of his time observing and investigating the nature and usage of those raw materials central to the commercial economy. Moreover, from 'contemporary observation' and from his historical studies, Ruskin was familiar with 'the actual processes by which large classes of goods were produced', a fact which gave him 'immense superiority over his opponents', who did not possess 'a tithe of this practical knowledge'.[48] The fact that Ruskin was unfamiliar with certain modern industrial processes was, in Hobson's view, not a disadvantage, as this was a deficiency he shared with most of the other so-called authorities on political economy.

A further advantage for which Hobson praised Ruskin was his 'mastery of language'. He used this ability to the full in his exposure of the 'verbal duplicity' of orthodox economists, who used 'ambiguity' to falsify the facts.[49] Although himself prone to literary diversion, Ruskin was never 'servile to authority' nor did he allow his views to be distorted by personal interest or by academic or political bias. He applied the same standard of intelligent observation to economics as he did to art, subjecting both disciplines to an unprecedented level of minute analysis and establishing the right of 'independent inquiry'.[50] Despite occasional weaknesses in his constructive reasoning, he was able to hold his own with trained economists and was always convincing in his exposure of the 'fallacious reasoning' of others.

These considerations alone, Hobson insisted, were enough to 'dispel the popular illusion' that Ruskin was ill-equipped as economic critic. He was 'quite competent to discuss economic problems with Senior, Fawcett, and J.S. Mill', and those defects that he did have were ones he shared with the previous generation of economists, who had little contact with the labouring classes and an 'insufficient grasp of evolution in the structure of industrial and political institutions'.[51] This latter point was Hobson's greatest criticism of Ruskin and the main point of difference between the two. As H.C.G. Matthew comments: 'Hobson got many things from Ruskin, but not his sense of evolution.'[52] In *Unto This Last*, Ruskin had outlined a static, utopian ideal of society, which did not accommodate progress. For Hobson, as Matthew comments, 'Progress towards organicism was of extreme importance; for Ruskin it was the restoration of a lost order.'[53] This factor apart, however, Hobson's support for Ruskin's credibility as economic critic was unequivocal, and Hobson had no hesitation in giving his own critical analysis of Ruskin's argument against *laissez-faire* economics.

On the subject of 'economic man', Hobson was equally supportive. Ruskin was prepared to accept that a hypothetical science, which based its assumptions on a theoretical man, totally dominated by selfish instincts, could be used to investigate laws of production and distribution of wealth. But hypothesis was its only value. Ruskin insisted that man was not an idle and 'covetous machine', motivated solely by material wealth, but was capable of taking pride in good work and had a capacity for self-sacrifice. What, therefore, as Hobson demanded pointedly, 'is the use of a science which begins by assuming that man is what he is not'.[54] Ruskin had put his finger accurately on the 'root-fallacy' of the economists' basic 'mode of reasoning'. Classical economic reasoning could only function where the problems were perceived as essentially mathematical, but as Hobson commented, 'It will work wrongly when the forces differ qualitatively and are combined not mechanically but organically.'[55] Considerations of humanity were alien to most manufacturers and this was the area in which Ruskin's teaching was most valuable.[56]

Ruskin had provided a more holistic, humane interpretation, with a special emphasis on the kind of work men were forced to do: 'Mr Ruskin had early come to recognise that work is not an evil to be shunned but a good to be desired, provided it is in kind and quantity desirable.'[57] In an educated and well-ordered society, this goal was attainable; in the present economic system, it was not even considered important. Ruskin had realised, more than most, the impossibility of separating social and economic issues. As Hobson noted, both in terms of production and consumption man is affected by factors other than 'getting and spending'. He is a social being, but with individual needs which cannot be accommodated in terms of simple material wealth. Paying lip-service to this fact was not enough. The 'occasional pious or humane reflections or aspirations' of early economists had been replaced largely by the writings of Mill, whose 'elaborate dissertations upon methods of social reform' were, for the most part, treated separately from economic factors. And the defectiveness of this system, which refused to acknowledge the total interdependence of social and economic functions, was further highlighted in 'the astounding diversity of meaning' locked into its key terminology.[58]

Every economist, claimed Hobson, had his own definition of 'wealth', and Ruskin was right to condemn Mill's declaration that there was one notion 'sufficiently correct for common purposes'.[59] Whatever definition was taken, 'the shifting character of industry and social institutions' created new difficulties. Was wealth to be classed purely in terms of material goods or did it include 'serviceable human qualities'? Should domestic labour and natural resources be excluded from calculations of wealth, because they were not exchangeable? Its very multifaceted nature confirmed how unsatisfactory it was to isolate wealth from the overall industrial system and to treat it as a science in its own right. This was not a true 'political' economy. If such a science existed, Ruskin considered it should be called what it actually is – 'mercantile' economy.[60]

Ruskin's distinction between 'mercantile' and 'political' economy was, considered Hobson, vital, and lay at 'the very heart' of Ruskin's social criticism.[61] His definition was distanced from current thinking on two major issues. Firstly, it 'breaks down the barrier separating industrial processes from other serviceable human activities'. It should become a 'science of human welfare [which] includes within its scope not merely the processes by which men gain a livelihood, but all human efforts and satisfactions'.[62] Mercantile economy assumes that man is simply 'a getter and spender', whose social and spiritual qualities and commitments are completely outside the sphere of economics. In Hobson's view, this was the key to Ruskin's seminality:

Mr Ruskin insists that the organic unity of man as a conscious, rational being, with a capacity for regarding his life as a whole and forming a plan for its conduct, imposes a corresponding unity upon the science which is to treat of human conduct, that the interaction of conscious forces within man is so constant and so intricate that it is not really convenient to make the separatist assumption required by mercantile Economy.[63]

The second factor, which for Hobson marked Ruskin's sharpest divergence with the exponents of orthodox economics, was in his interpretation of 'value'. The classical economists saw 'value' purely in terms of money or goods, whereas Ruskin insisted it should be estimated in terms of its life-enhancing properties. He wanted, in Hobson's words, to 'substitute for the money-measurement of wealth adopted by the business man and the mercantile economist a standard of human utility'.[64] Some economists had given slight attention to 'the vital services of goods', deploring, for example, 'the consumption of luxury by labourers', but this criticism was never an 'integral part of economic theory'. Ruskin's 'adoption of vital use as the standard and measure of value must therefore be regarded as the most revolutionary of his positions'. His famous maxim that 'THERE IS NO WEALTH BUT LIFE' was, claimed Hobson, both 'eloquent' and yet 'strictly scientific'. By insisting that 'that country is richest which nourishes the greatest number of noble and happy human beings',[65] Ruskin had 'substituted for the objective commercial standard of money a subjective human standard'.[66] He had thus imposed an ethical code which would completely transform the nature of economic science.

Another of Ruskin's great innovations, which Hobson identified in his biography and pursued in his economic writings, was Ruskin's reference to the term 'Political'. As has been indicated above, this was a crucial issue in Hobson's own political thinking. He was convinced that the exponents of *laissez-faire* completely failed to understand the organic structure of society. Ruskin's organicism was frequently commented on, and also frequently re-interpreted. This was partly because it was inspired by art rather than by science, and also because Ruskin never troubled to explain it thoroughly. The construction of Gothic architecture allowed for individuality of expression, yet at the same time relied for its completion on sustained communal effort. The end result thus had its own intrinsic moral dimension. Indeed, for Ruskin, the interwoven arches and natural forms of the Gothic cathedral mirrored the organic structure of society with its transcendent community spirit. Hobson took this organic metaphor from *Unto This Last* and turned it into a theory of social organisation. This helped both to eradicate existing prejudice against state intervention and to encourage the view that the community was itself a creator of values.

In summing up Ruskin's proposed economic reforms, Hobson revealed his own greatest concerns:

> The work of Mr Ruskin then consists in this, that he has 'humanised' Political Economy. Every fact and every process is stripped of its materialistic or its monetary garb and shown in its naked truth as vitality.[67]

The only standard of utility recognised by orthodox economists was 'a monetary measure of desire', whereas, for Ruskin, utility meant the 'promotion of life and happiness,' a goal which was attainable only if society changed its values. In trying to achieve this goal, Ruskin proposed a radical transformation of the whole structure and vocabulary of political economy by 'vitalising and moralising every term and every process'. He substituted the 'false short-range expediency of passing pleasures' for a 'just and orderly conception of social well-being'.[68] In so doing, he exposed himself to accusations of using sentimentalism as a substitute for science. But, argued Hobson, the defects of economic orthodoxy were 'primarily moral defects', and Ruskin's crusade was 'inspired by moral energy', not sentiment. He had attacked the economy on moral grounds precisely because it was in this area that it was so patently deficient. His reforms were essential to the 'orderly interpretation of economic phenomena' and in this sense they were entirely scientific.[69]

Hobson concluded this section of his analysis of Ruskin by claiming his significance in the advancement of social science. He commented that Ruskin would probably prefer to be seen as proposing an ethical basis for the study of socio-economics rather than a scientific one, but modern sociologists recognised the scientific nature of his work:

> By insisting upon the reduction of all economic terms, such as value, cost, utility, etc., to terms of 'vitality', by insisting upon the

organic integrity and unity of all human activities, and the organic
nature of the cooperation of social units, and finally by furnishing
a social ideal of reasonable humanity, Mr Ruskin has amply
justified his claim as a pioneer in the theory of Social Economics.[70]

But sociology was not purely a descriptive science. Its function, as Comte
recognised, was also to make practical suggestions for improvement. It
then began to acquire a moral dimension which, although not overtly
Christian, was the point at which Christianity and sociology converged.
Ruskin's socio-economic teaching, despite his crisis of faith, still retained
a largely Christian ethic, often bolstered by evangelical fervour. Hobson,
as a self-confessed religious heretic, was, like Harrison, content to
concentrate on Ruskin's essential humanitarianism.

It was, however, this particular humanitarian strain in Ruskin's writing
which made it so unacceptable to the upholders of economic orthodoxy. In
his social doctrine, particularly in the field of economics, Ruskin was,
wrote Hobson, both 'destructive' and 'constructive', a factor which had
'often proved a stumbling-block to the full comprehension and acceptance
of his teaching'. Ruskin's appeal to hearts as well as minds often caused
confusion and earned him the indictment of using 'literary' rather than
'logical' order. Also, his social criticism had to be gleaned from a wide
variety of sources, as there was no one single book which contained a 'full,
clear, and consistent statement of his social principles'.[71]

Hobson quoted *Munera Pulveris* as 'the most systematic' of Ruskin's
books, but even that contained many inconsistencies in the application
of basic principles. He was full of praise for Ruskin's insistence that the
examination of industry from a social standpoint required equal consideration of both the utility of goods and the kind of labour necessary to
produce them. The 'commercial economists,' Hobson claimed, 'look too
exclusively to the products and not sufficiently at the processes of
production.' People's prosperity was calculated by the aggregate of their
material goods with no regard for the 'increased duration, intensity,
monotony, and unwholesomeness' of the production process. In his
continued emphasis on the need for meaningful work for all, Ruskin had
'laid down as the foundation-stone of social theory the organic relation
between work and life, between production and consumption'.[72]

This was all very sound, agreed Hobson, but Ruskin did not carry his
analysis of wealth to its logical conclusions in terms of 'the interaction

between work and life'. Ruskin, Hobson admitted, took too narrow a meaning of wealth in *Munera Pulveris,* by omitting 'direct regard for labour cost' and giving undue emphasis to utility. His initial clear distinction between 'value' and 'cost' was not fully pursued in *Munera Pulveris,* as he rated goods in terms of value only: 'The value or "utility" side is worked out with admirable skill, but the "cost" side is slighted, while the organic relation between the two is left out of sight.'[73]

Three tests, Hobson insisted, must be applied to the utilities produced by a mercantile economy before they could satisfactorily fulfil the criteria of a more humane political economy. The first is to ask what is the nature of goods and services classified as utilities? Intrinsic value was the first essential component of 'wealth'; the second was its 'acceptant capacity' or 'the ability of the consumer to get out of the 'utility the good it contains'. Hobson quoted Ruskin in *Munera Pulveris* as commenting, 'As the aptness of the user increases, the effectual value of the thing used increases.' This was sound reasoning to Hobson, who commented: 'It has only just begun to dawn upon the minds of our most enlightened political economists that the prosperity of a country can be enhanced as much by educating the consumer as by improving the arts of the producer.'[74] And a third, related test, of the true nature of wealth which, said Hobson, Ruskin 'implies' rather than 'applies' in *Munera Pulveris,* was that the degree of utility of a product depends not only on its intrinsic value and the capacity of the consumer to make full use of it, but also on the quantity he possesses. In Hobson's terms – 'The greatest effectual utility is got from any article when it goes to satisfy the intensest human need.'[75] Distribution of goods was therefore also an important part of the evaluation of wealth.

These three tests then fulfilled the requirements of changing any analysis of 'commercial' into 'human' utility. But as Hobson stressed, Ruskin did not apply these tests to the problem of 'cost' or 'labour' in the same way that he did to 'intrinsic value'. He touched on the economics of labour in his earlier lectures on art,[76] but did not anywhere make a thorough analysis of the labour problem. To achieve the necessary balance between his treatment of the analysis of labour and the analysis of utility or value it was essential, Hobson claimed, to examine firstly 'the intrinsic nature of the work in relation to the worker'.[77]

Of all these considerations, Hobson noted, Ruskin was fully aware: 'Not one fails to find eloquent expression and illustration in his works.' But he never at any time drew them together. It was, claimed Hobson, this 'lack of systematic setting [which] has injured [Ruskin's] reputation as an economic thinker'. Had he set forth in *Munera Pulveris* or, indeed, in any of his works, 'these principles of the subjective political economy, their strictly scientific character could not have evaded recognition'.

> By neglecting formally to complete his statement of principles, by scattering his theory amid passages of passionate appeal, whimsical flights of philology, vigorous tirades against materialism and utilitarianism, Mr Ruskin has hidden the really consistent ground-plan of his economic teaching so that it is difficult to discover and apprehend as a perfect whole.[78]

Hobson identified other anomalies in Ruskin's social thought. In his concern for the lack of a 'sense of continuous development' in Ruskin's social views, he acknowledged that this might have something to do with the fact that Ruskin's intellectual principles were established before Darwin, Wallace and Spencer had inculcated notions of evolution into receptive minds. Or it may simply have been that Ruskin held 'the more abstract doctrines of the natural sciences' in some contempt, but he tended to cling to the notion of a possible specific ideal society sustained by certain immutable laws. This, claimed Hobson, was unfortunate, because an acceptance of the biological analogy of 'the modification of organism by environment'[79] may have convinced Ruskin that his concept of the immutability of certain values was untenable and given further ethical support for his views. His refusal 'to accept the teaching of evolution in human life' has led Ruskin 'to impart too statical a character to his 'Political Economy', and too uniform a type to his ideal society'.[80] Hobson dismissed such utopias, claiming that sociology embraced many different types of civilisation often with very disparate ideals and there could therefore be 'no single abiding, universal form of political or industrial society'. Ruskin was too inclined to see society as an 'accomplished order' rather than 'a means of progress'.

But, despite Ruskin's inconsistencies and the fact that he nowhere explained his economic 'science' in its entirety, Hobson remained insistent upon the 'fundamental excellence'[81] of Ruskin's economic ideas, and had no equivocation in admitting that he drew from him the 'basic thought' for his own 'subsequent economic writings'.[82] As to Ruskin's reputation, Hobson commented:

It has been humorous to hear the dull drudges of commercial economics speaking contemptuously of an economist whose logic is far keener than their own, and whose work will hereafter be recognised as the first serious attempt in England to establish a scientific basis of economic study from the social standpoint . . . Mr Ruskin's first claim as a social reformer is that he reformed Political Economy.[83]

Flaws in Modern Industry

Hobson's appraisal of Ruskin was not confined to the latter's critique of the 'mercantile economy'; it spanned the whole spectrum of Ruskin's social thought. Not content with exposing the false claims of classical economists, Ruskin had also turned his attention to what Hobson termed 'flaws in the structure of commercial science'.[84] Here, as in all his other social criticism, Ruskin had tended to obscure his acuteness of perception and intellect with scornful accusations aimed at 'honest specialists' such as Mill and Fawcett, which did nothing to encourage an acknowledgement of the rightness of Ruskin's thinking.

Ruskin's attitude toward Mill had always been one of undisguised contempt. In a letter to his friend, Charles Eliot Norton in 1869, he referred to Mill as the man looked up to as 'the greatest thinker', but who was in fact 'an utterly shallow and wretched segment of a human creature, incapable of understanding *Anything*'.[85] This rather excessive and ungenerous condemnation was directed toward a well-respected economist, who basically had a different concept of human nature. As James Sherburne comments: 'Mill's view of society reflects his view of human nature. Man is not an organic whole as he is for Ruskin and the Romantics.' Mill considered that human nature was capable of being split up into smaller elements or "properties"', which 'can be abstracted from one another and examined separately for purposes of deduction or prediction'. Unlike Ruskin, Mill did not see human nature as a 'tree', shaped by 'the inward forces which make it a living thing'.[86]

As Sherburne points out, the main difference between Ruskin and the Utilitarian economists 'lies less in ethical end than in choice of means to attain that end'. They had different sources of moral preference: 'the Judaeo-Christian softened by Romanticism and the Utilitarian modified by a strong attachment to individual liberty'.[87] In the case of Ruskin and Mill, these differences were heightened almost to the point of caricature.

Hobson was more selective than Ruskin in his criticism of Mill, claiming that one of Ruskin's greatest achievements was his 'convincing exposure of the fallacies of the teaching regarding capital for which J.S. Mill in particular was responsible'.[88] Hobson referred to the 'doctrine of the social utility of unlimited saving' – a particular *bête noir*. Among the myths that Ruskin successfully exploded, according to Hobson, were: the 'assumption that industry is limited by capital' and the view that 'demand for commodities is not demand for labour'.[89]

Ruskin had argued in *Unto This Last*, with his usual flair for botanical analogy, that capital was 'a root, which does not enter into vital function till it produces something else than a root: namely fruit.'[90] Hobson applauded this exposure of 'the folly of unlimited parsimony', saying that Ruskin's humorous gardening analogy, in which 'he points out the futile policy of postponing the production of the flower by an indefinite elongation of the stalk', should suffice to raise questions as to the quantity of saving which is 'socially useful'.[91] The 'intricate ambiguity of meaning' of the term 'capital' had blinded political economists to the truth, which is the fact that 'capital is limited by consumption', and that industry is limited by the three essential ingredients of capital, labour, and natural resources in equal proportion.

But Ruskin's most valuable contribution to this topic, in Hobson's opinion, was his 'refutation of Mill's proposition' that 'A demand for commodities is not a demand for labour.' If anyone was inclined to question Ruskin's ability in economic controversy, Hobson referred them to the second letter in volume one of *Fors Clavigera,* which contained 'his concise and thoroughly effective exposure of the three separate fallacies' contained in Mill's argument. Furthermore, Hobson commented that, while Professor Nicholson was the first British economist who had 'the courage in an authoritative textbook to admit the obvious falsehood of Mill's position', he made 'no acknowledgement whatever of the far more effective refutation given twenty-five years before by Mr Ruskin'.[92]

Trying to gauge whether Ruskin or Mill was right on this particular question is, claims James Sherburne, 'unprofitable' as it depends on a definition of terms and the point of departure from the economic process. The difference between Ruskin and Mill was, writes Sherburne, 'symptomatic of a crucial difference in vision'. Mill's proposals allow him to 'focus on production and neglect consumption in the belief that it will take care of itself', whereas Ruskin 'places consumption at the center of

the economy'. The difference is 'possibly semantic', but it is nonetheless
very significant as it forces a 'distinction between a quantitative and a
qualitative view of economics'.

> Ruskin's approach suggests more directly than Mill's that the real
> question is what *can* be supplied and *ought* to be demanded.
> Ruskin's crude refashioning of economic doctrines in terms which
> encourage a concern for quality is his greatest achievement.[93]

It was Ruskin's 'social imagination' that led him to expose another grave
defect of modern industry: the division of labour. Ruskin's condemnation
of over-specialisation was applauded by Hobson, who echoed Ruskin's
concern for its degrading effect upon the worker and endorsed his
opinion that it was in fact 'a denial of the reality of the consumer's
gain'.[94] Hobson did not equal Ruskin's eloquence on this topic[95] but
Hobson did emulate Ruskin's passionate disapproval. 'Over special-
isation,' he wrote, was 'one of the most destructive vices of our age and a
chief source of modern discontent'. Machinery had its place, even Ruskin
conceded this point; but when 'the product is severed from the process;
the product is all-valued [and] the process is ignored.'[96] This 'tyranny of
modern industry' was 'defended by orthodox Political Economy'. Again,
Hobson emphasised the seminality and significance of Ruskin's
particular mode of social criticism:

> When economic theory has accepted a really scientific setting of
> value, and comes to recognise the exact equivalence of cost and
> utility to terms of life, it will be once more forced to admit the
> fundamental sanity and importance of Mr Ruskin's criticism.[97]

Money, Ruskin insisted, meant 'power over labour, authority over men'. It
gave the power to demand work, yet its 'true vital significance' depended
upon 'the economic condition of the worker'.[98] Until this human element
was accepted, Hobson wrote, Ruskin's teaching on the truly organic nature
of political economy would continue to be undervalued.

Ruskin had thus introduced a moral principle into every area of
economic orthodoxy and industrial practice, which, despite some points
of discrepancy, gave Hobson the endorsement he needed for his own
growing critique of classical liberal policy. As H.C.G. Matthew com-

ments: 'Hobson's critique of Ruskin came at a timely moment' as it 'greatly broadened the basis of his writing'.[99] It raised Hobson's awareness of difficult questions about 'the relationship of moderated capitalism to the organic state'. It gave Hobson 'the moral core of his outlook' in which 'political economy' and his 'corrective theory of underconsumption' paved the way to 'a general reconstruction, as he saw it, of the understanding of what modern society could become'. In Matthew's opinion, the central theme of Hobson's work – 'The particular fallacies of orthodox political economy paralleling the moral vision of a different social, political and economic order – came from Ruskin.'[100]

Ruskin's vision of a post-capitalist organic society may have been too orientated toward Christian belief for its successful accommodation into secular politics but, like all utopias, it provided a standard towards which non-believers also could aspire. The concept of cooperation was central to these utopias and became the common keyword for social reformers, believers and non-believers alike.

Hobson, Ruskin and Competition

By the end of the nineteenth century, intellectual opposition to unfettered industrial competition was growing among many political persuasions. Although it was in economics that its influence was most keenly felt, the doctrine of *laissez-faire* spread its message over a wide social field and thus attracted some of the sharpest criticism. Ruskin's attitude toward competition was, Hobson comments, one of 'unqualified hostility'. Ruskin never tired of repeating the message, first pronounced in volume five of *Modern Painters* and then in *Unto This Last* the same year, that 'Government and Cooperation are in all things the Laws of Life; Anarchy and Competition the Laws of Death.'

Ruskin emphasised not only the quality of goods produced, but also the ability of the consumer to appreciate that quality, as when appreciating great works of art or music. As for modern political economists, he commented later in *Munera Pulveris*, that they have proved *'without exception, incapable of apprehending the nature of intrinsic value at all'*.[101]

How far Hobson felt it necessary to understand the aesthetic origin of Ruskin's economic theory is unclear, but Hobson was certainly able to empathise with Ruskin's circuitous route to that discipline, having himself had an unconventional beginning. And, as already noted, unlike some of his fellow liberals, Hobson keenly endorsed the use of the organic metaphor as providing moral justification for collectivism. Ruskin, he wrote, 'vehemently repudiates' both the morality and the utility of the 'competitive system' of industry. For Ruskin, 'what is immoral cannot be ultimately useful'; and 'the self-seeking motivations of 'economic man' did not generate 'a socially profitable line of conduct'.[102] By concentrating solely on profit instead of on quality, competitive industry was degrading to both the producer and the product. Thus, Hobson explained that Ruskin condemned unfettered competition as tending 'to glut markets with low-class commodities, and to debauch the taste and injure the persons and pockets of consumers'.[103]

On these points, Hobson was basically in agreement, although he considered that Ruskin 'painted too dark a picture' of man as 'a mere covetous machine'. It was, however, 'undeniable,' Hobson wrote, that there was a 'wide and glaring discrepancy between the higher teaching of ethics and Christianity, on the one hand, and the practice of industry on the other' and that 'the net moral result of competitive industry is to promote conscious discord between man and man.' Ruskin's hostility thus provided a timely warning:

> Mr Ruskin, therefore, even though he exaggerated the intensity of selfishness involved in commercial competition, and denounced in too unqualified terms its social inutility, must be held to have established his main charge, that a deep antagonism exists between our moral theory and our common practice in the affairs of life which most occupy our energies.[104]

But Ruskin was less precise, when substantiating these charges against commercial processes. Hobson acknowledged that, but praised Ruskin for exposing the hypocrisy of economists, who implied that bargaining was a fair means of exchange and distribution, the suggestion being that 'When an act of sale took place, seller and buyer made an equal gain from the transaction.' When Ruskin challenged current economic practice, it 'still rested on the assumption that competition harmonised the interests of the individual with the interests of society, all working together for the best'.[105] Instead, Ruskin exposed the 'elements of fraud and force' which were locked into this myth of orthodoxy. But while he was quite justified, wrote Hobson, in claiming 'that force lies at the root of bargaining', he found in Ruskin's reasoning 'two highly disputable doctrines'.[106]

Hobson firstly questioned Ruskin's insistence that there should be no profit in exchange. In *Unto This Last,* Ruskin maintained that 'In exchange, there is only one advantage, i.e., a bringing of vantage or power to the exchanging persons.'[107] Nothing is produced. Hobson instead noted that orthodox economists would argue that exchange produced utility as things were passed from those who did not need them to those who did. Ruskin did not call that 'profit'. And while Hobson did not blame Ruskin for 'narrowing the meaning of a word',[108] he was not sure what was gained by so doing. In fact, Ruskin's denial of 'profit' as the result of exchange had, wrote Hobson, 'misled' him into rather abstruse judgements on the entire subject. Ruskin implied that the whole 'advantage' of exchange depended on malpractice and there could only be gain on one side. 'He does not appear to recognise that, even in the cases of exchange where one party is immeasurably stronger or craftier than the other, a residuum of real gain or advantage must accrue to the weaker party.'[109]

The second error which Hobson identified was Ruskin's 'conviction of the illegitimacy of interest'. In this he was influenced, observed Hobson, by the pamphlets of W.C. Sillar,[110] which had convinced Ruskin by 1872 that all interest was wrong.[111] He set out his position in *Fors Clavigera* (letter 18) and concluded by letter 21 that 'Interest is a forcible taxation or exaction of usury.'[112] As Hobson observed, the real argument underlying Ruskin's condemnation of interest was that as 'capital is not productive, in the sense that it cannot grow', interest could not be seen as a reward for abstinence. There was certainly justification for Ruskin's disapproval of the 'modes by which the capital is often accumulated' but, wrote Hobson, 'the Ruskin of *Fors* has in fact abandoned the far sounder position of *Munera Pulveris*, which condemned only exorbitant interest due to oppression as one among various modes of oppressive dealing.' In this case, Hobson added, Ruskin's 'theological arguments' were sound, but his 'economical ones' were unconvincing.[113]

In his defence on this point, Hobson considered that Ruskin would have been in a stronger position had he 'confined his attack upon interest to the reassertion of the humane charitable duty of free lending to the poor.' As it was, like many opponents of the interest theory, Ruskin had failed to differentiate between the 'money lender' and the 'investor'. He had identified interest with usury. The chief harm done by such minor errors was only to himself, in giving further ammunition to his enemies.

The result was that Ruskin's socio-economic teaching had not got the attention it deserved. It was little wonder, Hobson commented, that Ruskin had bouts of madness. He poured both passion and intellect into his efforts to awaken people to 'the deadly injustice and inutility of the existing social order' and, although he was 'eagerly read' and 'passionately heard', he was not heeded enough by those who had the power to implement reforms:

> That people should gush over his beautiful writing about Art and Literature, should 'sympathise' with much that he has to say about the ugliness of industrial towns, the miseries of the poor, the dangers of luxury, the need of social solidarity, and should go their own way in comfortable self-complacency, giving their usual subscriptions to 'charities', and deprecating any radical change in this best of all possible worlds for the well-to-do – this surely is a more scathing indictment of his age and country than any that Mr Ruskin himself uttered in his most impassioned moments.[114]

Indeed, not all liberals shared Hobson's enthusiasm for Ruskin's incursion into sacred areas of economic policy. Writing in 1878, the liberal MP Justin McCarthy had remonstrated with Ruskin for 'intruding into fields where he was unfit to labour'.[115] Hobson was convinced, however, if not by the minutiae of Ruskin's attack on competition, but certainly by its underlying morality. This awakened in him a growing conviction of the pernicious effects upon society of the early liberal interpretation of the classical economic system. As he commented later in *Work and Wealth* :

> By laying the stress upon the competitive aspect of industry, this teaching stifled the growth of intellectual and moral sympathy between the various human centres of the industrial system, and impaired the sense of human solidarity…[116]

Hobson was aware of the practical limitations of Ruskin's critique in the context of new liberalism, but it was still Ruskin's basic humanism which provided the nucleus for Hobson's own condemnation of competition and prompted him to spend much of the rest of his life trying to reconcile organicism with a modified capitalist system.

Hobson, Ruskin and Utopianism

In his biography, Hobson commented extensively on Ruskin's ideal social order which he had set out in *Time and Tide* and *Fors Clavigera*. A man's property, he had argued, consisted of good things, honestly acquired and skilfully used. Nothing stolen or taken by force could rightfully be called 'property'.[117] In order to achieve this condition, society had a duty to educate its members. A healthy society was dependent upon the provision of education and the maintenance of morality, with a state prohibition on marriage between 'undesirables', a condition that Hobson considered 'one of the plainest demands of social welfare'.[118]

Education, Ruskin insisted, should also be state controlled and it should be 'free, liberal and technical' in orientation.[119] It was also to include a responsibility for the physical well-being of the children. As Ruskin commented in *Time and Tide*: 'I hold it for indisputable, that the first duty of a State is to see that every child born therein shall be well housed, clothed, fed, and educated, till it attain years of discretion.'[120] Schools should be situated, when possible, in the countryside and have enough land to enable physical exercise. Alongside the basic subjects, children should be taught moral conduct and principles of good behaviour, and in all cases their education should eventually be orientated toward the career they will pursue. Hobson had no equivocation in supporting Ruskin in this, commenting that:

> The pinchbeck policy which guides even our more liberal educationalists today, will furnish derision and amazement to a more enlightened posterity. For after this ideal, as after many other ideals of John Ruskin, history is slowly and dimly groping its way.[121]

As always, Ruskin concentrated on the nature of work as providing the key to the social order and Hobson commented that Ruskin's emphasis on 'clear lines of social and industrial demarcation' led to accusations of 'New Feudalism' by those who misunderstood his motives. Ruskin did not want a 'stereotyped caste system'. There were always to be opportunities for those indicating a special aptitude to develop their particular skills. Indeed, he was one of the earliest advocates of 'equality of opportunity' through education, despite his unshakeable conviction of innate differences of ability and class, 'a principle of social stratification' that he had developed from Plato.[122]

Hobson observed that Ruskin had completely dismissed 'the false and foolish thesis that all work is in itself equally worthy and ennobling', a ploy used to 'dignify manual labour' and to 'assuage discontent'. Ruskin considered that some jobs were totally mindless and degrading but that there were some persons who were suitable for nothing else. As Hobson remarked, it seemed here that Ruskin, like Carlyle, was considering 'slavery', although Ruskin's essential humanity rebelled against the harshness of this 'necessity', and he hoped that, in an improved society, degrading work would be reduced to a minimum level.[123]

With his assembled ranks of craftsmen, Ruskin anticipated a reciprocal arrangement whereby the workers would produce the quality of goods, which an educated society of consumers would demand. Quite how this would function effectively, Ruskin did not make clear, but Hobson noted that it was 'implied both in *Fors* and *Time and Tide* that voluntary cooperation of individuals should be the basis of action'.[124] Trade Unions should be transformed into Labourers Unions or Guilds, each responsible under the direction of elected advisors for the quality of the goods produced and the conditions of the workforce. This, Hobson found 'a harking back to mediaevalism', and he was uncertain as to its practicality as a system but he approved the underlying motivation of quality control of goods. He refers to Ruskin's words in *Time and Tide*:

> Advisable improvements or varieties in manufacture would have to be examined and accepted by the trade guild: when so accepted, they would be announced in public reports; and all puffery and self-proclamation on the part of tradesmen absolutely forbidden, as much as the making of any other kind of noise or disturbance.[125]

Membership of guilds, Ruskin insisted, should be 'entirely optional', leaving consumers free to buy from outsiders 'at their pleasure and peril'. Guilds were also to control the retail trade, and all necessary public works were to be owned and administered by the public for the benefit of the public. No private speculation was to be allowed.

In the organisation of agriculture, Hobson commented, Ruskin was 'eminently a practical reformer', and 'his insistence upon fixity of rent and security of tenants' improvements as the most urgent needs, indicates a firm grasp of the existing agricultural situation.' He was well qualified to comment, decided Hobson, on the grounds of Ruskin's 'wide and close' observation of continental agricultural processes. *Fors,* in particular, was for Hobson full of 'shrewd criticism and suggestion'.[126]

Ruskin's greater plan for agriculture within his ideal state was, however, in Hobson's view 'fraught with peculiar difficulty'. Ruskin tempered feudalism with security of tenure and freedom to cultivate for the 'peasant class'.[127] Hobson was less convinced, when Ruskin argued that 'great old families' should be maintained by the state and not live off the rent of tenants. Hobson commented:

> What the actual status and the occupation of this feudal aristo-cracy, in the midst of a population of virtually independent peasant occupiers, paying rent to the State, would be, we are not told; nor is it easy to conceive how, otherwise than by existing beautifully, they would justify the State incomes they receive.[128]

Moreover, Ruskin's reforms for agriculture, in Hobson's view, differed vitally from those for commerce and manufacture. The quasi-feudalistic system that Ruskin advised in agriculture was not consistent with the 'growth of a voluntary state within a state', which he advised for industry. The changes that he advocated for the land system would require 'State coercion', and a 'practical nationalisation of the land', subject to state control. This, wrote Hobson, was evidence of the way in which Ruskin tended to 'oscillate between voluntary cooperation and State action'.[129]

This, to a certain extent, was due to a genuine development in Ruskin's thinking. As Hobson pointed out, the preface to *Unto This Last* showed the government in control of functions which later, in *Time and Tide* and *Fors,* Ruskin 'assigns to voluntary guilds'. However, it became obvious through an examination of Ruskin's idea of the governing role of the 'upper classes', Hobson wrote, that Ruskin 'never definitely abandoned the idea of limited State Socialism for a thoroughly thought-out scheme of voluntary cooperation'.

Hobson criticised Ruskin for seemingly accepting the 'upper classes,' imperfect as they were, and seeking to 'moralise and elevate them into a condition which will justify their social and industrial supremacy'.[130] His reasoning, wrote Hobson, was 'based upon curiously simple and defective generalisations of history and heredity'. There was also an inconsistency in Ruskin's advocacy of 'fixed pay for fixed appointments' and his later insistence in *Fors* that the professions formally ascribed to his upper classes should be paid anything but a pittance, as they were peripheral to the real business of sustaining life.[131]

Ruskin's reference to feudalistic hierarchies could only be excused, determined Hobson, through an understanding of his interpretation of anarchism. In Ruskin's terms, an anarchic society, in direct contrast to a feudal one, was an individualistic state, where people took no responsibility for anyone but themselves and their immediate family. This was a very dubious form of liberty for the underprivileged and Hobson echoed Ruskin in a poignant plea for government intervention:

> Never perhaps in the world's history has the particular form of helpless, hopeless 'liberty' which shows itself in the poorer life of our modern great cities, elsewhere appeared; where families, grown up in want and ignorance, struggle for a bare subsistence, live in disorder and degradation, and die without society giving to them any systematic recognition whatever. The casual and arbitrary interference of the police, the equally casual enforcement of a few social regulations respecting the rudiments of sanitation, hygiene, and education, the legal registration of a few cardinal facts of life and death – at certain odd intervals this machinery of social order impinges upon the 'liberty of the citizen'. But there is no pretence of any genuine social education and social supervision. The State, the city, the parish have no real official knowledge or control of the lives of the great mass of the population. So long as this is so, there can be no government that is worthy of the name. The responsibility of all to each and of each to all is the essential of true citizenship.[132]

Hobson did regret that Ruskin had obscured the importance of this message, as he so often did, with his 'fancy for names', which exposed him to the ridicule of many who had neither 'the humour or the sense' to follow his 'dialectics of reform'.[133] Yet Ruskin's proposals, though not always 'clear and consistent', had yet a 'powerful coherence and a genuinely practical value'. This could be observed in the way in which society had begun to move toward an adoption of his schemes. Indeed, Hobson urged that any inconsistencies in Ruskin's thinking could largely be explained by the course of events between his earlier and later writings. When he published *Fors Clavigera,* he had become very disillusioned and convinced that no one was listening to him: hence the note of despair. As a form of catharsis, he concentrated on small practical schemes. But Ruskin never lost sight of his greater vision of 'an enduring and united Commonwealth'.[134]

Hobson, Ruskin and the Political Arena

Any assessment of Ruskin's influence has to include an analysis of his political persuasion, for, despite his denial of any form of categorisation, the orientation of some of his most prominent disciples is a significant indicator to the contrary. In his biography, Hobson considered how far Ruskin could be labelled a socialist. Hobson provided his own questionable description of socialism as:

> An organic view of social life, which accords to society a unity not constituted of the mere addition of its individual members, but contained in a common end or purpose, which determines and imposes the activities of these individual members.[135]

In that sense, wrote Hobson, Ruskin was a committed socialist. But socialism meant more than a 'simple adhesion to some organic view of social life'. It also demanded a recognition of significant social activity in politics and industry either under state control or through voluntary cooperation. In this 'general economic sense' which approved greater state control of industry, and in his humanitarian critique of a capitalist economy, Ruskin could also be ranked as a socialist. Hobson compared Ruskin's economics with continental socialism, which also called for the abolition of the competitive system in favour of publicly organised industry, the eradication of rent and interest, and the establishment of a labour basis of exchange.[136] In Ruskin's insistence in *Unto This Last,* that every 'man or woman, boy or girl out of employment' should be given a fixed rate of pay while retraining for suitable work in a government school, Ruskin was also, decided Hobson, [obviously thinking of Fourier] 'in close sympathy with the tenets of revolutionary Socialism'.[137] There were, however, certain areas of disagreement.

Hobson referred to *Fors* (Letter 18) where Ruskin stressed free ownership of land with hereditary tenure, a principle antagonistic to revolutionary socialism. The same applied to his insistence that houses were the private property of the occupants. Also at odds with social democracy, noted Hobson, was Ruskin's inconsistency on the question of public ownership and control of industry. But what really distanced him from mainstream economic socialism was his reversion to medievalism in advocating a guild system which was to be voluntary and self-governing. Although even there, Hobson conceded, there was evidence that continental socialists had flirted with similar notions.

But if Ruskin did not comply entirely with continental socialism, Hobson found an appropriate place for him among the more radical school of Christian Socialism, which tended to eschew close economic analysis in its reforming policy in favour of a concentration on charitable action. Although Ruskin was meticulous in his own analytical critique of the economy, there were many traces of sentimentality in his writing, which were often isolated and exploited in the Christian cause by those who were 'smitten with social compunction', but could not risk following Ruskin in cutting away 'the economic roots of poverty'.[138]

Hobson acknowledged that some Christian Socialists, inspired by the process of rationalism and a greater concentration on the quality of life on earth, would accept Ruskin's advocacy of both spiritual and temporal leaders, while others would be less enthusiastic about his virtual abandonment of doctrine and dogma. It was, however, Ruskin's emphasis on authority which distanced him from any form of democratic government. There was some justification for Hobson's reservations here. Ruskin's call for cooperation was moral rather than political and could not, he felt, be achieved in a corrupt climate. He supported the concept of cooperative workshops and indeed, followed the Owenite principle of trying to establish small communities, but he did not see this as the sole answer to existing evils. He completely mistrusted people's abilities to protect their own interests and equated liberty and equality with anarchy, a conviction, said Hobson, which 'brought him into strange company and into strange historic judgements'.[139] Hobson referred here to the case of Governor Eyre in which Ruskin unashamedly followed Carlyle's support for the cruel suppression of Jamaican rioters in 1865-6, an action very much at odds with Ruskin's usual humanitarian stance.[140]

Hobson added some further interesting observations on Carlyle's influence upon Ruskin. Organic unity for Ruskin, whether in art or society, depended on the cooperation of 'unequals'. This theory was endorsed by Carlyle's proclivity for 'hero-worship', which Ruskin had 'eagerly absorbed', although it was 'more consciously ideal' in Ruskin as he was well aware of the many defects of 'great men'.[141] Nevertheless, he equated anarchy with modern liberalism and was repelled by the implications of all that it represented to him in terms of the levelling of social distinctions and the disintegration of moral and practical authority.

In this aspect, as in his economic criticism, Ruskin was thus opposed to liberalism. Nineteenth-century conservative and socialist thinkers were united in using the organic metaphor for their critique of the *laissez-faire* society. The 'common enemy,' as Raymond Williams points out, 'is liberalism' and Ruskin's role in this scenario is very significant: 'Ruskin, like Carlyle, was one of the destroyers of liberalism: this may now be seen as his merit. It is for his destructive social criticism that he is important.'[142] Williams had argued that both Ruskin and Carlyle could only find their organic metaphor by looking back. This is almost certainly true in Carlyle's case, but not consistently so with Ruskin. *Unto this Last* was remarkably free of medieval reference and Ruskin's organic imagery came initially from his theory of art and nature. But it was almost certainly Carlyle who reinforced Ruskin's Platonic rejection of democracy. Indeed, Hobson remarked upon 'the overbearing influence of Carlyle on his [Ruskin's] politics', but still argued that Ruskin was closer to new liberalism than he would probably care to admit.

Hobson observed also that Ruskin's fiercest opposition to radicalism was reserved for J.S. Mill, yet in some ways Ruskin was closer to Mill than he was to Carlyle. Indeed, Ruskin himself did not seem to realise how far he was removed from Carlyle in both 'historic and economic criticism'. Carlyle, despite some 'intuitive glimpses' of corruption among the governing classes, did not even begin to analyse the intricate connection between politics and industry as Ruskin did.

In his attention to detail, Hobson compared Ruskin with Mazzini, although Ruskin was for Hobson far more thorough and perceptive. Their main difference, Hobson decided, lay in their plans of reform. Mazzini suggested that the people should basically be responsible for both economic and political government, but Ruskin, even though he could see the results of economic injustice more clearly than did Mazzini, could never accept popular government. This rather surprised Hobson, who commented on how close Ruskin came at times to admitting the inevitability and even the rightness of democracy. He certainly was not wedded to the idea of benevolent despots, unlike Carlyle. Instead, Ruskin continued to pin his hopes on 'the voluntary self-reformation of the governing classes' and the encouragement of individual effort among the 'lower orders'. Democracy was never really on the agenda in Ruskin's thinking, which led him to a strange form of socialism:

> In a word, the Socialism, to which Mr Ruskin looks, is to be imposed by an hereditary aristocracy, whose effective cooperation for the common good is to be derived from the voluntary action of individual land-owners and employers. There must be no movement of the masses to claim economic justice; no use of Parliament to 'nationalise' land or capital, or to attack any private interest.[143]

The governing classes, who were, in Ruskin's view, living idly upon the fruits of economic exploitation, were therefore to be invited to become aware of their moral and social obligations. In this, as Hobson observed, Ruskin shared a doctrine with the Comtist movement who, as already noted, also wished to impose an educated aristocracy on their ideal society. Hobson quoted the example of Frederic Harrison as representative of a small body of dissident intellectuals, who followed Ruskin in wishing to bring much needed moral reflection into the arena of social reform. Although Harrison was neither a Christian nor a socialist, his aspirations for society had many points in common with those who claimed to be both.[144] His authoritarianism was, like Ruskin's, intended ultimately to generate greater social harmony, albeit at the expense of individual liberty. Hobson, however, was much more aware of the fragile political balance between liberty and welfare.

In trusting reform to an enlightened capitalist aristocracy, Hobson identified what he saw as two fatal errors in Ruskin's thinking. The first was the difficulty of persuading 'captains of industry' that their present conduct was dishonest. The great majority of them would, wrote Hobson, remain 'intellectually incapable' of following the economic analysis of Ruskin or any other reformer, and those who were capable would 'refuse to do so'. There was, he wrote, a great deal of difference in seeing the right and doing it, especially if it involved the abandonment of 'a customary and agreeable line of conduct'.[145] Ruskin's aspirations were commendable, but he was over optimistic if he sought to reverse the 'whole spirit of industry'. Moreover, commented Hobson, a moral injunction to individuals would not overcome the ills of society – 'Social evils require social remedies.'[146] The general will must be the engine of reform even if the appeal in the first instance was to the higher principles of the individual. Ruskin's invocation to the social conscience of 'captains of industry' would not solve the problem of economic injustice; they would simply answer that they could not raise wages without raising prices, nor improve the quality of their goods for the same reason. Manufacturers were too closely bound within the processes of competitive trade and risked losing their position in the business world, if they did not conform.

Hobson was critical also of Ruskin's desire to educate the consumer. Indeed, Ruskin's whole assumption that society could be reformed privately through an appeal to individual action was, decided Hobson, untenable. Moral awareness was important, but it must stimulate organic cooperation if it was to be effective. State intervention did not preclude the requirement for voluntary reform by individual groups with their own special expertise: 'The advocates of State action are not the enemies of private reform agencies, but the friends.'[147] These agencies should rather direct their activities to the general good.

Ruskin's fear of democracy and his insistence on a ruling elite was thus, considered Hobson, 'a radical defect in his social thinking'. A new order could only come from the 'enlightened, rational, freewill of the people':

> A so-called Socialism from above, embodying the patronage of emperor or of a small enlightened bureaucracy, is not Socialism in any moral sense at all; the forms of government must be animated by the social spirit, must be the expression of the common organic genius of the people, if it is to have true vitality and meaning.[148]

Ruskin, Hobson concluded, was deluded about the true nature of democracy. He interpreted it as meaning absolute equality with no room for 'reverence'. His peculiar predilection for total servility obscured his moral judgement and led him to believe that any respect for superior qualities in others was incompatible with democratic government. But a rational democracy would depend for its successful functioning on a recognition of these qualities. Therefore Ruskin's fears were unfounded.

Absolute equality was not essential to democracy – the role of government leaders was to express the general will of the people. Ruskin's own formula of a hierarchically structured organism, in his words: 'The true strength of every human soul is to be dependent on as many nobler as it can discern, and to be depended upon, by as many inferior as it can reach,'[149] was in fact, claimed Hobson, little different from Mazzini's democratic principle: 'The progress of all through all, under the leadership of the best and the wisest.'[150]

Hobson was aware that the freedom advocated for craftsmen in Ruskin's *The Nature of Gothic* did not realise its obvious potential in Ruskin's later social thought, but this did not detract from the essential rightness and impact of his thinking. Despite some areas of disagreement, and the resulting difficulty of placing him accurately among either new liberals or socialists, Hobson was never in any doubt as to the huge importance of Ruskin's moral and economic critique. He made frequent reference to Ruskin in other major works where he reinforced his views on many issues. In *The Evolution of Modern Capitalism* (1894), Hobson referred to Ruskin's strictures on the inadvisability of over-saving,[151] and in *The Social Problem* (1901), Hobson consolidated Ruskin's theory of value:

> So long as there are persons who are ignorant, or vicious, or vulgar, and who are willing and able to back their ignorance, vice, or vulgarity, by the use of money, these things rank as wealth. Ruskin presses this point with keen and accurate insistence, that the human value or true worth of a thing consists in, and is measured by, its life-sustaining and life-improving qualities.[152]

In 1902 Hobson commented that 'Ruskin was one of the first men to recognise the impotence – nay, even the mischievousness – of political revolution unaccompanied by economic revolution.'[153]

Hobson's own influence on both new liberals and socialists was also profound but difficult to analyse because of the complex nature of liberalism itself. Primarily, he sought to redefine the whole negative concept of liberty, embraced by earlier liberals, into one which would tolerate state intervention. Indeed, the part he played in eliminating the doctrine of unfettered *laissez-faire* can be seen, as John Allett comments, as a significant factor in preparing the way for the foundation of the Welfare State:

New Liberals sought to undermine the doctrine of *laissez-faire* and therefore disabuse old liberals of their distrust in the state. In this task Hobson took on the main responsibility for attacking the premises of classical economics, while Hobhouse, Samuel, Ritchie, and others concentrated on the political philosophy of old liberalism.[154]

Ruskin's part in this process was covert and unwitting but nonetheless important. He may have denied any political affiliation but his influence was far reaching, embracing both new liberals and socialists with equal intensity. Through Hobson, he helped facilitate a liberal-socialist synthesis, a compromise in which competition was minimised but still retained, in which a level of subsistence was at least attempted,[155] and a national health and employment scheme was ultimately initiated. If Hobson is rightly seen as the bridge between nineteenth- and twentieth-century social and economic thought, Ruskin must be acknowledged as the inspirational factor. Hobson's organic perspective, his insistence on social goals, and his underlying humanism undoubtedly came from Ruskin. Hobson himself was very clear on the extent of his debt: 'To clarify the vision, to elevate the aim, to humanise, and so to dignify, the needs of conduct, are the persistent endeavours of John Ruskin's teaching.'[156]

7

RUSKIN AND THE SOCIALISTS

'The book which made me a Socialist was *Unto This Last*.' F.W.
Jowett, M.P. (Bradford, West).

'Among the books of John Ruskin the one *Unto This Last* was most
useful to me.' J. Johnson, M.P. (Gateshead).

'Probably those [books] that I love the most and have received the
greatest advantage from are Ruskin's works, particularly *Unto This
Last*.' John T. Macpherson, M.P. (Preston).

'John Ruskin's *Unto this Last* was lent me, and it had much to do
in forming opinions.' J.W. Taylor, M.P.
(Durham, Chester-le-Street).[1]

'Ruskin, the man whose spirit inspired British Socialism.'
E. Halevy (1939)[2]

In the period of economic depression which characterised the last twenty-
five years of nineteenth-century Britain,[3] there was a socialist revival. As
the wave of mid-Victorian prosperity ebbed, new strategies were needed
to address the problems of indigence, yet the Liberal Party was still
reluctant to abandon the principle of *laissez-faire* individualism. Without
state intervention the problems of poverty and disease were not being
addressed other than by the selective and unsystematic efforts of various
churches and charities.[4] Positivism had ultimately failed to address the
needs of the working man and there was an overwhelming requirement
for the creation of a separate party to represent the working-class cause.
Ruskin was, by the 1880s, ill and disillusioned, still opposed to democracy and still adamant about his apolitical stance. So why did so many
working-class sympathisers look to him for inspiration?

Defining Socialism

One of the problems confronting would-be socialists was defining the movement, a situation which was not speedily resolved. Writing on socialism in 1887 Charles Bradlaugh commented that his greatest difficulty was in discovering any general agreement in England on what was meant by the term 'Socialism'.[5] There were, he wrote, 'so many grades and shades of diverse opinion loosely included in, and attacked, or defended, as Socialism' that in the absence of 'any authoritative, or official, or even generally accepted definition' he would provide his own which, if in error, was because he has been 'misled by Socialist writers'.[6] His attempt at definition by no means covered the spectrum, however, and he concluded his analysis by identifying socialism with communism. This was not surprising as the two ideologies had initially much in common. Indeed, Marxism was a significant part of the nineteenth-century socialist renaissance. Nonetheless, while there were obvious similarities between Marxist communism and other forms of socialism in terms of a critique of capitalism, there were also many important discrepancies. Stanley Pierson observes in his book *Marxism and the Origins of British Socialism*:

> By the early nineties three different versions of Socialism had emerged – British Marxism, Fabianism, and a much less coherent school of thought that I have labelled Ethical Socialism. The last, strongly utopian in spirit, became the dominant form of British Socialism.[7]

It is in the context of this latter form that the extent of Ruskin's influence begins to emerge.

Ruskin, like other middle class reformers, wanted a revolution of values; Marx, however, rejected this aspiration as utopian dreaming. His critique of capitalism, which he considered to be scientific, was predicated on the idea that by raising the workers' consciousness of their role in history they would become aware that they were victims of capitalist exploitation. Only political revolution would free them from this condition and deliver them into communism.

Marx, like Ruskin, perceived a society which was essentially organic, but his perception differed in several crucial aspects. His attitude to work, an issue on which many socialists based their critique of capitalism, echoed Ruskin's concerns about unity and self-fulfilment but omitted the moral dimension. Ruskin, like Carlyle, considered that work contained a spiritual element, present in all good craftsmanship and that industrial processes, in denying the opportunity for creativity, were thus producing dissatisfied workers who took no pride in the end product. Marx considered the 'gospel of work' to be merely a further ploy for exploitation of the workforce. Ruskin stressed the need for a reconsideration of values, which persisted even after his orthodox Christianity had ebbed; Marx's emphasis was on class conflict and the necessity of proletarian revolution. As he observed in 1847:

> Modern industry has converted the little workshop of the patriarchal master into the great factory of the industrial capitalist. Masses of labourers, crowded into the factory, are organised like soldiers . . . Not only are they slaves of the bourgeois class, and of the bourgeois state, they are daily and hourly enslaved by the machine, by the overlooker, and, above all, by the individual bourgeois manufacturer himself.[8]

Ruskin's words on the same subject, written some six years later, long before Marx became a political force in England, pressed home Ruskin's all-pervading sense of morality. Because of their significance to the socialist movement and to Ruskin's place in its philosophy, they merit repetition:

> It is verily this degradation of the operative into a machine, which more than any other evil of the times, is leading the mass of the nations everywhere into a vain, incoherent, destructive struggle for a freedom of which they cannot explain the nature to themselves . . . We manufacture everything except men . . . To brighten, to strengthen, to refine or form a single living spirit, never enters into our estimate of advantages.[9]

The juxtaposition of these extracts illustrates the reasoning behind Keir Hardie's comment that 'a mere abstraction, be it ever so demonstrable scientifically, will never move masses of people'.[10] Both Marx and Ruskin considered their critique of capitalism to be scientific, but in Britain only Ruskin seemed able ultimately to touch the hearts as well as the minds of socialist sympathisers.

Religion and the Working Classes

Ruskin's 'socialism' filled a gap in the consciousness of the British working classes, exacerbated by a widespread disillusionment with orthodox religious observance. This was particularly true of the self-educated, more intellectual, members of the labouring classes. In 1869, the rationalist Leslie Stephen examined this phenomenon with more than a little humour. He commented on the fact that some 'unusually observant' clergymen actually noticed that 'the more intelligent of the working classes do not go to church or chapel, do not like going there, and profess to get little or no good when they do go.'[11] They therefore invited a group of skilled artisans to the London Tavern to tell them 'the reason why'.

The meeting consisted on one side of 'dignitaries of the Church' and 'eminent Nonconformist ministers of various sects' and on the other 'a number of genuine working men from different trades and occupations – engineers, carpenters, hawkers, gilders, porters, ex-scavengers, plasterers, and railwaymen.' The 'plain and concise directness' with which these men answered questions must, commented Stephen, 'have not a little startled,' and, he hoped, 'enlightened, their reverend hearers'. He felt that he would be doing his readers a 'welcome service' by condensing and classifying the reasons these men gave for their con-tinued refusal to patronise either church or chapel or to have anything to do with 'ministers and religious ministrations'.[12] There was no question of disputing the truth of the situation, it was generally acknowledged and the men questioned did not consider themselves to be 'infidels'. But Stephen considers it is too bland to simply say that the 'labouring classes' did not attend church; it was necessary to place them in 'distinct categories'.

He stressed that, while the agricultural poor continued to attend church or chapel, 'according to the influence of their superiors',[13] in the towns and cities there was a marked division in religious observance between skilled and unskilled labourers. Apart from the vast numbers of urban poor who were 'too ignorant, too restless, too dissolute, or too lazy and self-indulgent to care for religion in any shape', there were two other distinct groups. The first was composed of 'mechanics and operatives' who belonged to either the church or one of the dissenting sects – 'sometimes Baptists, oftener Weslyans' – and were regular churchgoers. These people were 'sober, industrious, domestic, thriving, and in every

way estimable' but in Stephen's opinion, they did not 'constitute the
intellectual portion of the skilled artisan class, the eager politicians, the
lecture-goers, the supporters of mechanics' institutes, and the like'.
These are the men 'who think, the men who aspire, the men who investigate' and they do not for the most part 'attend church or chapel'. The
first group 'seek to save their souls', the second, 'the intelligent, strive to
improve their minds; and naturally, therefore, they do not go to church'.[14]
Why they did not attend their church had great political as well as social
significance.

The intelligent artisan, in Stephen's view, no longer believed that the
teachings of Christ were preached – 'the common people do not hear it
gladly.' The clergy had so far ignored this fact, blaming poor attendance
on fatigue or a reluctance by the indigent to sit in the pews ascribed to
them. This Stephen rejected; the skilled workman was never too fatigued
to attend political meetings nor too poor to afford a pew. He simply had
no incentive to be forced to listen to a lot of unsympathetic and irrelevant
cant. The English skilled operative was 'eminently practical' and not
given to 'metaphysics or to dogma'. In religion, he was 'ethical rather
than either doctrinal or aesthetic'. He was attracted to the human, for-
giving side of Christianity not to 'crude metaphysics'. In effect, Stephen
concluded, 'the hard headed mechanic, weary of "astounding pro-
positions" and "awful denunciations", given by "a shallow and narrow
preacher whose intelligence was hard for him to respect" found his faith
"shaken to the very foundations".' His love of 'clearness, sincerity and fair
play' was frustrated by a clergy who 'seldom display any of these qualities';
the intelligent artisan thus tended to become a secularist.[15]

These were reasons enough for disaffection, but one final factor had
deep repercussions for the government. While Stephen agreed that the
clergy had the right to 'stand aloof from party controversies', there were
some great social problems to which it was their duty to alert public
attention. These were 'questions of life and death to the poor', issues on
which conservatives and liberals exhibited 'precisely the same views'. It
was the neglect of these social problems which made the working man
so resentful. Finding little help from the state and no solace in religion
he was forced to reinterpret his values and look elsewhere for the strength
of practical assistance. This was a sharp analysis, which, while it
underestimated working-class liberalism, pointed to crucial issues for
late nineteenth-century politics.[16]

Marxist socialism, while it proposed a practical solution for inequality, offered few people a moral or spiritual replacement for lost Christian values. It was not wholly in tune with the English working-class mentality. Even Engels, who was the leading authority on British Marxism and had closely observed the living conditions of the working classes, was not always at ease with them. In a letter dated 11 June 1890, he commented that he was frequently annoyed by 'the insular stiff-necked obstinacy' of English workers,[17] but impressed by their independent spirit. Stanley Pierson comments:

> While Engels came to recognise something of the tenacity of traditional working-class attitudes and the difficulty of bringing the 'Socialist instinct' to the full consciousness, his Marxism provided no answers to these problems . . . Until his death in 1895 Engels remained wedded to notions which prevented him from understanding the actual development of the British workers.[18]

Ruskin's position was different. His relationship with the working classes may have been less direct than that of Engels, but his effect on them was ultimately more profound, albeit through a very circuitous route. Ruskin was sympathetic as a young man to the plight of the labouring classes but had little direct engagement with them other than through the Working Men's College, where he taught drawing during the mid-1850s. It was there, also, that he became aware of the early concept of Christian Socialism, but at this time his identification with the movement was slight. F.J. Furnivall had introduced Ruskin to the College in 1854 and used his famous essay on 'The Nature of Gothic' as a blueprint for its aims. Ruskin taught there for four years and introduced other artists such as Rossetti, Ford Madox Brown and Burne-Jones as teachers, but found himself impatient with the aims of both Maurice and Christian Socialism, feeling that the principles of 'self-help' and cooperation, although admirable, were doing little to address the underlying causes of industrial and economic exploitation. Writing on Ruskin's association with the early Christian Socialists, G.J. Holyoake commented in 1879 on the dismissive nature of Ruskin's tone in referring to the 'amiable sentimentalism' of Maurice. Holyoake, however, added:

It is right, however, to say that the spirit shown by Mr Maurice's disciples was free alike from condescension or assumption. They were not dogmatic; they asserted but did not insist on other persons adopting their views. You felt that it would be a pleasure to them if you could think as they did; but they made it no offence to you if you did not.[19]

Maurice, like Ruskin, despised the practice of *laissez-faire* but did not lay the blame upon the economic system. He saw capitalism and social deprivation as largely separate issues.[20] Ruskin's concerns, as has been demonstrated, were even at this early stage of social protest, more complex, more radical, and difficult to align with any one political ideology. He was also, at this time (late 1850s), experiencing his own personal crisis of faith, which was to further distance him from some members of the original Christian Socialist Movement, but ironically, made his teaching the inspiration of the second wave of Christian Socialism in the last two decades of the nineteenth century. By the mid-1870s Ruskin's Christianity, stripped of its doctrine and dogma, had re-emerged unbidden in 'socialist' garb. One of the men who helped to facilitate this process was William Morris (1834–96).

Morris, Marx and Ruskin

Morris was undoubtedly one of the key players in the late nineteenth-century socialist revival, and, following Ruskin's example, he drew his social inspiration from his aesthetic studies and his own experiences of craftsmanship. As with Ruskin, the nature of creative activity in medieval society provided Morris with the metaphor for his critique of capitalism, and also, as with Ruskin, the division of labour was a focal point of Morris's attack. Despite these very strong links, however, which were often acknowledged by Morris, his later adoption of the Marxist explanation of exploitation, class struggle and the inevitability of revolution has led to an underestimation of Ruskin's influence, as already indicated. Yet much of Morris's political writings pre-dated the publication of Marx's work in England and Morris's concentration on the nature of work, which was his major contribution to socialist thought, was undeniably an echo of the Ruskinian ethic.

Morris first became familiar with Ruskin's writing when he went up to Oxford in 1850. He was so impressed by *The Stones of Venice*, published a year later, and in particular, by 'The Nature of Gothic', that Morris printed this chapter as a separate item in 1854, with a more prestigious reprinting by the Kelmscott Press in 1892. The ideas that Ruskin so eloquently expressed in this work became pivotal to Morris's ideology, as he explained in his preface:

> The lesson which Ruskin here teaches us, is that art is the expression of man's pleasure in labour; . . . that unless man's work once again becomes a pleasure to him, the token of which change will be that beauty is once again a natural and necessary accompaniment of productive labour, all but the worthless must toil in pain, and therefore live in pain.[21]

'The Nature of Gothic,' claimed Morris, 'is one of the most important things written by the author, and in future days will be considered as one of the very few necessary and inevitable utterances of the century.'[22] His motivation for this generous appraisal did not lie purely in aesthetics; he considered this chapter more significant for its 'ethical and political' implications than for its 'artistic side' and he emphasised its enduring qualities. In the same preface he also praised *Unto This Last*, which he considered marked the culmination of the ethical and political ideas inherent in 'The Nature of Gothic'.[23] Ruskin was, indeed, a lasting source of inspiration for Morris. One of his contemporaries, J.W. Mackail,[24] commented in 1899:

> Among the great prose authors under whose influence [Morris] had fallen at Oxford, Carlyle and Ruskin were the two who had continued to hold him most strongly. For the latter, whose influence over him was indeed much the more profound and far-reaching, his admiration was sometimes crossed by that defiance which had been observed in his Oxford days to mingle with his enthusiasm for Tennyson . . . But this was the caprice of a momentary impatience; and all his serious references to Ruskin showed that he retained towards him the attitude of a scholar to a great teacher and master, not only in matters of art, but throughout the whole sphere of human life.[25]

There is little doubt that the central principle embodied in Ruskin's contrast between the Gothic artisan and the modern labourer was both pivotal to Morris's own thought and a fundamental factor in his incipient socialism. In 1884 he gave a lecture to the Hampstead Liberal Club, entitled 'Useful Work versus Useless Toil', in which Morris condemned the latter as the dehumanising consequence of capitalist production methods. The parallels with Ruskin's exhortations in 'The Nature of Gothic' were very apparent:

> To compel a man to do day after day the same task, without any hope of escape or change, means nothing short of turning his life into a prison-torment. Nothing but the tyranny of profit-grinding makes this necessary.[26]

Ruskin's concern for the degradation of the modern labourer sprang from a quasi-religious ethic, which took its point of reference from the past. Morris's pursuit of the same ethic is often interpreted as Marxist. Indeed, any attempt to diminish the extent of Ruskin's influence on Morris is usually justified by an affirmation of Morris's Marxism. But many of Morris's so-called Marxist tendencies can equally well be traced to Ruskin, whose notions of alienation and concern for exploitation can in turn be traced to the romantic tradition which pre-dated Marxism. Morris may have moved away from romantic notions of society redeemed by art, but his political writings developed out of art and a socialist theory of culture which was very similar to that of Ruskin, when stripped of its Biblical symbolism. Marxist theory made Morris a revolutionary, but his recognition of the interactive nature of the forces of work, culture and capitalism and his moral critique of capitalist values can more directly be traced to Ruskin. On the founding of the Arts and Crafts Society, Mackail observed:

> The way here, as in so many other instances, had been pointed out by the far-ranging genius of Ruskin long before any steps were, or could be, taken towards its realisation. The prophet had, as usual, been long before his age. The whole of the Socialism with which Morris identified himself so prominently in the eighties had been implicitly contained, and the greater part of it explicitly stated, in the pages of *Unto This Last* in 1860, when Morris had just begun the work of his life as a manufacturer.[27]

Thus, although Morris's critique of capitalism may subsequently have achieved greater recognition than did that of Ruskin, that was because Morris, unlike Ruskin, eventually tempered aestheticism with political realism. Morris moved on from social criticism to political action. Ruskin was probably only too aware of the logical implications of his own doctrines but he favoured moral reconstruction within the existing society. In a letter that he addressed to Mr Frederic Pickles, a working man, in 1884, Ruskin's point of departure from Morris was made clear:

> Morris is quite right as to the things to be gained, but be sure they cannot be got by fighting as nothing but desolation comes of that – being flat denial of Heaven's power to begin with . . . Determine what you want first abolished of evil. State that plainly – and send men to Parliament to have it done. What have you got the franchise for, *but* that?[28]

Morris's full response illustrated a synthesis of purpose if not of method. His analysis deserves quotation at length:

> As to Ruskin's note to you, the subject matter of it is very serious, and I would not by any means if I can help it exaggerate my views on it, or evade the subject . . . If you send members to parliament they must be sent with the express purpose of overthrowing it as it exists at present; because it exists for the definite purpose of continuing the present evil state of things. And now as to active *force*: supposing a parliamentary victory for the Socialists and the Bourgeois outvoted: how is the vote to be carried out when it must mean a change in the basis of society? Would not the Bourgeois say 'You have outvoted us, try now if you can outfight us.' I do not say that the Bourgeois would fight, they might be cowed by the people, if the people are only *solid enough in combination*: all depends on that: but the bourgeois will not be convinced *as a class* they *can* only yield to force, actual or potential. Ruskin is quite sound in his condemnation of rent and usury, but he does not understand this matter of classes. The class struggle is really the only lever for bringing about the change. Of course you understand that though I would not shrink from a civil war if that be the only necessary means, I would do all I could to avoid it: in point of fact the

question of peace or war does not rest with us but with our opponents: my belief is that when we begin to seem dangerous to them they will attempt to repress our propaganda forcibly: recent events in London certainly point to that. Meantime at present to meddle with parliament is clearly not our game: we must put the issue clearly before the country first and make people understand our principles definitely unmuddled by political opportunism. This I admit is the long game and is very trying to the patience, but it is the sure game; and if we have not a full stock of patience we are not fit for revolutionists.[29]

Morris's desire for social revolution was, certainly at this stage, a significant point of divergence with Ruskin. But was it simply a question of Ruskin misunderstanding the concept of 'class'? Ruskin believed that a revolution would not work for the same reason that he rejected democracy, because, in the words of P.D. Anthony, 'Political action requires the abandonment of irreconcilable ethical positions.'[30] In a class war, Ruskin felt that the very values he sought to overthrow would be absorbed rather than eliminated. His working-class readers seemed to understand this, as Morris himself noted:

> . . . my experience so far is that the working man finds it easier to understand the doctrine of the claim of Labour to pleasure in the work itself than the rich or well-to-do man does. Apart from any trivial words of my own, I have been surprised to find, for instance, such a hearty feeling toward John Ruskin among working-class audiences; they can see the prophet in him rather than the fantastic rhetorician, as more superfine audiences do. That is a good omen.[31]

Ruskin's position remained moral and idealistic, because he simply did not believe that revolution was the answer to social and moral injustice. As he commented in one lecture: 'So far from being a common cause, all anarchy is the forerunner of poverty, and all prosperity begins in obedience.'[32] Morris's contrasting position here was a mark of his growing frustration, a stage that Ruskin had already gone through twenty-five years earlier when he wrote *Unto This Last*. Morris took Ruskin's ideas to what seemed to him to be their natural conclusion. In particular, Ruskin's moral critique of classical economy contained those quintessential higher principles of collectivism, which were absorbed and developed by Morris and later persuaded him to identify with revolutionary Marxism.[33]

There were indeed superficial points of similarity between Ruskin's thought and early Marxist aesthetic theory, as already noted. These similarities have often obscured the underlying points of divergence. What distinguished Ruskin from Marx was the former's essentially moralistic interpretation of society and his emphasis upon the quality of life. These factors were also central to Morris's argument. As P.D. Anthony comments:

> Those qualities for which Morris was once berated and for which he came to be praised, of moralism, idealism, utopianism, are his inheritance from Ruskin. What he got and acknowledged from Ruskin was moral criticism of capitalist values added to despair at the prospects for art in a capitalist world.[34]

This Ruskinian legacy had presented something of a problem for Morris, who never abandoned his aesthetic ideals but became equally enthusiastic about the Marxist explanation and solution for existing evils. In effect, as he explained in 'How I Became a Socialist', he was able to accommodate the two by allowing an ideal to push him toward a form of 'practical socialism'.[35] He quoted Ruskin as being his 'master toward the ideal aforesaid' and wrote that 'it was through him that he was able to give form to [his] discontent'.[36] All that he needed to do was to 'hook' himself on to the practical movement.[37]

It was this process of accommodation that made Morris's influence in the socialist revival both powerful and unique. In a lecture at Oxford in 1883 entitled 'Art under Plutocracy', he declared himself 'one of the people called Socialists' and was pleased that this announcement was made with the 'first comer', Professor Ruskin, in the chair.[38] The lecture perpetuated the Ruskinian ethic that art could not be considered in isolation from society:

> Art is man's expression of his joy in labour. If those are not Professor Ruskin's words they embody at least his teaching on this subject. Nor has any truth more important ever been stated; – the chief accusation I have to bring against the modern state of society

is that it is founded on the art-lacking or unhappy labour of the greater part of men . . . it is a token of the unhappy life forced on the great mass of the population by the system of competitive commerce.[39]

This considerably displeased the University authorities, who did not specifically object to socialist ideas but did dislike the fact that Morris had used his lecture as a platform to appeal for funds. Ruskin followed with an impromptu speech. The *Pall Mall Gazette* reported that: his appearance was the signal for immense enthusiasm, speaking of the lecturer as 'the great conceiver and doer, the man at once a poet, an artist, and a workman, and his old and dear friend'. Ruskin agreed with Morris in 'imploring the young men . . . to seek in true unity and love one for another the best direction for the great forces which like an evil aurora, were lighting the world.'[40] Ruskin continued to offer moral support, but at arm's length. Now aged 63, he knew that his health was failing and wrote to Morris:

It is better that you should be in a cleft stick than make one out of me – especially as my timbers are enough shivered already. In old British battles the ships that had no shot in their rigging didn't ask the disabled ones to help them.[41]

Morris was by the early 1880s moving closer to a form of Marxism, which he found complementary rather than antithetic to Ruskin's teaching. Bringing with him the early ideas of Robert Owen, that saw the working classes as instruments of change, Morris tempered his Marxism with the fundamentally Ruskinian emphasis on division of labour as the capitalist-induced canker of modern society. Like Owen, Morris clung to utopian notions of small communities, where technology would only be allowed when it was useful to lessen the burden of labour. But he was more concerned than was Owen to restrict the size of these communities and more interested in egalitarianism.[42] Morris also clung to his aesthetic ideals. Delighting in good craftsmanship himself, he felt the need to share his experiences and never ceased to believe that socialism would have a liberating effect on the workforce. In his own company he not only successfully revived medieval crafts, but also encouraged his workers to rotate their tasks, thus improving their skills and counteracting the monotony induced by the division of labour. His eulogies on the pleasures of craftsmanship were perhaps too narrow but his underlying central emphasis that the quality of life was considerably enhanced by work-satisfaction came directly from Ruskin. This philosophy, along with his distrust of political centralisation, distanced Morris from mainstream Marxism. In an 1889 review of Edward Bellamy's utopian novel *Looking Backward*, he commented:

> It is necessary to point out that there are some Socialists who do not think that the problem of the organisation of life and necessary labour can be dealt with by a huge national centralisation, working by a kind of magic for which no one feels himself responsible; that, on the contrary, it will be necessary for the unit of administration to be small enough for every citizen to feel himself responsible for its details and be interested in them; that individual men cannot shuffle off the business of life on to the shoulders of an abstraction called the State, but must deal with each other; that variety of life is as much an aim of true Communism as equality of condition, and that nothing but an union of these two will bring about real freedom.[43]

If Morris was indeed a Marxist, he was thus a particularly British one who carried the early ideas of Owen, filtered through the aesthetic romanticism of Carlyle and Ruskin, and gave it contemporary relevance. As E.P. Thompson comments:

> The moral critique of capitalist process was pressing forward to conclusions consonant with Marx's critique, and it was Morris's particular genius to think through this transformation, effect this juncture, and seal it with action.[44]

Morris acknowledged the humanitarian core of Ruskin's economic critique, applauded and endorsed his dominant condemnation of the division of labour, but was unable to come to terms with the inherent contradictions of trying to reconcile socialism with even modified capitalism. Entrepreneurial success had made him a capitalist and most of his goods were going to the homes of the rich, because they were the only ones who could afford them. If therefore Morris was to remain true to his [primarily

Ruskinian] principles, how could he ethically continue to make a profit from money which was in effect surplus value 'stolen' from the poor? The answer was not accommodation, but social revolution, a conclusion to which he had been unwittingly led by Ruskin:

> I know that I come to these [socialist] conclusions a good deal through reading John Ruskin's works, and that I focused so to say his views on the matter of my work and my rising sense of injustice, probably more than he intended . . . [thus] I was quite ready for Socialism when I came across it in a definite form, as a political party with distinct aims for a revolution in society.[45]

Morris was in no way a complete revolutionary. Inconsistency was another trait that he shared with Ruskin. As Peter Stansky comments, Morris was 'humanly inconsistent in that when arguing with parliamentarians, he veered in an anarchist direction, and when disputing with anarchists he tended to be somewhat sympathetic towards traditional political measures'.[46] Certainly, Morris was insecure about state control and more in tune with Ruskin than were many of his socialist comrades on the question of the significance of the human element in any programme of social and economic reform. Thus, Morris's *News from Nowhere* (1891) was written as a utopian response to *Looking Backward*, because Morris felt that Bellamy's emphasis on centralisation and lack of human values was totally at odds with the humanitarian-organicist teaching of Ruskin. 'The essential of monopoly is,' wrote Morris, 'I warm myself by the fire which you have made, and you (very much the plural) stay outside in the cold.'[47]

Ruskin also distrusted governments, urging in 1871 the workers to take control of their own fate. Their prosperity, he wrote in *Fors Clavigera*, lay in their own hands: 'Only in a remote degree does it depend on external matters, and least of all on forms of government.'[48] He did not suggest filling the Houses of Parliament with dung as Morris did later in *News from Nowhere*, but Ruskin's sentiments were not dissimilar. And Morris's insistence to the end that art, using the word in its widest and due signification, was not a mere appendage of life but was the necessary expression and essential instrument of human happiness secured his enduring alliance with the Ruskinian tradition.

Ruskin's influence does not, however, diminish Morris's achievements, but rather gives them a deeper historical and ideological perspective. There is little doubt that Morris was an inspirational contributor to socialism. His *News from Nowhere*, although largely a work of fantasy, was a key text among early socialists, and his political activism is well documented. He brought with him the essence of Ruskin's thinking, adding political practicality to romanticism. Morris, in the verdict of E.P. Thompson, 'transformed a tradition'. Ruskin taught him the significance of art and work in the equation of human happiness – that 'the art of any epoch must of necessity be the expression of its social life'.[49] This was, stressed Thompson, 'please note, what Ruskin taught, and not Marx.'

Ultimately, the important fact was the difference between Morris and a strict interpretation of Marxism. The difference, writes P.D. Anthony, 'lies in Ruskin' and it 'represents the measure of Morris's attachment to an English, romantic, utopian, moralistic tradition'.[50] However strong the measure of Morris's later flirtation with Marxism, it was in *The Stones of Venice* and *Unto This Last*, and not in *Das Capital*, that Morris discovered the embryo of his socialist vision.

The Christian Socialist Revival

Morris was not a Christian and Ruskin was not a socialist, but a large part of the socialist revival of the 1880s was, if not orthodox Christian, at least ethical in nature. Christianity as preached by the established church was perceived to have failed the working classes and was further challenged by the emergence of numerous politically and socially active groups and individuals. One disparate group of reformers worked under the common banner of a revived Christian Socialism. They took their inspiration from the first Christian Socialists of the 1850s, led by Maurice, Kingsley, and Ludlow. The revived movement's leaders were primarily non-conformist in their beliefs. They operated in most large cities and they exerted influence among the working classes, although for some socialists the linkage of politics with religion was always a tenuous one. One article in the *Clarion* in 1901 stated firmly:

To my mind 'Socialism' is enough to express our aim, whether we be Christians or Atheists or whatever our theological opinions may be. We are Socialists and as such we have certain ideas in common, and in our Socialist work there is no need to endeavour to foist upon Socialism and each other our own particular theological creed. A man's creed is a personal matter.[51]

And even for those who professed both a religious and a political affiliation to Christian Socialism, there was a certain wariness about the term. E.V. Neale commented:

> Christian Socialism was a name which I never liked, but regarded as a mistake, tending to alienate on the one hand Christians who were not socialists, and on the other socialists who do not like to call themselves Christians. But being myself a Christian as well as a socialist, I find no personal reason for objecting to the name.[52]

By contrast, some orthodox clergymen considered that socialism posed a threat to Christianity. An editorial in *The Times* in 1887, commenting on a meeting of the Church Congress, observed that 'The Bishop of Derby claimed in his opening paper that Socialism is essentially of Christian origin.' Undoubtedly there were external features in common, continued the editorial, but he 'is on firmer ground when he resists the demand of Socialism to be regarded as so far fulfilling and completing Christianity as to be entitled to take its place.' Socialists, claimed the Bishop, 'taunt Christianity in general, and the Church of the State in particular, with the deplorable distance between its aspirations and results'. But, he asked, with what did they propose to replace it? It seemed to him that socialists hoped 'to destroy and obliterate [society] not to reform it'. Their 'plans of amelioration start with revolution' and they commanded the Church to 'assist them in their experiment'.[53]

Some socialists also considered socialism and Christianity to be incompatible and were very wary of reforms proposed under the mantle of religion. E. Belfort Bax[54] commented in *Justice* in 1895 on the 'middle class organisations professing social ends with a quasi-religious colouring'.[55] This did not, however, indicate a revival of the 'old dogmatic basis' of religion but rather indicated a new code of ethics which had its origins in Christianity. 'New social ideals,' wrote Bax, 'have taken the place of old personal and theological ones, and the full truth of modern Socialism is yearly absorbing larger and larger masses of the proletariat, and even of the better elements among the cultivated middle classes.' In his view, organised religion had to a large extent destroyed faith among the working classes. But the Christian message of community and friendship still prevailed and provided the impetus for much socialist sermonising. Bax felt that to be a triumph for modern socialism, rather than for old-style religion:

> We see such a strong tendency in the present day among social reformers, and more or less inchoate Socialists to adopt Christian phraseology in working for their respective ends. But we should be in error in attributing the energy and enthusiasm often shown by such persons as indicating a revival of 'religion' in the old sense. What really animates them is undoubtedly the contagion of the Socialist atmosphere in which they live, and not the superficial coating of Christian sentiment which is put forward, and to which they and other people might be disposed to attribute their zeal, but which never showed such results in the palmy days of Christian theological belief.[56]

This provoked a continuing argument in *Justice*. An article in 1896, signed 'George', endorsed Bax's concerns and added that 'illogical minds' think that 'by making Christ a Socialist they obtain Divine sanction for Socialism, and thus permeate the mass of Christians'. 'George' also warned that the more intelligent sector of the clergy would not be slow to take advantage of this opportunity to push their cause, for: 'Just at a time when religion is being discredited by scientific and historical discoveries the attempt is made to give it a new lease of life by tacking it on to a young and vigorous movement.'[57]

Ruskin was to some extent a victim of this scenario, as his own faith had been badly shaken by a surfeit of bleak religion. An Anglican theologian, A.L. Moore, commented in 1890: 'John Ruskin, like J.S. Mill, might have been a loyal member of the Church of Christ if, when he was asking for the bread of Christ, Calvinistic teachers had not given him a stone.'[58] It was hardly surprising that Ruskin was able to empathise with the poor and that in this spiritually impoverished climate his eloquent injunction to a doctrine of communal welfare found a very receptive audience. In his study of the late Victorian Christian socialist revival, Peter Jones comments that it is this 'aesthetic reaction' which links 'countless British late Victorian reformers and socialists, and John

Ruskin in particular was one of the writers most widely quoted in the literature, newspapers, and journals of the working-class movement'.[59] His teaching went straight to the heart of socialist thinking.

> Ruskin's doctrines of *meaningful* labour, his hatred of *laissez-faire* liberalism, his cutting distinction between 'wealth' and 'illth', his experimentation with a cooperative community in Sheffield, all made him very attractive to the moral and utopian type of socialist and, understandably, to Christian socialists generally.

William Morris has been seen as 'the leading socialist exponent of Ruskinian ideals during the revival years'[60] but Morris's atheism did not endear him to all reformers, and his influence waned rapidly after his death in 1896. British socialism in the 1880s was faction-ridden, isolated and in need of a coherent identity, if it was to attract the working classes who had as little interest in organised secularism as they did in conventional religious observance.[61]

The writings of Ruskin, much of it by now twenty years old, struck a chord with many disenchanted British labourers and found its spiritual home among politically active Christians, who were acutely aware of the social requirements of the period. These requirements were eventually addressed in the Labour Churches, founded by John Trevor in 1891. This, writes John Gorman, 'was not an act of spontaneous creation'. 'It was an evolutionary development of the socialist challenge to the role of the churches in a capitalist society.'[62] The five principles on which the Labour Church rested were a clear expression of Ruskinian thinking in an insistence on non-sectarian religion and that 'the Emancipation of Labour can only be realised so far as men learn both the Economic and Moral Laws of God, and heartily endeavour to obey them.'[63] It would be wrong, however, to imply that this increased social awareness of church and chapel was entirely political. All the denominations at the end of the nineteenth century experienced a shift of theological emphasis, away from the doctrine of atonement and hellfire in the afterlife, toward a greater emphasis on brotherhood and forgiveness on earth.[64]

Some individual examples make the Ruskinian connection clear. George Dawson (1821–76), described in 1877 by R.W. Dale in the periodical the *Nineteenth Century* as a 'politician, lecturer, and preacher,' was an enthusiastic supporter of Ruskin's teaching and 'a great influence on the religious thought and the general public life of the town'. Dawson was heavily involved in the municipal and political affairs of Birmingham and it was here that Ruskin's influence was apparent. Dale quoted approvingly from the *Spectator* on 2 December 1876, which described Dawson as 'a kind of literary middleman' whose 'chief function in life was to popularise for the middle classes of Birmingham some of the best ideas of contemporary thinkers'. Dawson's influence was ascribed 'partly to his moral earnestness, and partly to his power as "a very effective retailer" of the thoughts of such men as Mr Carlyle and Mr Ruskin.' Politically, wrote Dale, Dawson was a radical, but 'a Radical of a type which has only recently become common in England'. Like Ruskin, he rejected the false concept of freedom favoured by early liberals, and called for greater state intervention. 'The old Radicals made the limits very narrow within which they thought the State could act wisely and effectively – Mr Dawson, on the other hand, believed in free libraries and in national education.'[65]

The Christian Socialists were, for the most part, not actively radical, but rather combined their politics with their preaching as a matter of course, many of them preferring to remain detached from direct political action. An article in the *Commonweal* in 1886, submitted by a 'sympathetic subscriber', highlighted extracts from a sermon preached in St Vincent Street Unitarian Church in Glasgow, by the Rev A. Lazenby, which 'made a good impression on a congregation that contained a large number of well-to-do folks'.[66] The extracts did not mention Ruskin specifically but they were very much along the lines of *Unto This Last* in the similarity of their attack on social and economic injustice, enunciated in scriptural tones.

Lazenby referred to the report of the N.E. Railway for the latter part of 1884, where 'One million pounds went to the workers who carried on the line, and one million and a half to those who never lifted finger save to hand over capital.' Similarly, he quoted the figures of a London matchmaking company where ten capitalists divided between them as much as was shared by 'the 990 who do the work'. Looked at from a moral point of view, Lazenby demanded whether that was 'equitable'? The financial risks taken by the capitalists might have been considerable but they were outweighed by the human cost to the poor in a period of trade depression. Lazenby echoed Ruskin's sentiments, that 'there is no wealth but life', in his closing remarks: 'There is nothing in all God's universe more ruthlessly wasted than man and woman – and for what? To satisfy the world's passion for wealth!'[67]

This Ruskinian ethic was echoed again in the words of A.E. Fletcher, editor of the *Daily Chronicle*, who wrote in 1886 in support of a fixed minimum wage as suggested to Ruskin by the Parable of the Vineyard. Fletcher commented:

> You must have a fixed minimum wage, below which there shall be no discussion. You may say that it is contrary to the laws of political economy. No; it is not. It is sound science and has been proved to be sound science by the greatest political economist still living, John Ruskin, who founds his economic philosophy upon this parable, and takes from it the title to the greatest of all his works, '*Unto This Last*.'[68]

Listening to Ruskin, wrote Fletcher, might help the government to solve the problem of unemployment if they, like Ruskin, would only 'face it honestly'.[69] But the links between Christian morality and political economy were never again to have quite the same impact as they had had, when so powerfully exposed by their original author in 1860.

Even Stewart Headlam, one of the more radical members of the Christian Socialist Union, did not see his own role as being that of a political activist but rather as a social commentator.[70] This earned him a strong endorsement from Ruskin. The *Church Reformer*, described as 'An Organ of Christian Socialism and Church Reform', was edited by Headlam and its advertisement carried the legend: '*I never yet looked through a paper I thought so right, or likely to be so useful. John Ruskin.*'[71] Headlam was an enthusiastic follower of Ruskin, not only for his obvious humanitarianism, but also for his attempts to moralise the economy. In 1884, a difference of opinion arose between Headlam and a fellow member of the Guild of St Matthew, the economist Rev John Elliotson Symes. At a meeting chaired by Headlam in January 1884, Symes fiercely defended the principle of private property in capital and later published a book on the subject. This angered Headlam, who felt moved to 'censure his former ally for publishing an "obsolete" economics textbook on the old pre-Ruskinian lines . . . which ignores the existence of "illth" side by side with wealth'.[72] As he was to write later:

... it is especially worth noting that the teaching which has revolutionised Political Economy in England was founded on Christ's saying, 'I will give unto this last even as unto thee.' It is to be hoped that, now that Mr Ruskin's epoch-making little book can be obtained for a few pence, it will be read far and wide as a text-book of Political Economy which is essentially Christian.[73]

Headlam, like many other Christian Socialists, favoured the moral tone of the economic works of that other pro-Ruskinian, J.A. Hobson,[74] especially for Ruskin's argument that it was the over-saving of the wealthy minority which was the root cause of unemployment.[75] Ruskin's analysis of the true economic structure of society appealed to Headlam as both ethical and sound:

... the true classification of Society is not so much Matthew Arnold's, a materialised upper class, a vulgarised middle class, a brutalised lower class – but John Ruskin's into Beggars, Robbers, and Workers; the workers being all those who are not living on the charity of others, or preying on the hard-won earnings of others – all those in fact, who are not living on rent or interest – unless indeed those who are so living are of their own accord conferring a benefit on the community equal to the rent or interest they get from the community.'[76]

The membership of the Guild of St Matthew may have been small but Headlam's influence was profound and his admiration for Ruskin undisguised. The question remains, however, why Ruskin's quasi-religious, aesthetic moralising finally struck home in the late 1880s and just how strongly he can be identified with Christian Socialism in the light of his own religious and political ambiguity. Was it simply a question of adding practicality to romanticism? Or were there other reasons why Ruskin's social writings had a delayed positive response among the classes they were designed to help?

The logistics of publishing played a large part in the originally restricted circulation of Ruskin's work and to a large extent this was politically manipulated. But in the *Commonweal* in June 1886, one contemporary, Thomas Shore, Jnr., implied that Ruskin had kept his writings from the working classes quite deliberately. Shore quoted from the 1885

Report by the Master of the Guild of St George:[77] 'Unreasonable in so
much, but yet so full of pity for the evils all around and so sincere in
desire to remove them, it is much to be regretted that this writer has
prevented the full knowledge of his works to be spread.' Ruskin
professed communism but seemed to have 'some amount of dread at the
spread of socialism'. His 'peculiar contradictions', added Shore, were
nowhere more apparent than in his 'ideas on publication and selling his
books'. Why did Ruskin 'pour out his wrath on capitalists, landlords,
financiers' yet not make his writings more accessible? He referred to
Ruskin's letter in *Fors Clavigera* of June 1871, where Ruskin wrote 'The
retailer charges what he ought to charge, openly; and if the public do not
choose to give it, they can't get the book.'[78] Why did Ruskin thus
consciously keep his books from the poorer classes? Shore believed that
he had the answer. 'I have sometimes thought that his method of issuing
his books was to prevent too many of the workers knowing the truth;
that he felt compelled to write the truth, but hoped it would not spread
too fast.'[79] Shore was probably right: Ruskin wanted to help the workers,
but at the same time mistrusted them, fearing the effect of his writings
on minds made susceptible through years of poverty and exploitation.

This situation gradually changed, however, as Ruskin had in time to
'give in to his surroundings'. Shore commented on one of Ruskin's
circulars, dated July 1882, 'announcing that in future a discount would
be allowed to booksellers and librarians'. The connection might seem
remote to some, Shore observed, but to him, 'It seems a very positive
proof that in the long run environment is the stronger, and what a farce
freedom of contract is in relation to the worker really depending on his
work for bread.'[80] Ruskin had created a monster of revolutionary
economic and social criticism, which could, and should, no longer be
held back from the reading public: 'We must use great names,' wrote
Shore, 'if they help us to attack great abuses.'[81]

Timing, then, was a crucial factor in Ruskin's acceptance as a forerunner of socialist thought. Economic depression in the 1880s with its
corollary of physical and spiritual deprivation, plus Ruskin's willingness
to disseminate his works among a wider readership, all contributed to his
gathering significance in the Christianising of socialism. Although
Ruskin was neither an orthodox Christian nor a socialist, his teaching
made possible an ethical synthesis between the two. His function and
influence lay essentially, to quote Pierson, in assisting an 'alteration of

consciousness' and a 'reordering of values'.[82] The impact of Ruskin's moral critique of capitalism became even more apparent as socialism took on greater political significance in the last two decades of the nineteenth century. 'No one,' notes Pierson, 'can read extensively in the autobiographies of the Socialist and labour leaders of the end of the century without being struck by the frequent references to the influence of Carlyle and Ruskin.'[83]

Ruskin and the Socialist Leaders

Carlyle's role in providing a moral/aesthetic influence upon socialist philosophy was undoubtedly important; but in terms of influence upon prominent individuals in the socialist movement Ruskin's writings had a far more immediate impact. As Pierson comments later: 'Some of the new Socialist leaders, like Fred Jowett or Katherine Conway, looked back to their reading of *Unto This Last* as an event which changed their lives.' And others 'like Tom Barclay and Tom Mann, brought a strong commitment to Ruskinian ideas into their early work as Socialist propagandists'.[84]

Much groundwork, however, had to be done before the actuality of socialist representation in parliament could be achieved. The problems of establishing a separate working-class political party in the 1880s were numerous. The trade unions and cooperatives, initiated for the protection of the labour force, saw themselves as negotiating within the existing system, not in opposition to it. There was an inbuilt resistance to any form of violent change, and much criticism of the radical extremes of Marxism.

One of the key figures in this scenario was Keir Hardie (1856–1915), who, along with Robert Blatchford, the editor of the *Clarion*, did most to promote the socialist cause at the end of the century. Hardie recognised the need for a redistribution of power, but also sought to operate within the present parliamentary system. He never lost his interest in class conflict but, like Morris, he was too concerned about the moral aspect of socialism to become an outright revolutionary. Marxism for Hardie was not a moral doctrine, whereas socialism, he claimed, should be both practical and moral:

Socialism, like every other problem of life, is at bottom a question of ethics or morals. It has mainly to do with the relationships which should exist between a man and his fellows. Civilisation, even at its lowest form, necessitates that people should live together as an organism since only thus is life with any degree of security and of intellectual companionship possible.[85]

Hardie was born to secular parents but had experienced a personal conversion to Christianity at an early age. He became a lay preacher in a local chapel in Cumnock, but eventually, like Ruskin, dropped formal religious observance while retaining its ethical centrality.[86] He had been influenced from the age of sixteen by the moral and religious works of Carlyle, but later found a more acceptable alternative to his harsh Calvinistic pessimism in the teachings of Ruskin, in whose writings Hardie located the catalyst for his particular form of ethical socialism. In an appendix to his autobiography Hardie itemised *Unto This Last* and *The Crown of Wild Olive* as being significant among 'a selection of writings for the guidance of those who desire to learn more about Socialism and the Modern Labour Movement'.[87] He admitted to quoting Ruskin very frequently in his lectures, selecting those works which best illustrated Ruskin's moral centrality.[88] Hardie also exhibited a Ruskinian distaste for the Darwinian concept of life as an unmitigated struggle for existence. 'Darwinism,' he wrote, 'with its creed of a pitiless struggle for existence . . . appeared to give new life to The Manchester School of Economics.'[89] What later became known as Social Darwinism 'gave a fillip to the competitive system by appearing to stamp it with the sign manual of scientific approval'. This, asserted Hardie, was in fact a mis-interpretation of Darwin's work, because it ignored the 'greater fact that life did not depend upon struggle but upon adaptation to environment'. 'The Darwinian apologists for Capitalism made little if any reference to the fact that no matter how fierce the struggle, life could not be kept alive unless it could be made to harmonise with its environment.' And with an echo of Ruskin's words, Hardie concluded that 'It is sympathetic association and not individualistic competition which makes for progress and the improvement of the race.'[90] Although he did not always refer directly to Ruskin, Hardie's writings and speeches were liberally peppered with Ruskinian sentiments. As one of Hardie's biographers, Kenneth Morgan comments:

Ruskin's essays entitled *Unto This Last*, with their passionate critique of self-interest and of the values of commercial society, provided something of the moral framework for Hardie's shadowy political philosophy. For Hardie, as for Ruskin, the quality of living was to be the ultimate touchstone for any creed and any society: 'There is no wealth but life.'[91]

Ruskin's teachings were strongly endorsed by Robert Blatchford, who was, in the words of A.J. Davies, 'probably the most successful British socialist propagandist of all time'.[92] In his publication, *Britain for the British* (1902), Blatchford insisted:

I would say, then, that wealth is all those things which we use. Mr Ruskin uses two words, 'wealth' and 'illth'. He divides the things which it is good for us to have from the things it is not good for us to have, and he calls the good things 'wealth' and the bad things 'illth'. or ill things . . . Thus opium prepared for smoking is illth, because it does harm or 'works ill' to all who smoke it; but opium prepared as medicine is wealth, because it saves life or stays pain . . . Mr Ruskin is right, and if we are to make the best of our country and of ourselves, we ought clearly to give up producing bad things, or 'illth', and produce more good things, or wealth.'[93]

Blatchford used the Ruskinian ethic quite freely in the pages of the *Clarion,* which in its direct appeal to the working man was a popular alternative to Hardie's more earnest stance in the *Labour Leader.*

Tom Mann (1856–1941) was another prominent socialist[94] who made strong claims for Ruskin's influence. Like Hardie, Mann found the ethical strand of socialism the most appealing and also the most effective in reaching the working-class audiences of his speeches. His method of address as president of the Dockers' Union was very much in the Ruskinian mode. In early life Mann had hoped to become a religious missionary and his later socialism reflected much of Ruskin's thinking. In 1891 and 1892 Mann and Ben Tillett, another important docker's leader, were often to be seen preaching in Congregational chapels or to the Brotherhood and Pleasant Sunday Afternoon groups. Their appeal was largely to the sentiments of those working-class men and women who still adhered, for whatever reason, to Nonconformist religious observance.[95]

Moreover, Tom Mann, like Keir Hardie, did not view Ruskin simply as a suitable vehicle for the dissemination of popular socialism, but acknowledged the value of Ruskin's economic critique for its detailed analysis and moral centrality. This fact Mann acknowledged clearly in his memoirs, saying that he 'quoted Ruskin and Thorold Rogers more often than any other authorities'.

> In appealing for independent thought and self-reliance instead of leaning upon capitalist advice and instruction, I quoted John Ruskin's eighty-ninth letter in *Fors Clavigera* – 'Whose Fault is it?' – to the trade unions of England, and especially that portion where Ruskin states that he at one time had confidence in the 'learned and the rich'.[96]

The particular passage to which Mann referred left the reader in little doubt as to Ruskin's political orientation at that time. The letter was dated 31 August 1880, and in it Ruskin made clear his intent to address the workers as a separate body. 'I have never before acknowledged the division,' declared Ruskin, 'but I recognise the distinction today.' This was partially brought about by a review of *Fors,* which had appeared in the *Bingley Telephone* on 23 April 1880, expressing the wish that Ruskin 'would write more to and for the workmen and workwomen of these realms'.[97] Ruskin was moved by this request and tried in his letter to explain his reasons for withholding a more direct acknowledgement of the 'separate' nature of the poorer classes:

> As a separate class, I knew scarcely anything of you but your usefulness, and your distress; and that the essential difference between me and other political writers of your day, is that I never say a word about a single thing that I don't know, while they never trouble themselves to know a single thing they talk of.[98]

It was shortly after this letter that Ruskin made his work more easily available to the working classes (a development welcomed by Thomas Shore in the *Commonweal* in June 1886, as has already been noted). The extract particularly favoured by Mann began:

> And now I turn to you, understanding you to be associations of labouring men who have recognised the necessity of binding your-selves by some common law of action, and who are taking earnest

council as to the conditions of your lives here in England, and their relations to those of your fellow workers in foreign lands. And I understand you to be, in these associations, disregardent, if not actually defiant, of the persons on whose capital you have been hitherto passively dependent for occupation, and who have always taught you, by the mouths of their appointed Economists, that they and their capital were an eternal part of the Providential arrangements made for this world by its Creator . . . Whose is the wealth of the world but yours? Whose is the virtue? Do you mean to go on for ever, leaving your wealth to be consumed by the idle and your virtue to be mocked by the vile?[99]

'Many hundreds of times,' wrote Mann, 'have I made some portion of the above serve as my text for a speech on *The Condition of England* question.' And he added 'In dealing with unemployment, for a long time I supported the establishing of Municipal Workshops. Here again I made use of Ruskin, but this time it was *Unto This Last*, and especially the preface.'[100] Mann was here referring to the passage where Ruskin insisted 'that any man, or woman, or boy, or girl, out of employment, should at once be received at the nearest Government School, and set to work as it appeared, on trial . . . at a fixed rate of wages.' And Ruskin's further insistence that, if 'being found incapable of work through sickness, [they] should be tended.' 'This,' Mann declared, 'with variations, dealing with the apathy of the trade unions, and urging them to definite action, gave me a good jumping-off ground at open-air meetings.'[101] Mann had a tendency to make use of convenient ideologies to further the socialist cause, but that did not detract from his influence. Engels remarked in 1889 that, with certain reservations, he regarded Mann as 'the finest' of the socialist leaders.[102]

Another socialist leader who demonstrated a strong commitment to Ruskin's moral centrality was Tom Barclay (1852–1923). In his autobiography, he referred to the first Labour Club in Bedford Street, London, where he taught and managed to obtain a free set of Ruskin's works for the use of his members.[103] He remembered also taking a course in Political Economy in 1880, when he was given books by Adam Smith, J.S. Mill and Marshall. 'But he soon threw over the Manchester School after reading *Progress and Poverty* by Henry George, *Communal and Commercial Economy* by Carruthers, *The Cooperative Commonwealth* by

Gronlund, *Unto This Last*, by Ruskin, and something or other by Belfort Bax.'[104]

In July 1887, Barclay assembled what he considered to be the most significant aspects of Ruskin's social writing and published them in a pamphlet. He explained how this came about in his autobiography:

> I made a kind of abridgment of *Unto This Last*, and got a local printer to print off a number of copies. It was in pamphlet form and sold at a penny. I never made a penny by it, and didn't want to; my object was propaganda purely. The title of the pamphlet was THE RIGHTS OF LABOUR, *According to* JOHN RUSKIN, then in smaller type 'Arranged by Thomas Barclay.' A friend meeting me some days later asked me whether I had had Mr Ruskin's permission. Well, I hadn't: I never thought about it. In some trepidation I sent a copy to him, as well as a letter explaining, offering at once to stop further publication if he demanded it. Instead of demanding suppression of publication, here is an extract from the letter he sent me.[105]

The following is the extract of Ruskin's letter which Barclay printed triumphantly at the front of his edition:

> Your pamphlet is the best abstract of all the most important pieces of my teaching that has yet been done; and I am entirely grateful to you for doing it, and glad to have your letter. The time is certainly drawing near for the workmen who are conscious of their own power and probity, to draw together into action.[106]

Barclay was delighted that Ruskin had taken time to write to a mere 'proletarian working man' and Barclay's introductory remarks on Ruskin's significance as a social thinker stressed his greatness. 'The object of this pamphlet,' Barclay explained, 'is to place before the workers in a cheap form, the main views of one of the greatest thinkers of the age, on a subject that ought to interest them more than any other.' That subject was 'Political Economy', and 'until working men understand thoroughly what this relation is, all hope is vain of bettering their conditions as a *class*.'[107]

The extracts in this pamphlet were all taken from *Unto This Last* and Barclay commented upon its initial poor reception: the 'bitter opposition from all the usual enemies of the working man – including Press, Priests, and Professors.' It was not surprising, added Barclay, that Ruskin had difficulty in getting it published, considering its 'revolutionary character, combined with the logic, grace, and vigour, of which he is so capable'. Barclay therefore decided that Ruskin was aptly called 'the Modern Plato' for his 'analytic mind' and 'lofty morality', which constituted 'a reproach to bishopdom':

> He lashes the hypocrite and scourges the oppressor; meanness and injustice fall back from his terrific onslaught. Sweet to the innocent and good; gentle to the erring and unfortunate. True Philosopher; mighty Poet without the name; Prophet too; not a visionary, but one who sees the very truth – no will o' the wisp, but a beacon light to lighten men's darkness – a great teacher, whose clear, brilliant, and powerful language, is but the fitting conductor of original and valuable thought. Such is Ruskin![108]

Barclay was obviously moved by Ruskin's rhetoric and determined to bring it to a wider audience among the working classes. But his subsequent breakdown of Ruskin's objectives in *Unto This Last* also demonstrated a healthy respect for his logic. Barclay gave a very perceptive analysis of Ruskin's main points, including a section on *The True Function of the Capitalist*. He quoted Ruskin's insistence that it was the manufacturer's function in a state 'to *provide* for it', just as it was the soldier's duty to defend it, the physician's to keep it healthy, and the lawyer's to enforce justice. Everyone had work to do 'irrespective of fee'. The stipend of a teacher 'is a due and necessary adjunct, but not the object of his life, if he is a true teacher'. All this might sound very strange, Ruskin had argued, but the only real strangeness was that people found it so, because it was all true:

> . . . not partially nor theoretically, but everlastingly and practically; all other doctrine than this respecting matters political being false in premises, absurd in deduction, and impossible in practice, consistently with any progressive state of national life.[109]

This, for Barclay, and for many other socialists, represented the essence of Ruskin's teaching. Barclay accordingly urged anyone interested in political economy, which was 'essentially the science of the working man', to 'cooperate to get his books and study for themselves'.[110] 'What working man is there,' he concluded, 'that will not reverence these far-seeing and noble utterances of a great and good man devoted to the cause of the poor and downtrodden.'[111]

Ruskin's Influence upon Socialist Thought

Just how widespread, however, *was* Ruskin's influence upon socialist ideology? Ruskin's reputation as a social and political critic rested primarily on the reception of *Unto This Last*. When it was first published in 1860, his was a lone voice protesting to a country at the high point of commercial success. Owen had been largely forgotten, and the socialist revival was not to begin for another twenty years, when the economy was in depression. Only then did Ruskin's social and moral intensity make sense to working class sympathisers and provide them with the ethical, utopian socialism, which under the banner of the Independent Labour Party was to become the dominant form. *Unto This Last* with its quasi-religious combination of moral and practical economic reform became a major source of inspiration and Ruskin's ideas were disseminated through numerous small societies, including the Tolstoyan movement, which emphasised the empathy of these two revolutionary thinkers.[112] As an unwitting contributor to British socialist ideology, Ruskin thus ranks in significance with Owen, Morris and Marx.

This point was further endorsed by George Bernard Shaw (1856–1950), a gifted speaker and powerful promoter of the socialist cause, who frequently drew on Ruskin's thinking to underpin his own propagandist speeches.[113] Shaw joined the Fabian Society in 1884, having rejected Marxism as ultimately unethical. Shaw claimed that Ruskin was not only very ethical, he was also revolutionary; and Ruskin's appeal, although addressed primarily to the working people, cut across the class divide and found its strongest disciples 'among the few who were at war with commercial civilisation'.[114] His appeal was 'to the educated, cultivated, and discontented'. Shaw continued that he had met many 'extremely revolutionary characters' in his lifetime and, when he asked them if it was Marx who put them onto the revolutionary track, most of them answered: 'No, it was Ruskin.' 'Generally,' responded Shaw, 'the Ruskinite is the most thoroughgoing of the opponents of our existing state of society.'[115] Such a person attacked society with a 'magnificent thoroughness' and without hatred, so that when Ruskin was compared with Marx and Cobbett it seemed somehow that Ruskin 'beats them hollow'. His main problem was that 'respectable' people thought he could not possibly be talking about them, so they ignored him. Yet Ruskin's influence endured and his contribution to economics was important, because 'he knocked the spurious law of value into a cocked hat'. He was the first to expose the fallacy of classical economics, by showing that its value basis was 'unreal and inhuman'. Shaw added that Ruskin did not understand the law of rent; but then neither did Marx, who had a 'weakness for posing as a mathematician' and whose own 'celebrated theory of value' was now a 'celebrated blunder'.[116] In Shaw's estimation, Ruskin ranked with Jevons as one of the great economists, and in political terms, Ruskin was equally important. In Shaw's view, Ruskin was a communist but not a democrat, believing that the reconstruction of society must be 'the work of an energetic and conscientious minority'. In terms of both economic and political reform, decided Shaw, Ruskin had been both misunderstood and – particularly – underestimated.

There was good reason for Shaw's interpretation of Ruskin's politics. The message of the Sermon on the Mount from which Ruskin drew his terminology was indeed ultimately one of communism. But Ruskin's was not the revolutionary communism of Marx. It was a mixture of the economic communism of Robert Owen and the utopian, ethical and hierarchical communism of Thomas More, to whom Ruskin referred in some detail in Letter 7 of *Fors Clavigera*.[117] This Letter, written in 1871 at the time of the Paris Commune, was designed to illustrate the difference between 'old' and 'new' communism and to provide a guide to Ruskin's own theory of social organisation. It was his insistence on a just economic system, underpinned by a broad Christian ethic of cooperation, which ultimately found its appeal in a working-class audience.

It was not, therefore, simply a case of Ruskin's homiletic style and obvious compassion striking a chord with a spiritually impoverished underclass. His influence also took the shape of 'moral righteousness', which drew strength from the fact that it was deeply antithetic to the central tenets of Marxism.[118] There was undoubtedly much truth in this; but it was only a partial truth. Ruskin's teaching in fact blurred the boundaries between utopian and scientific socialism, for while it certainly served to rekindle the evangelical spirit in an increasingly secular world, it also acted as a catalyst for many socialist leaders. It was a filter for the early economic experiments of Robert Owen, and the inspiration which caused Morris to fuse aesthetic vision with Marxist revolutionary optimism. John Ruskin, announced an obituary in *Justice*, was the 'companion spirit' of Owen and Morris, and as such the working man could 'ill afford to lose him'.[119] In fact, as the testimony of the Labour members of 1906 confirmed (as cited at the head of this chapter), the organised labour movement did not lose him. Ruskin's influence, dispersed and perpetuated by radical ideals and practical reform, endured well into the twentieth century.

In another obituary in 1900, Robert Blatchford considered in the *Clarion* why Ruskin's true significance had been overlooked by many historians. 'Is it true,' he asked, 'that John Ruskin is no longer a living influence in the world?' 'Is it true that John Ruskin's economics are the ravings of an amiable crank?' But no:

> . . . the enduring effect of [Ruskin's] life and his teachings upon modern ethics would be hard to overestimate. Ruskin's genius has become part of the national thought, his high ethical ideals have entered into and coloured the national conscience. So with Ruskin's economic theories. The nation has learned his lesson, has assimilated his gospel, although we do not always repeat his words between quotation marks.[120]

Ultimately, however, links were less important to Ruskin than the ideas to which he devoted his life. Thus Ruskin's friend and biographer, W.G. Collingwood, observed that 'When, long after *Fors* had been written, Mr Ruskin found other writers advocating the same principles and calling themselves Socialists, he said that he too was a Socialist.'[121] The key thing was to reject the oversimplified 'economic man' of the classical economists and to reintroduce culture and society into economic thought. As Sydney Ball pointed out in a Fabian publication: 'Readers of *Unto This Last* will remember . . . the economist who has best understood the real significance of the pre-established harmony between ethics and economics.'[122]

8

CONCLUSION:
MORAL RECONSTRUCTION
IN A CAPITALIST SOCIETY

On receipt of Mr West's letter I left for Natal. I had taken Mr Polak into my fullest confidence. He came to see me off at the station, and left with me a book to read during the journey, which he said I was sure to like. It was Ruskin's Unto This Last.

The book was impossible to lay aside, once I had begun it. It gripped me. Johannesburg to Durban was a twenty-four hours' journey. The train reached there in the evening. I could not get any sleep that night. I determined to change my life in accordance with the ideals of this book.[1]   M.K. Gandhi (1927)

If further evidence were needed of the far-reaching impact of Ruskin's social thought, the above extract from Gandhi's autobiography should fulfil that requirement. *Unto This Last* is still published in India and no one doubts the extent of Gandhi's own influence. This indicates the widening impact of Ruskin's thought over time. Responses can be examined both at the time of Ruskin's death in 1900 and in the years immediately following.

Obituaries, as Stefan Collini points out, can be a 'curiously hybrid form of writing'.[2] They have to strike a balance between the requirement for a tone of respectfulness and the accommodation of often widely divergent opinions. In Ruskin's case, they have an additional and important dimension as the stature and political orientation of his obituarists sheds further light on the true nature and significance of his influence.

Ruskin died on 20 January 1900, aged 80, after a bout of illness recorded on his death certificate as 'influenza'. The response to this event was immense. *The Times,* which had taken a keen interest in his health in his last years, was inundated with tributes and opinions for some five years after his death. Hardly one month passed in that period without some reference to Ruskin's work and legacy.[3] Comments varied considerably, the obituary in *The Times* being more perceptive than many on the value of his social thought. Published two days after his death it ran:

> The new Political Economy is not quite that of *Unto This Last*, but it was borrowed not a little from that book and its successors. And if Ruskin's ideas have made way in the realm of social order as they have lost ground in the realm of art, his position as master of English prose has become more and more assured.[4]

Despite its unusual format, *Unto This Last* gained increasing respect from those who began to recognise its areas of acute analytical plausibility. In 1923, J.A.R. Marriott[5] commented in the *Cornhill Magazine,* some sixty years after that magazine had curtailed publication of Ruskin's essays:

> If [Ruskin's] destructive criticism was unfair and irrelevant, his constructive contribution to economic thought was far from negligible. More particularly in his insistence upon the significance of *Consumption* as a department of Economic Theory, and in his analysis of *Value*.[6]

The 'irrelevancy of his attack on the Economists', considered Marriott, did not 'essentially detract from the value of his ethical teaching', nor, indeed, even more remarkably, 'from the real importance of his own constructive contribution to Economic Theory'. The fact that the significance of the latter was to a large extent missed by his contemporary critics was, claimed Marriott, largely Ruskin's own fault. The 'brilliant exaggeration' in which he habitually spoke on economic subjects 'has unquestionably directed attention from the grains of sound doctrine'.[7]

Ruskin could no longer be ignored. *Palgrave's Dictionary of Political Economy* was guarded about Ruskin's seminality but acknowledged his significance, commenting in the 1926 edition that '*Unto This Last* has had a very wide circulation both in its complete form and in a penny pamphlet of extracts from it called *The Rights of Labour*, and many of the labour leaders of today have been among his readers.'[8] And, another sixty years after that, Lawrence Goldman observes in the 1987 edition of the *Palgrave's Dictionary of Political Economy*:

> [Ruskin] sought to redefine all the basic categories of political economy – not only wealth but value, labour and capital as well – as a prelude to the construction of harmonious social relations in an ideal, moral society to be characterised by cooperation, justice and hierarchic order rather than competition, avarice and flux.[9]

He was not a 'systematic thinker', concedes Goldman; nor was Ruskin's critique entirely novel, yet 'he was read and revered throughout the emerging labour movement at the turn of the century'.[10]

Ruskin had achieved a growing reputation as a reputable economist especially among working-class sympathisers, but there were always some who felt that he had strayed from his rightful territory in entering the field of economic criticism. Leslie Stephen, who admired him in many ways but who obviously had not read Hobson, commented that Ruskin's assault on the political economists had 'succeeded in irritating if not in convincing'.[11] Even the obituary in *Justice,* while praising Ruskin's efforts on behalf of the workers, rated *Unto This Last* as 'a literary rather than an economic masterpiece'.[12]

This was a scenario predicted by Robert Blatchford in the *Clarion* with an impressive degree of accuracy. 'There will,' he commented, 'be thousands of columns thrown off by the pens of ready writers on John Ruskin and his work.' 'And the great mass of this outpouring will contain gross error, weak criticism, and shallow impertinence.' That, at least, said Blatchford, had been his experience to date. Ruskin, he wrote, was too great a man for the shallow pens of 'young pressmen' who have 'never studied nor understood either the economics of Ruskin or the old and discredited "dismal science" which his powerful attacks so shook and shattered.'[13]

This was perhaps too extreme, as the debate still continues as to whether 'economic man' is too narrow an abstraction, but in one respect Blatchford was right: the inability to appreciate the value of Ruskin's

economic criticism, or to find a neat political category for him, has
perpetuated an underestimation of his significance.[14] This is due, in large
part, to the fact that Ruskin's own economic criticism was ultimately
incompatible with his theory of political organisation. Ruskin's rejection
of democracy, or rather his rejection of *his perception* of democracy, was at
odds with the undeniably communistic elements of *Unto This Last*. As
Hobson commented in 1902:

> It is worthy of notice that whereas in *Unto This Last*, and elsewhere,
> Ruskin has applied with remarkable insight and skill the 'organic'
> conception of Society as an economic structure, deducing therefrom
> the laws of sane distribution alike of work and wealth, he never
> realised the necessity of applying the same principles to Society as a
> political structure. To him, political Society was an orderly arrange-
> ment of individuals and classes, not mechanical, indeed, for it was
> to be maintained by vital bonds of sympathy and brotherhood; but,
> on the other hand, not resting on any organic principle of self-
> growth. His ideal was a harmony of human forces, but it did not bear
> within itself any capacity of progress. It was an organisation and not
> an organism.[15]

As Hobson argued, Ruskin was 'deluded' about the nature of
democracy.[16] Like the Gothic cathedrals from which he frequently drew
his metaphor, his organic communities were to be composed of
mutually-sustaining but unequal parts. This had generated confusion as
to his political stance, which, like his economic writings, must be viewed
in context. The modern concept of democracy, Hobson decided, could
endorse much of Ruskin's organic approach but not his 'benevolent
oligarchy'.[17] But when Ruskin first wrote *Unto This Last,* he could see no
alternative. He saw more clearly than most the 'trend of modern
industrial forces' and the 'gathering of a new industrial feudalism',[18]
which in a secular society made the location of authority more significant
than ever. Only the infusion of 'true sentiments of authority and
obedience', commented Hobson, would avoid the 'Scylla of anarchic
mob-rule and the Charybdis of industrial boss-rule'.[19]

Ruskin was not alone in combining a desire for radical reform with a
fear of democracy. His adherence to a principle of wise leadership, which
was his substitute for democracy, was not unusual among those who

proposed an otherwise collectivist philosophy. Indeed, the concept of Plato's 'Guardians' resonates through many so-called democratic utopias, from the moral elect of Thomas More to the scientific absolutism of Auguste Comte. 'In antiquity,' writes M.I. Finley, 'it is hard to find any Utopian thinking which is not hierarchical.'[20] In the precarious political climate of the nineteenth century, the concept of a guiding intellectual elite still held its appeal for many utopian writers.

Utopianism itself, however, was the target of much criticism. Robert Owen was commonly held as the father of British socialism but his small-scale communism did not protect him from attacks from others of the same persuasion. His enduring belief in moral and social revolution led to accusations of utopianism from Marx and Engels, who favoured what they considered to be a more scientific approach. But as Ruskin's argument has proved, the rigid distinction between practical socialism and utopian socialism is untenable. Socialism must be underpinned by pragmatism, but it also needs a vision of a future perfect society. Owen preached the 'New Moral world' to give practical reform a visionary context.[21]

Nevertheless, in the nineteenth century, utopianism had a pejorative image, and Owen, Ruskin, and later William Morris, perceived the need to combine ethics with practicality in their reforming visions. Utopianism, not being a political ideology, or indeed an ideology at all, can embrace a variety of forms of social organisation. It does, however, demand the fulfilment of certain precepts before it can be classified as utopianism. Firstly, it must contain an over-riding disapproval of existing society, and secondly, there must be a plan of reform which addresses all aspects of human life, both public and personal. On these counts, Ruskin can be classified as a utopian thinker, not like Owen for his practical interpretation – Ruskin's practical experiments were not a resounding success – but for his vision of economic justice, as expressed primarily in *Unto This Last,* which included many workable suggestions for reform.

These elements of utopianism did not make Ruskin a socialist, however. His insistence on an organic community with greater state intervention predisposed him to socialism, but, ultimately for Ruskin, individual moral regeneration was to be the saviour of society. Also, while not totally anti–collectivist,[22] Ruskin lacked the Spencerian and Comtist sense of evolution and this, combined with his fear of the possible outcome of democracy, meant his organic society was to be static and hierarchical. Yet, as Hobson has indicated, and the approbation of the Labour members would appear to confirm, Ruskin's key emphasis could be accepted despite his misconception of the nature of democracy. As Hobson observed in 1902:

> The attitude which modern Socialists adopt towards John Ruskin is peculiarly interesting. Gratefully, enthusiastically, admitting and adopting his magnificent services in economic criticism, accepting many of his constructive suggestions and the social spirit which animates them, they calmly set aside his pronounced Illiberalism, his vehement Anti-Democracy, as a perverse intellectual freak which had no organic relation to his economics and did not deserve serious consideration.[23]

In 1889, the positivist, Frederic Harrison, who tried so hard to establish a linkage between Ruskin and Comte, gave a very perceptive explanation of the difficulties of establishing Ruskin's political orientation:

> In many things Ruskin is in direct conflict with Socialism. He is all for kings, captains of industry, and powers that be in Church and State. But in so far as the Sermon on the Mount savours of Socialism, so far as St Bernard of Clairvaux and St Francis of Assisi fostered Socialist tendencies – and it is certain that neither Gospel nor friars encouraged a millennium of capital and unlimited competition – so far Ruskin is really the apostle of a sort of moral and religious Socialism.[24]

It was this religious or ethical dimension, which, when added to Ruskin's powerful attack on economic orthodoxy, allied him with the socialist cause. Despite his anti-democratic stance, Ruskin's continuity with Owen, which was economic rather than communitarian, forged links between early socialist development in England and the Christian Socialist revival of the 1870s and 1880s. With the weighty endorsement of Hobson, Ruskin's impact was both considerable and dual-edged, as has been shown above. In his social critique Ruskin was important not only for his passionate emphasis upon ethical centrality, but for the germs of sound economic analysis which permeated his writings and made *Unto This Last,* in particular, essential reading for many socialist sympathisers. The wider impact of Ruskin's influence can be seen in the fact that, by the end of the nineteenth century, the organised working class was no longer content to allow economics to be isolated as a separate issue, devoid of ethical implications. By 1900, decided M. Beer:

> The working classes have grown in moral and intellectual stature, and are asking the nation to regard and treat them as free personalities. It is an appeal on economic as well as on moral grounds.[25]

Ruskin's influence was both direct, and indirect, via those he influenced and those influenced by him. This diffuse influence permeated not only left-wing politics but also the world of trade-unionism.

A further aspect of Ruskin's influence on socialist thought is to be found in his relationship with Guild Socialism, a movement that emerged in the first two decades of the twentieth century.[26] The central ethos behind such guilds or collective organisations was the promotion of individual creativity, which was perceived as being destroyed in the nineteenth century processes of industrialisation. The idea was to give workers a stronger sense of community and greater control over production through the medium of trade unions, thus giving Ruskin's guild principle a practical basis. Taking its *raison d'être* from the Guild of St George, the Guild of Handicraft, for example, emerged from what was originally a reading class inspired by Ruskin's thinking.

A.J. Penty, assisted by A.R. Orage and S.G. Hobson, was instrumental in establishing guild socialism through the promotion of principles attributed to both Ruskin and Morris. In wishing to emphasise the ethic of community, however, Penty favoured Ruskin's medieval Christian idiom and reinforced the central organicist message of *Unto This Last.* After his break with the Fabians,[27] Penty protested:

> When we remember that twenty years before the Fabian essays were written, Ruskin had exposed the fallacies inherent in the divorce of economics from morals, it is difficult to absolve Fabians from the charge of stupidity in imagining that they could afford to ignore his teachings. Yet, strange as this may seem, it is stranger still that from the very start it has been behind the frequent quarrels and splits in the Socialist movement.[28]

Penty, who was an architect, followed Ruskin in his dislike of the Renaissance, favouring instead the romantic concept of imperfection and incompletion, which Ruskin had located in Gothic architecture and injected into his vision for society. This organic approach was not original; it continued a tradition established by Wordsworth, Coleridge, Southey and Carlyle. Ruskin, however, took the organicist ethic to greater depths and was, as J.C. Sherburne points out, a more 'sensitive register of changes in his society's largely unconscious assumptions'.[29]

Ruskin valued the romantic tradition because it stressed an almost physiological interdependence, emulating the example of the natural world. But romanticism also valued individual fulfilment. It was for this reason that Ruskin attacked what he perceived as the negative, alienating effects of the division of labour. This, for him, and later for the guild socialists, had wider repercussions in terms of economic exploitation of the workforce. As Penty commented in 1917:

> It is to be observed that though the system of division of labour cheapens production, it does not allow the workers to take advantage of the resulting cheapness. The skill of the craftsmen is an asset like property. It gives him an effective bargaining power in the market, and so enables him to get a decent wage. But the system of division of labour demands little or no skill of the individual worker, and the capitalist finds it easy to exploit the unskilled worker. Deprived of his skill, the worker can offer no effective resistance to the tyranny of the capitalist, who can bring in the competition of boy and woman labour to drag down his wages to mere subsistence level. And there can be no remedy so long as this diabolical system is allowed to endure.[30]

As Penty continued, Ruskin had called attention to this 'evil' some sixty years earlier in *The Stones of Venice* and the world would have been much happier had it listened to him. The problem had not been seriously addressed. Despite an increase in social reform, Labour representation in Parliament had done little to remedy the personal and social implications of the division of labour, or to curtail the growing discrepancy between the cost of living and the real wages of the workman.[31]

This concern for wages was further emphasised in the writings of one of Penty's colleagues, A.R. Orage, the Fabian editor of the *New Age*

(1907–22). Orage shared with Penty the Ruskinian view that man was naturally imperfect and that the nation was in need of total spiritual regeneration. Indeed, early guild socialists shared a belief in Ruskin's recognition of a symbiosis of moral and economic functions and this, in turn, greatly influenced the trade unions and the thinking of the Independent Labour Party. Orage also shared Penty's opinion, however, that the Labour Party was failing the workers by perpetuating the wage system. Only in the conception of National Industrial Guilds, Orage and his colleagues believed, would the solution be found to 'the problems now vexing one-twentieth of our population and ruining the remainder'.[32]

'Some twenty years ago,' wrote Orage, 'the intelligent workman, fed on Carlyle, Ruskin, William Morris and others . . . said "it is political power we must secure" and the Labour Party was born.' Labour had, however, been too easily diverted into 'political preoccupations' and had 'lost its grip on the industrial machine.' Is it any wonder, Orage commented, that 'politics now stink in the workman's nostrils and that he has turned firmly to direct action'?

> Had a living Socialist Party found itself in Parliament, instead of the present inert Labour Party, led by charlatans and supported by Tadpoles and Tapers, the energies of Labour might possibly for a slightly longer period have been fruitfully employed in the political sphere. But the lesson would have been learnt in due season that the Socialist conquest of the industrial system is an economic and not a political operation: that economic power must precede political power.[33]

Further support for these theories was evident in the writings of one of the leading socialists of the next generation, G.D.H. Cole (1889–1959). His guild socialism emphasised also the need for a moral basis for the economy and the achievement of a Ruskinian reconciliation between the interests of the producer and the consumer. Cole also stressed the linkage of guild socialism with 'the Owenite experiments of 1832–4', where the 'attempt was made to build the structure of Cooperative or Guild production directly upon the Trade Unions and to enlist Trade Union support to the fullest possible extent'.[34] Although guild socialism lost much of its practical influence after 1920, it remained, in Cole's view, the 'outstanding contribution to the new non-Communist theories of socialism during and immediately after the first world war'.[35]

In the requirement to reaffirm Ruskin's position within the guild socialist movement, Cole's work is very significant, because, as P.D. Anthony points out, 'He exhibits the strongest evidence of Ruskin's influence.'[36]

> Cole's concern with industrial as well as political democracy contradicts Ruskin's scepticism on the ultimate value of that political characteristic. But his [Cole's] reasons for emphasising its importance reveal the same values and concern as Ruskin and his conception of democracy was not dissimilar.[37]

Anthony stresses that Cole attributed much of his inspiration to Morris but is at pains to emphasise that the qualities Cole admired were those which '[Morris] got and acknowledged from Ruskin: . . . moral criticism of capitalist values added to despair at the prospects for art in a capitalist world'.[38] This indicates how Ruskin's influence was refracted not only via his own works but via those of other thinkers he had inspired and influenced. Penty admitted in 1922, in the context of discussions between workers and industrialists post WW1, when finding that all sides were conversant with the writings of Ruskin: '. . . I never realised before how far the influence of Ruskin had penetrated'.[39]

Ruskin was convinced that the only method of 'practical' change was through the moral reformation of society. Cole maintained these same moral convictions to the end of his life.[40] The charge that Ruskin's influence has been seriously underestimated remains intact. Henry Pelling observes:

> [Morris] believed that the immediate role of the Socialist was to educate people for the great inevitable change which would bring back the simpler, sounder society of medieval times, when craftsmen took pride in their work and when there was no capitalist exploitation or industrial ugliness. In this there is clear evidence of Ruskin's influence, shaping a criticism of contemporary society that was to form the basis of Syndicalism and Guild Socialism in the twentieth century.[41]

This emphasis on moral or ethical centrality has, of course, wider, more enduring implications. It is, as P.D. Anthony comments, where Ruskin 'escapes the test of the ballot box' by his 'assertion that industrial society is so manifestly contrary to the laws of God and to the accumulated moral judgement of civilisation that it will destroy itself or that it must be destroyed'.[42] What is known as industrial capitalism supports an affluent society at the expense of the environment and of growing third world poverty. It is 'not preoccupied with morality' and 'has no sympathy with the understanding of aesthetic considerations'.[43] The peripheral status of moral concerns in a capitalist society was ultimately Ruskin's major concern.[44]

It is not enough, however, to say that Ruskin's all-pervading sense of morality was his sole contribution to social reform. Neither would it be true. His sharp analysis of the terms 'wealth' and 'value' shook the complacency of the classical economists and forced them to re-evaluate the status of economics as an exact science. Ruskin's organic approach and his insistence on government intervention in health, education and the general quality of life, were all evident in the subsequent concept of a welfare state. And, although his concern for the loss of individual creativity in an increasingly mechanised world has never seriously been addressed by any British government, that may well be something for the future. Despite all Ruskin's eccentricities, in the working class appreciation of his close analytical exposure of current social injustice, his place in the development of collectivist economic thought is secure.

Finally, then, the circumstances behind the changes in Ruskin's reception have been assessed in detail, to show that it was largely a question of timing. His thoughts were absorbed over the years, but he had no political party to implement them. Christian Socialism came closest to fulfilling that requirement, and, with Ruskin's help, its membership greatly increased in the later nineteenth century.[45] But Christian Socialism never really resolved the tension between the acceptance of even modified capitalism and the ethic of brotherhood, underpinning Christian belief.[46] The endorsement of Hobson, however, gave Ruskinian thinking unquestionable plausibility and by the early twentieth century greater state intervention in social concerns had become a moral obligation. Ruskin's undoubted influence and latent popularity lay in the fact that he achieved what Marx and other critics of capitalism neglected: Ruskin successfully injected humanitarian,

Christian-based ethics into a close analysis of economic malpractice. This led to misunderstandings but also to a lasting legacy.

In 1862, H.H. Lancaster dismissed Ruskin's social writings as 'baseless discontent', commenting complacently: 'It is no true philanthropy to demand for the working classes conditions of happiness which are impossible.'[47] By 1906, the political context was beginning to change fundamentally and the working classes were reading Ruskin avidly. In 1919, on the centenary of Ruskin's birth, Hobson tried to set the record straight:

> I am disposed to think that [the] literary cover for [Ruskin's] ideas was itself a sound operation for the self–protective instinct of a mind which in its depth was conscious of harbouring thought for which the times were not yet ripe. The heavy price [Ruskin] paid in contemporary neglect will, I think, be refunded to his memory in years to come in an England enriched by the fruits of many of those thoughts rejected by the blindness of his generation.[48]

The case for this reassessment of Ruskin's importance has rarely been so clearly and so justly stated.

NOTES

Chapter 1
Introduction

1   J.H. Whitehouse (ed.), *Ruskin the Prophet and Other Centenary Studies* (1920), p. 10.

2   A.J. Penty, *A Study of the Post-Industrial State* (1917), p. 79. Penty was referring specifically here to Ruskin's attack on the division of labour.

3   Ernest Barker, *Political Thought in England, 1848 to 1914* (!st pub. 1915; repr., 1930), p. 196. Barker's testimony is important not only as an early assessment of Ruskin's significance but as a verdict enshrined in what remained for many a standard textbook. For later interpretation of the period more generally, see esp. W.H. Greenleaf, *The British Political Tradition*, Vol. 1: *The Rise of Collectivism* (1983) and Vol. 2: *The Ideological Heritage* (1987).

4   Raymond Williams, *Culture and Society* (1982 edn), p. 141.

5   Royden Harrison, *Before the Socialists: Studies in Labour and Politics, 1861–81* (1965), p. 2.

6   An 1862 edition of *Unto This Last,* held at the London Library, bears the copperplate inscription by a reader: 'He who agrees with this book is a socialist.'

7   See, for example, J. Ruskin, *Fors Clavigera* (1871–84), Letter 1, 1 Jan. 1871, where Ruskin commented that 'Men only associate in parties by sacrificing their opinions, or by having none worth sacrificing.'

8   P.D. Anthony, *John Ruskin's Labour* (1983), p. 2.

9   There are, however, some similarities in their views on work.

10   Anthony, *Ruskin's Labour*, p. 2.

11   Ibid., p. 198.

12   Ibid., p. 201.

13   J.C. Sherburne, *John Ruskin, or the Ambiguities of Abundance: A Study in Social and Economic Criticism* (Cambridge, Mass., 1972), pp. 298–9.

14   The principal exponents of the classical system in England were James Mill, T.R. Malthus, David Ricardo, J.S. Mill, N.W. Senior, and J.R. McCulloch: See F. Crouzet, *The Victorian Economy* (1990).

15   Richard Altick, *Victorian People and Ideas* (1973), p. 131, comments '*Laissez-*

faire, in short, sanctioned the policy of benign neglect which perfectly suited the convenience of bustling entrepreneurs.'

16   Williams, *Culture and Society*, p. 22. Williams also argues that Southey's social critique is often underrated and that he had strong links with Owen in his criticism of orthodox political economy 'on the grounds of its exclusion of moral considerations': ibid., p. 24.

17   Sherburne, *Ambiguities*, p. 98.

18   Ibid., p. 99.

19   Robert Southey (1774–1843), was an English poet and historian. His most important work of social criticism was *Sir Thomas More: Or, Colloquies on the Progress and Prospects of Society* (1829).

20   There were, however, important points of departure.

21   Thomas Carlyle, *Critical and Miscellaneous Essays* (1887 edn), Vol. 1, p. 480.

22   M. Levin, *The Condition of England Question: Carlyle, Mill, Engels* (1998), p. 43.

23   A.L. Le Quesne, 'Carlyle' in A.L. Le Qesne and others, *Victorian Thinkers: Carlyle, Ruskin, Arnold, Morris* (Oxford, 1993), p. 87.

24   Ibid., p. 87.

25   Ibid., p. 89.

26   Sherburne, *Ambiguities*, p. 99. The Ricardian Socialists were a group of radicals who, in the 1820s and 1830s, tried to demonstrate that, under the existing capitalist system, workers were being exploited. Among this group, who were not given a generic identity at the time, must be included John Bray, John Gray, William Thompson, and Thomas Hodgskin. See G. Claeys, *Machinery, Money and the Millennium: From Moral Economy to Socialism, 1815–60* (Oxford, 1987), pp. xxiv–xxv. Also N. Thompson, *A People's Science: The Popular Political Economy of Exploitation and Crisis, 1816–34* (Cambridge, 1984).

27   See Claeys (ed.), *Selected Works of Robert Owen*, Vol. 1, p. xxxviii.

28   William Thompson, *An Inquiry into the Principles of the Distribution of Wealth Most Conducive to Human Happiness* (1824), p. 178.

29   Ibid.

30   Ibid., p. 369.

31   Ibid., p. 12.

32   The Christian Socialist Movement was established in April 1848 by J. M. Ludlow, Charles Kingsley, and F.D. Maurice, in response to a failed Chartist march. Together, they produced a manifesto: 'To the Working Men of England' which confirmed their role as Christian Socialists, although they did not use the term until 1850. They were not socialists in the later political sense and their efforts to attract a working class readership with their pamphlets failed, their style being too moderate to satisfy the mood of growing unrest. In fact, despite a belief in cooperation, they can be seen more as enlightened Tories than as political radicals. The movement did not survive beyond 1854 but one of its achievements was the establishment of the Working Men's College the same year, with Maurice as its principal. Another achievement was the provision of a radical alternative to the prevalent Christian orthodox

message of an unquestioning acceptance of social and economic injustice. For this movement, see E.R. Norman, *The Victorian Christian Socialists* (1987).

33   A.M.C. Waterman, *Revolution, Economics and Religion: Christian Political Economy, 1798–1833* (1991), pp. 3, 4.

34   Norman, *Christian Socialists*, p. 16.

35   Ibid., p. 62.

36   Ibid.

37   Ibid., p. 9.

38   In this, Ludlow had the support of Maurice and Kingsley, who, while accepting the central structure of political economy, rejected the principle of competition and Malthusian ideas on population.

39   See K. Taylor, *The Political Ideas of the Utopian Socialists* (1982).

40   Charles Raven observes that Ludlow's Fourierist influence on Maurice's circle was tempered by the introduction of Lloyd Jones into the group. Jones was a master tailor and an Owenite Socialist, who, despite his religious scepticism, 'threw himself wholeheartedly into the plans of the Christian Socialists' and reinforced the English socialist tradition. See Raven, *Christian Socialism*, (1920), p. 140.

41   Norman, *Christian Socialists*, p. 12.

42   Robert Williams, '*Laissez-Faire*', *Fraser's Magazine*, Vol. 81 (Jan. 1870), p. 83.

43   As indeed was Frederic Harrison, whose intellectual relationship with Ruskin is discussed below. Also sympathetic was Patrick Geddes (1854–1932), who was very interested in communitarian development and published *John Ruskin, Economist* (1884).

44   Harrison, *Before the Socialists*, p. 252.

45   Ibid., p. 333.

46   Even Ernest Barker, who has a very positive approach to Ruskin's influence, categorises him under 'Political Theory of Literature': see Barker, *Political Thought*, p. 183.

Chapter 2
The Emergence of a Social Critic

1   E.T. Cook, 'Mr Ruskin in Relation to Modern Problems', *National Review* Vol. 22 (Feb. 1894), p. 823.

2   See P.J. Corfield, 'The Rivals: Landed and Other Gentlemen', in R. Quinault and N.B. Harte (eds), *Land and Society in Britain, 1700–1914* (1996), pp. 1–33.

3   J. Ruskin, *Praeterita* (1885–9). This text is taken from the three volume edition of 1899, republished in 1949 with an introduction by Kenneth Clarke (ed.), *Praeterita* (1949), Vol. 1, p. 17.

4   Charles Dickens, *Bleak House* (1852). Dickens' works are saturated with a loathing of evangelical hypocrisy.

5   Ruskin, *Praeterita* Vol. 1, p 133.

6   Ibid.

7   Ibid., Vol. 1, p. 22.

8   Ibid., Vol. 1, p. 36

9   In Ruskin, *Fors*, (1871), p. 3, Letter 1: Ruskin spoke of his anguish at 'the material distress' around him.

10   E.T. Cook, 'Mr Ruskin in Relation to Modern Problems', *National Review* (Feb. 1894), p. 824.

11   Ibid: Cook quoted Charles Eliot Norton, who likened Ruskin's nature to an 'Aeolian harp' with the 'strings quivering musically in serene days' but as the storm clouds gathered 'vibrating in the blast with a tension that might break the sounding-board itself.'

12   Leslie Stephen, 'John Ruskin,' in *National Review*, Vol. 35 (Apr. 1900), p. 240.

13   John Ruskin, *Praeterita* (1949 edn), p. 56.

14   See Michael Wheeler, *Ruskin's God* (1999), p. 5.

15   Ruskin, *Praeterita* (1949 edn), p. 62.

16   Ibid., pp. 64–5.

17   See Wheeler, *Ruskin's God*, pp. 25–6.

18   See R. Altick, *Victorian People and Ideas* (1973), pp. 65–202.

19   Ruskin, *Praeterita* (1949 edn), p. 175.

20   Ruskin, *Modern Painters*, ed. David Barrie (1987), p. 28.

21   From a letter to Charles Eliot Norton, 3 Apr. 1871 in J. Bradley and Ian Ousby (eds), *The Correspondence of John Ruskin and Charles Eliot Norton* (Cambridge, 1987).

22   *The Times,* 12 Feb., 1878.

23   Ibid.

24   Wheeler, *Ruskin's God*, p. 150.

25   Ruskin, 'The Nature of Gothic', in idem, *The Stones of Venice* (1906 edn), Vol. 2, pp. 162–3.

26   Ruskin never actually used the word 'alienation' as Marx did, but their sentiments are very similar.

27   Gervase Rosser from 'Crafts, Guilds and the Negotiation of Work in the Medieval Town', *Essays in Criticism* (Jan. 1997).

28   This was also true of Social Darwinism which Ruskin later rejected on the grounds that it was not feasible to extend the laws of the animal world into the realm of humankind.

29   See D. Knoop and G.P. Jones, *The Medieval Mason* (1967 edn), p. 3.

30   Ruskin, *The Crown of Wild Olive* (1906 edn), p. 65, lecture 2 : 'Traffic'.

31   Frederic Harrison, although a keen supporter, also disputed Ruskin's dogmatic approach to the social context of art. See F. Harrison, *John Ruskin* (1902), p. 65.

32   Ruskin, *The Two Paths* (1904 edn), pp. vii–viii: Preface to The First Edition (1859).

33   Ruskin, *Praeterita* (1949 edn), pp. 34–5.

34   Phyllis Rose considers the question of Ruskin's sexuality in some detail: P. Rose, *Parallel Lives: Five Victorian Marriages* (1984), pp. 51–94.

35   E.T. Cook , *The Life of John Ruskin* (1911), Vol. 1. pp. 476–7.

36   See T. Carlyle, *Past and Present* (1843), Proem to Book 1: 'England is full

of wealth, of multifarious produce, supply for human want in every kind;
yet England is dying of inanition.'

37   Ruskin, *Fors* (1906 edn), Vol. 4, pp. 120–1, Letter 78.

38   Ibid.

39   Idem, *Modern Painters* (1987 edn), Vol. 1, p. 29.

40   Idem, *The Seven Lamps of Architecture* (1906 edn), pp. 53–4.

41   See M. Wiener, *English Culture and the Decline of the Industrial Spirit, 1850–
     1980* (1981), pp. 27–9.

42   Ruskin, 'The Opening of the Crystal Palace, Considered in Some of its
     Relations to the Prospects of Art' (1854).

43   Ibid.

44   See Asa Briggs, *The Age of Improvement, 1783–1867* (1979 edn), p. 303.

45   See Weiner, *English Culture*, pp. 64–5, 67.

46   Ruskin, Letter to the *Pall Mall Gazette* (15 Mar. 1872).

47   H.H. Lancaster, 'The Writings of John Ruskin', *North British Review*,
     Vol. 36 (Feb. 1862), p. 31.

48   Ibid., p. 12.

49   *Westminster Review*, Vol. 5 (Jan. 1854–Apr. 1854), p. 315.

50   Ibid., p. 316.

51   Ibid.

52   Ibid.

53   Anon., 'Classic or Gothic: The Battle of the Styles', *Blackwood's Magazine*,
     Vol. 91 (Jan.– Jun. 1862), p. 295.

54   Ibid., p. 296.

55   Anon., *Westminster Review* (Jan. 1854 – Apr. 1854), p. 317.

56   Ibid., p. 318.

57   Ibid.

58   See David McLellan, *Karl Marx: The Legacy* (1983), p. 23.

59   Ruskin, 'Nature of Gothic', from idem, *The Stones of Venice* (1906), p. 161.

60   Ibid.

61   Ibid.

62   *Westminster Review* (Jul. 1866 – Oct. 1867), p. 227.

63   Ibid., p. 229.

64   J. Ruskin, 'Nature of Gothic', in idem, *The Stones of Venice* (1906 edn), p. 163.

65   The Working Men's College was founded in London in 1854 by the Rev
     F.D. Maurice. 'The Nature of Gothic' was used as its manifesto. Ruskin was
     asked to take charge of the drawing class but in fact his main objective was
     to educate the workmen. The experience prompted him to widen his own
     views on the social production of art and he included some of these ideas
     in the third and fourth volumes of *Modern Painters*, which he published in
     1856.

66   Anon., *Westminster and Foreign Quarterly Review* (Jul. 1854 – Oct. 1854),
     p. 297.

67   Ruskin, *A Joy Forever* (1857 edn), p. x, Preface.

68   Ruskin, from a speech delivered at the Mechanic's Institute, Bradford, 1
     March 1859, published in *The Two Paths*, in idem, *Works*, Vol. 16, Lecture 3.

69 Ruskin had, however, obviously read widely round the subject, including the writings of Xenophon and Thomas De Quincey. For a list of the most likely influences on Ruskin's economic thought, see above, chapter one.

70 Ruskin, *A Joy Forever* (1857 edn), pp. xi–xii, Preface.

71 H.H. Lancaster, 'The Writings of John Ruskin', *North British Review* (Feb. 1862), p. 3.

72 Ibid.

73 E.T. Cook, 'Mr Ruskin in Relation to Modern Problems', *National Review*, Vol. 22 (Feb. 1894), p. 827.

74 Ibid., p. 827.

75 Ruskin, *A Joy Forever* (1904 edn), p. 4.

76 Anthony, *Ruskin's Labour*, p. 176.

77 Ibid., p. 188: 'Ruskin rejected Darwin on the one hand, Mill on the other and Spencer cohabiting with both.'

78 Ruskin, *The Queen of the Air* (1869; in 1906 edn), p. 90.

79 See Anthony, *Ruskin's Labour*, p. 188.

80 Ruskin, *The Two Paths* (1859; 1904), p. vii.

81 Ibid., p. ix.

82 Ruskin's organicism was complex, however, and confined to superficial organisation rather to an acknowledgement of underlying growth and development. Some of his most committed disciples, including the economist J.A. Hobson, found this a flaw in his social thought. It also, as J.C. Sherburne points out, allowed Ruskin to escape the 'suggestions of natural determinism which disturbs a Burke or a Coleridge': Sherburne, *Ambiguities*, p. 10. Ruskin's 'static organicism', writes Sherburne, 'bears a superficial resemblance to the neo-classical ideal of harmony' but as he 'becomes aware of the far-reaching aesthetic and social implications of the shift from neo-classic to Romantic, he finds himself more firmly tied to the Romantic fold.' See ibid., p. 11.

83 Ruskin, *Stones of Venice* (1906 edn), Vol. 3, p. 180.

84 E.T. Cook, *National Review*, Vol. 22 (Feb. 1894), p. 828.

85 Ruskin, *A Joy Forever* (1904 edn), pp. 119–120: Lecture 2, 101, 13 Jul. 1857.

86 Ruskin, *The Two Paths* (1904 edn), p. 131: Lecture 3, 97, 1 Mar. 1859.

Chapter 3
Ethics and Economics:
The Reception of *Unto This Last* and *Munera Pulveris*

1 H.H. Lancaster, 'Writings of John Ruskin', *North British Review*, Vol. 36 (Feb. 1862), pp. 2–3.

2 For J.A. Hobson's assessment of Ruskin as an economist, see chapter six.

3 The papers, which were published in 1862 as *Unto This Last,* first appeared in serial form in the *Cornhill Magazine* in 1860, but they aroused such hostility that the editor, W. Thackeray, informed Ruskin that publication would have to cease after the fourth instalment: see Cook, *Life of Ruskin*,

Vol. 2, pp. 6–9. Cook referred to the particularly vitriolic response to *Unto This Last* in the *Saturday Review*.

4   J. Ruskin, *Munera Pulveris* (1872 edn; repr. 1904), pp. xxvii–iii: preface to 1872 edition, dated 1871.

5   Ruskin, *Unto This Last* (1862 edn), pp. viii–ix.

6   Idem, *The Stones of Venice* (1873 edn), Vol. 2, p. 165.

7   G. Claeys, *Machinery, Money and the Millennium,* p. 186.

8   *Literary Gazette* (3 Nov. 1860), as quoted in E.T. Cook, *Life of John Ruskin*, Vol. 2, p. 6.

9   Anon., 'Leading Article', *Manchester Examiner and Times* (2 Oct. 1860).

10 Ruskin, *Unto This Last* (1862), p. vii.

11 Lancaster, 'Writings of John Ruskin', *North British Review*, Vol. 36 (Feb. 1862), p. 28.

12 Ludlow, rather than Maurice, made a close analysis of socio-economic concerns.

13 P.D. Anthony, however, comments that the attack on Ruskin 'came from the press and from opinion formers rather than from economists': Anthony, *Ruskin's Labour*, p. 73.

14 See W.J. Barber, *A History of Economic Thought* (1967), p. 79.

15 Ruskin's affinity with Comte, a factor which Ruskin vehemently denied, is considered in some detail in chapter five.

16 Ruskin, 'The Roots of Honour', *Unto this Last* (1862), p. 1.

17 Idem, *The Two Paths* (1904 edn), p. 129.

18 See Barker, *Political Thought*, p. 9 and Greenleaf, *The British Political Tradition*, Vol. 1, *The Rise of Collectivism*, p. 128.

19 Unsigned article, 'Political Economy in the Clouds', *Fraser's Magazine*, Vol. 62 (Nov. 1860), p. 653.

20 Ruskin's break with Evangelicalism came in 1858. He recorded this turning point in *Praeterita* (1885–9): see *Praeterita* (1949 edn), pp. 460–1. For a modern interpretation, see also Wheeler, *Ruskin's God*, pp. 148–52.

21 See Richard D. Altick, *Victorian People and Ideas* (1973), pp. 168–9.

22 J. Ruskin, *Modern Painters* (1987 edn), p. 615.

23 The Census of 1851 indicated a considerable lack of interest in church attendance among the working classes: see J.R. Moore (ed.), *Religion in Victorian Britain* (1988), Vol. 3. p. 313.

24 Anon., 'Political Economy in the Clouds', *Fraser's Magazine* (Nov. 1860), pp. 652–3.

25 James Keir Hardie, *From Serfdom to Socialism*, ed. Robert E. Dowse (1907 repr. 1974), pp. 38–9. Hardie was an enthusiastic disciple of Ruskin.

26 *Fraser's Magazine* (Nov. 1860), p. 652. This was a view also taken by Walter Bagehot, who ridiculed Ruskin for pressing 'St Matthew into the service as the warranter and endorser of his nonsense.' See N. St John-Stevas (ed.), *The Collected Works of Walter Bagehot* (1986), Vol. 14, p. 316: 'Aesthetic Twaddle versus Economic Science'.

27 Ruskin, *Unto This Last* (1862), p. 41.

28 Ibid., p. 42.

29 The logical extension of this theory would be opposition to overseas trading, but Ruskin was sufficiently in thrall to Carlyle to endorse imperialist expansion, although in Ruskin's case it was for moral, not for economic, reasons. See Sherburne, *Ambiguities*, pp. 203–6.

30 Ruskin, *Unto This Last* (1862), pp. 45–6.

31 Ibid., p. 47.

32 Ibid., p. 60.

33 *Fraser's Magazine* (Nov.1860), p. 656.

34 Ibid.

35 Ibid.

36 Ruskin, *Unto This Last* (1860), p. 62.

37 Anthony, *John Ruskin's Labour*, p. 81.

38 Ruskin, *Unto This Last,* p. 70. Ruskin here drew an interesting parallel with the highwayman robbing the rich 'because he is rich,' but this would be less attractive to the merchant, because being 'less profitable and more dangerous than the robbery of the poor, it is rarely practised by persons of discretion.'

39 *Fraser's Magazine* (Nov. 1860), p. 653.

40 H.H. Lancaster, in *North British Review* (Feb. 1862), p. 34.

41 *Unto This Last* (1862), p. 102.

42 *Fraser's Magazine* (Nov. 1860), p. 659.

43 Anon., 'Contemporary Literature', *The Home and Foreign Review*, Vol. 1 (Jul. 1862), p. 559.

44 Cook, *Ruskin* , Vol. 2, p. 16.

45 Ruskin, *The Crown of Wild Olive* (1906 edn), p. 31, Lecture 1.

46 *Westminster Review,* Vol. 22 (Jul.– Oct. 1862), pp. 530–1.

47 Ruskin, *Unto this Last* (1862), pp. 118–19.

48 Thomas De Quincey identified 'utility' and 'demand' and suggested that more emphasis be placed upon utility: T. De Quincey, *The Collected Writings* (Edinburgh, 1890), Vol. 9, p. 179.

49 Walter Bagehot, 'The Merchant's Function,' first published in the *Economist* (1860), repr. in Bagehot, *Collected Works*, pp. 322–4.

50 Ibid.

51 Ruskin, *The Two Paths* (1906 edn), p. 130.

52 Ruskin, *Unto This Last* (1862), p. 155.

53 Sherburne, *Ambiguities,* p. 129.

54 Anon., *Westminster Review,* Vol. 22 (Jul.– Oct. 1862), pp. 531–2.

55 Ibid.

56 From the *Christian Life* (20 Dec. 1879).

57 *Westminster Review* (Jul.– Oct. 1862), p. 532.

58 *Home and Foreign Review* (1862), p. 558.

59 Ruskin Library, Lancaster, Ms 33, Diary of John James Ruskin, 1845–64.

60 'Political Economy in the Clouds,' *Fraser's Magazine* (Nov. 1860), p. 652.

61 J.H. Whitehouse, 'Ruskin as a Pioneer Force in Modern Life', *Ruskin Centenary Address* (8 Feb. 1919), p. 58.

62 *Fraser's Magazine* (Nov. 1860), p. 652.

63 Ruskin, *Unto This Last* (1862), pp. 102–3.
64 Ruskin Library, Lancaster University, Ms. 12, Transcript of Ruskin's Diary, 1861–3, p. 42.
65 Whitehouse, *Ruskin Centenary Address*, p. 58.
66 Ruskin, *Munera Pulveris* (1904), p. xxviii.
67 Cook, *Ruskin*, Vol. 2, p. 55.
68 Ruskin, *Munera Pulveris* (1871), p. viii.
69 Ibid., p. viii.
70 Ibid., p. xiv.
71 Ibid., p. xxix.
72 Ibid., pp. xxix–xxx.
73 Cook, *John Ruskin*, p. 56.
74 Ibid.
75 Ibid., p. 57.
76 Sherburne, *Ambiguities*, p. 101.
77 In Ruskin's case, however, there were other reasons for this.
78 Cook, *Ruskin*, Vol. 2, p. 13.
79 Ibid., p. 14.
80 This is a successful example of Ruskin's communitarian spirit and is also redolent of Owenite economics.
81 E.T. Cook, *Some Aspects of Mr Ruskin's Work* (1890), p. 201.
82 Ruskin, *Munera Pulveris* (1904 edn), p. 6.
83 Norman, *Victorian Christian Socialists*, p. 139.

Chapter 4
Vindication: A Changing Society and a
More Favourable Reception

1   Barker, *Political Thought*, p. 196.
2   Anon., 'Belles Lettres', *Westminster and Foreign Quarterly Review*, Vol. 28 (Jul.– Oct. 1865), p. 574.
3   Ibid.
4   J. Ruskin, *Sesame and Lilies* (1907), p. xi: preface to the small edition of 1882.
5   The publisher's note at the front of this particular edition recorded 'one hundred and fiftieth thousand in original form'.
6   Ibid., pp. viii–ix.
7   Anon., ' Belles Lettres', p. 575.
8   Ibid.
9   Thomas Dixon was not a fictitious character. He was indeed a working man who often sought the advice of famous people, sometimes to their annoyance. See T. Hilton, *John Ruskin: The Later Years* (Bath, 2000), p. 116.
10 Ruskin, *Time and Tide* (1906 edn), pp. 221–2: Appendixes.
11 Ibid., p. 222.
12 See P. Thane, *The Foundations of the Welfare State: Social Policy in Modern Britain* (Essex, 1982), p. 14.

13   From 1833, a series of 40 Factory Acts to improve working conditions was passed by Parliament.

14   See Barker, *Political Thought*, p. 206 and Greenleaf, *The Rise of Collectivism*.

15   Weiner, *English Culture*, p. 82.

16   Weiner referred to the discussion by Arnold Toynbee, 'Are Radicals Socialists?', in idem, *Lectures on the Industrial Revolution of the Eighteenth Century in England* (1884; repr. 1923), p. 237.

17   Anon., 'Men of the Day,' *Vanity Fair*, No. 40 (17 Feb. 1872), p. 55.

18   See Norman, *Victorian Christian Socialists*, p. 10.

19   G. Stedman Jones, 'Utopian Socialism Reconsidered' (Ruskin College Position Papers, 30 Nov.– 2 Dec. 1979), sect. 1: 5.

20   J. Ruskin, *Fors Clavigera* (1871), p. 2: Letter 1.

21   Ibid.

22   Leslie Stephen, 'Mr Ruskin's Recent Writings', *Fraser's Magazine*, Vol. 9, No. 49 (Jun. 1874), p. 688.

23   Ibid.

24   Ibid., p. 689. Stephen included a footnote explaining that 'the monthly numbers of Mr Ruskin's *Fors Clavigera* are to be obtained for the sum of tenpence each on application to Mr George Allen, Orpington, Sunnyside, Kent.' This, in theory, made them accessible to the working man to whom they were addressed.

25   W.G. Collingwood, *The Life and Work of John Ruskin* (1893), Vol. 2, p. 125.

26   Collingwood, *Life and Work of John Ruskin*, p. 126.

27   *Westminster Review*, Vol. 40 (Jul.– Oct. 1871), p. 217.

28   Ibid., p. 523.

29   Ibid., Vol. 41 (Jan.– Apr. 1872), p. 233.

30   Ibid., Vol. 42 (Jul. – Oct. 1872), p. 234.

31   Ibid., Vol. 43 (Jan.– Apr. 1873), p. 266.

32   Jeffrey L. Spear, 'These are the Furies of Phlegethon': Ruskin's Set of Mind and the Creation of *Fors Clavigera*', in idem., *Dream of an English Eden: Ruskin and his Tradition in Social Criticism* (Columbia, 1984), p. 157.

33   Ruskin, *Fors* (Jan. 1871), p. 5: Letter 1.

34   Leslie Stephen, 'Mr Ruskin's Recent Writings', *Fraser's Magazine* (Jun. 1874), p. 692.

35   Ibid., p. 692.

36   Ibid., pp. 692–3.

37   Ibid., p. 694.

38   Frederic Harrison, *John Ruskin* (1902), p. 170.

39   Stephen, 'Recent Writings', *Fraser's Magazine* (1874), p. 700.

40   Ruskin, *Fors* (Nov. 28, 1875; in 1906 edn), Vol. 3, p. 231: Letter 61.

41   Anon., *Westminster Review*, Vol. 40 (Jul.–Oct. 1871), pp. 307–8.

42   He was later to become Sir Herbert Warren, President of Magdalen College, Oxford.

43   Herbert Warren, 'Communication', in J.H. Whitehouse (ed.), *Centenary Addresses* (Oxford, 1919), pp. 45–6.

44 Ruskin is referring to: *Aratra Pentelici*; *The Eagle's Nest*; and either *Val d'Arno* (Orpington, 1874) or *Lectures on Art* (Oxford, 1870).

45 Letter from Ruskin to *Glasgow Herald* (5 Jun. 1874), reprinted in *The Times* (6 Jun. 1874). Also published in A.D.O. Wedderburn (comp.), *Arrows of the Chace* (1880), a collection of Ruskin's letters.

46 E.T. Cook, 'Mr Ruskin in Relation to Modern Problems', *National Review*, Vol. 22 (1894), p. 834. The context of this remark was a reference to the scheme Ruskin had financed to enable Octavia Hill to oversee the housing of poor tenants and to improve their general living conditions. In so doing, wrote Cook, Ruskin provided a permanent and enduring example of 'model landlordism'.

47 See Barker, *Political Thought*, p. 196.

48 W.H. Greenleaf, *The British Political Tradition*, Vol. 1: *The Rise of Collectivism* (Cambridge, 1983), p. 128.

49 Ibid., p. 127.

50 Ibid., p. 128.

51 Mill's relationship to the individualist/collectivist debate is discussed in Stefan Collini, *Public Moralists*, pp. 334–5.

52 E.T. Cook *Studies in Ruskin* (1890), p. 192.

53 Stephen, 'Recent Writings', p. 698.

54 Ibid.

55 Sherburne, *Ambiguities*, pp. 139–40.

56 Ruskin, *Unto this Last* (Doves Press, 1907), p. 105: Notes. For further details on the Doves Press see P. Stansky, 'Morris', in *Victorian Thinkers* (Oxford, 1983), p. 405.

57 Stephen, 'Recent Writings', p. 699.

58 Ruskin, *Munera Pulveris* (1904 edn), p. 1.

59 *Westminster and Foreign Quarterly Review*, Vol. 147 (Jan.– Apr. 1879), pp. 186–7.

60 Ibid., Vol. 22 (Jul. – Oct. 1862), p. 530.

61 Ibid., Vol. 147 (1879), p. 187.

62 This particular extract was part of an address, entitled *The Present Position and Prospects of Political Economy*, given in Dublin in 1878.

63 William Stanley Jevons (1833–82) English economist and logician. From 1876–80, he held the chair in political economy at University College, London.

64 *Westminster Review*, Vol. 147, pp. 187–8.

65 Ibid., p. 189.

66 Ibid.

67 Ibid., Vol. 147, p. 191.

68 Ruskin, *Unto This Last* (1862), p. 5.

69 *Westminster Review*, Vol. 147, p. 191.

70 For a discussion of Mill's reputation, see S. Collini, *Public Moralists*: pp. 319–23.

71 Anon., 'John Stuart Mill', *Fraser's Magazine*, Vol. 8 (Jul.–Dec. 1873), p. 663.

72 Ibid.
73 Ibid., p. 676.
74 Ibid., p. 681.
75 Ibid.
76 See Frederic Harrison, *Tennyson, Ruskin, Mill and Other Literary Estimates* (1899), pp. 286–9.
77 Signed G.S., 'Starvation Wages and Political Economy', *Fraser's Magazine,* Vol. 99 (Jan. 1879), pp. 32–3.
78 J.S. Mill, *The Principles of Political Economy* (1848), p. 7.
79 *Fraser's Magazine,* Vol. 99 (Jan. 1879), p. 33.
80 Ibid., p. 33.
81 *Letters of John Ruskin to Charles Eliot Norton* (1905) Vol. 1, p. 245: letter dated 12 Sept. 1869.
82 Ibid., Vol. 1, p. 230: letter dated 18 Aug. 1869.
83 Ibid., pp. 248–9: letter dated 21 Sept. 1869.
84 This was not, of course, all due to Ruskin; some state intervention was evident as far back as the 1830s with the introduction of the Factory Acts. Ruskin, however, certainly raised awareness of the need for further action.
85 E.T. Cook, 'Mr Ruskin in Relation to Modern Problems', *National Review,* Vol. 22 (Feb 1894), pp. 832–3.
86 Whitehouse, *Centenary Addresses,* pp. 64–5.
87 Malcolm Hardman, *Ruskin and Bradford: An Experiment in Victorian Cultural History* (Manchester, 1986), pp. 212–2.
88 Cook, *Studies in Ruskin,* p. 200.
89 Sherburne, *Ambiguities,* p. 139.

Chapter 5
Frederick Harrison: Positive Thinking

1 F. Harrison, *Tennyson, Ruskin, Mill and Other Literary Estimates* (1899), p. 101.
2 For a brief account of Harrison's life and work, see: Christopher Kent, 'Frederic Harrison', J.O. Baylen and N.J. Gossman (eds), *Biographical Dictionary of Modern British Radicals,* Vol 3: 1870 – 1914 (1988), pp. 389–94.
3 See Martha Vogeler, *Frederic Harrison: The Vocation of a Positivist* (Oxford, 1985).
4 Royden Harrison, *Before The Socialists,* pp. 251–2. Harrison stressed that 'positivism' (with a small 'p') was the most distinctive intellectual tendency in England between 1860 and 1880, with a following which exceeded that of Christian socialism.
5 This was an aspiration Frederic Harrison shared with Patrick Geddes: see R. Harrison, *Before The Socialists,* p. 252.
6 Frederic Harrison, *Autobiographic Memoirs* (1911), Vol. 1, p. 4.
7 Ibid., Vol. 1, p. 63.
8 Ibid., Vol. 1, p. 81.
9 Ibid., Vol. 1, p. 95.

10 Frederic Harrison on 'The Making of a Positivist', (1850–61): see J.R. Moore (ed.), *Religion in Victorian Britain,* Vol. 3 (Manchester, 1988), p. 450.

11 Harrison was referring to the Broad Church contributors to *Essays and Reviews,* among whom can be numbered: A.P. Stanley, F.D. Maurice and Samuel Taylor Coleridge.

12 B. Jowett (1817–93), created Master of Balliol, Oxford in 1870, was a theologian and scholar with great personal influence.

13 F. Harrison, 'Apologia pro Fide Mea: Introductory' (1907), in idem, *The Creed of a Layman: Apologia pro Fide Mea* (1907), pp. 13–25, 27, 30, 38–42.

14 The book which best explained the basic tenets of positivism in English was E.S. Beesly (ed.), *The Fundamental Principles of the Positivist Philosophy* (1905).

15 Archdeacon William Paley argued in his *Natural Theology* (1802) that the proof of God's existence lay in the evidence of a grand design. Using the analogy of a watchmaker, Paley demonstrated that the complexity and interdependence of nature was proof of an intelligent creator. Another of his works justified the Christian religion in terms of miracles: W. Paley, *The Evidence of Christianity* (1794).

16 Harrison, *Autobiographic Memoirs*, Vol. 1, p. 146.

17 Ibid., Vol. 1, p. 230

18 Ibid. F.J. Furnivall (1825–1910) was an enthusiastic Christian Socialist who was renowned for his lack of tact and had an uneasy relationship with Maurice. See: C.E. Raven, *Christian Socialism: 1848–54* (1920), pp. 121–3.

19 Harrison, *Autobiographic Memoirs*, Vol. 1, p. 231.

20 Ibid., Vol. 1, p. 282.

21 Harrison was referring to Ruskin's father whom he had also met.

22 Ibid., Vol. 1, p. 231.

23 Ibid., Vol. 1, p. 232.

24 Ibid., Vol. 1, p. 233.

25 London School of Economics Archives, Ms 1/101, Letter from Ruskin to Frederic Harrison, 8 Jul. 1868.

26 Ibid.

27 Frederic Harrison, 'The Limits of Political Economy', *Fortnightly Review*, Vol. 1 (Jun. 1865), p. 356.

28 Ibid., pp. 356–7.

29 Harrison, *Autobiographic Memoirs,* Vol. 1, p. 271.

30 Ibid.

31 The positivists objected to the practice of *laissez-faire* but based their argument primarily on their insistence on scientific observation and the desirability of a managerial elite. See C. Kent 'Frederic Harrison', in Baylen and Gossman (eds), *Biographical Dictionary of Modern British Radicals*, p. 391.

32 Harrison, *Autobiographic Memoirs*, Vol. 1, p. 272.

33 Harrison, 'Limits of Political Economy', p. 357.

34 Ibid.

35 Ibid.

36   L.S.E. Archives, Ms 1/101, Letter from Ruskin to Harrison, dated 12 Dec. 1865.

37   Prof. Cairnes (1823–75), who held the chair of political economy at University College, London, belonged to the same school of thought as did J.S. Mill.

38   Frederic Harrison, 'Professor Cairnes on M. Comte and Political Economy', *Fortnightly Review* (Jul. 1870), p. 52.

39   J.E. Cairnes, 'M. Comte and Political Economy', *Fortnightly Review* (May 1870), p. 580.

40   Ibid., pp. 41–2. Harrison did not mention Ruskin here, but the analogy with the construction of the Gothic cathedral becoming something more than the sum of its parts clearly alluded to Ruskin's teaching.

41   Ibid., p. 45.

42   Harrison, *Autobiographic Memoirs,* Vol. 2, p. 274.

43   Ibid., Vol. 2, p. 275.

44   Ibid.

45   Harrison, *John Ruskin,* pp. 97–8.

46   Ibid., p. 98.

47   Ibid., p. 100.

48   Harrison, 'Limits of Political Economy', p. 362.

49   Ibid., p. 375.

50   Ruskin, *Unto This Last,* p. 156.

51   Harrison, 'Limits of Political Economy', p. 375.

52   Harrison, *John Ruskin,* p. 107.

53   Ibid.

54   Ibid., p. 102.

55   Ibid., p. 103.

56   Harrison's determination to establish a linkage between Ruskin and Comte was further endorsed by the communitarian interests of another positivist, Patrick Geddes. Geddes was very interested in the practical experiments of Robert Owen, and was also greatly influenced by Ruskin's proposals for economic cooperation: see Philip Mairet, *Pioneer of Sociology: The Life and Letters of Patrick Geddes* (1957), p. xii and p. 23.

57   Harrison, *John Ruskin,* p. 104.

58   Ibid., p. 106.

59   Ibid., p. 165.

60   See T. Hilton, *John Ruskin: The Later Years* (Bath, 2000), pp. 109–11.

61   Harrison, *John Ruskin,* p. 166.

62   Ibid., Harrison recorded that after the capture of Paris in January 1871, Ruskin joined a 'Paris Food Fund,' to which he gave £50. In November of that year he gave the university of Oxford £5000 to endow a mastership of drawing. He also gave a relative £15,000 to set him up in business. And at Christmas Ruskin gave the tithe of his remaining capital to found the St George's Company, into which so much of his money and his energies were destined to be absorbed. John James Ruskin at his death in 1864 had left to his son £157,000 in money, besides pictures and houses. In seven years

the son had but half of this left after his lavish gifts; and that half not long afterwards followed the first. Ruskin recorded the state of his finances in some detail in *Fors* (1906) pp. 85–91: Letter 76.

63 Frederic Harrison, *Realities and Ideals, Social, Political, Literary and Artistic* (1908), p. 364.

64 Ibid.

65 Ibid., p. 168.

66 Ibid., p. 169.

67 Ibid. This was a significant factor in Ruskin's reception among the working classes. There were, however, other factors involved.

68 Ibid., p. 366.

69 Harrison, *John Ruskin*, p. 181.

70 Ibid., p. 185

71 Ibid., p. 194.

72 Harrison, *Realities and Ideals*, p. 365.

73 Idem, *John Ruskin*, p. 195.

74 Ibid., p. 196.

75 Ruskin, *Fors,* (1906 edn), p. 337: Letter 66, dated 14 May 1876.

76 Ibid, Letter 69, dated July 1876.

77 Frederic Harrison, 'Past and Present', *Fortnightly Review*, Vol. 20 (Jul. 1876), p. 93.

78 L.S.E. Archives, Ms 1/101, Letter from Ruskin to Harrison, dated 11 Jul. 1875.

79 L.S.E. Archives, Ms 1/101, Letter from Ruskin to Harrison, dated 25 Jul. 1876.

80 L.S.E. Archives, Ms 1/101, Letter from Ruskin to Harrison, dated 27 Jul. 1876.

81 Harrison, *John Ruskin,* p. 196.

82 Leslie Stephen, 'The Comtist Utopia', *Fraser's Magazine* (Jul. 1869). Leslie Stephen (1832–1904), was a lapsed Christian and influential man of letters. He was a supporter of Comte and friend of Frederic Harrison: See Baylen and Gossman (eds), *Dictionary of Modern British Radicals*, Vol. 3. pp. 792–6.

83 Stephen, 'Comtist Utopia', p. 2.

84 Ibid., p. 10.

85 Harrison, *John Ruskin*, p. 170.

86 Stephen, 'Comtist Utopia', p. 11.

87 Ibid., p. 12.

88 Ibid.

89 Vogeler, *Harrison*, p. 60.

90 Ruskin, *Daily News* (19 Jun. 1880).

91 Stephen, 'Comtist Utopia', p. 12.

92 Harrison, *John Ruskin*, p. 195.

93 Harrison, *Autobiographic Memoirs,* Vol. 2, p. 240.

94 L.S.E. Archives Ms I/101, Letter from Ruskin to Harrison, dated 30 Jul. 1876.

95   L.S.E. Archives Ms 1/101, Letter from Ruskin to Harrison, dated 9 Aug. 1876.

96   For a comparison between the thinking of Ruskin and Mill, see Sherburne, *Ambiguities*, pp. 119–20.

97   In his paper 'Thoughts on Government', Harrison wrote: 'The political teaching of Comte comes in effect to results, analogous to, but not the same as, those of Carlyle; but it reaches similar results on very different grounds and by widely contrasted methods.' In effect, Harrison commented that although these two thinkers agreed in rejecting direct democratic government, Carlyle invested his ruling heroes with 'superhuman' powers, whereas 'Positivism regards the ruler as the minister of Public Opinion.' This argument was expanded in 'Carlyle and Comte on Government', in Harrison's *Order and Progress* (1875), p. 32.

98   Stephen, 'Comtist Utopia', p. 15.

99   Ibid., p. 18.

100   Herbert Spencer (1820–1903) supported the principle of *laissez-faire* using the evolutionary language of Darwin as a justification: see D. Wiltshire, *The Social and Political Thought of Herbert Spencer* (Oxford, 1978).

101   Harrison, *John Ruskin*, p. 177.

102   Stephen, 'Comtist Utopia', p. 21.

103   Frederic Harrison, 'The Revival of Authority', *Fortnightly Review*, Vol. 19 (1 Jan. 1873), p. 1; also repr. in idem, *Order and Progress* (1875), p. 348.

104   Harrison, 'The Revival of Authority', p. 2.

105   Ibid., p. 2.

106   Ruskin, *Unto This Last* (1862), p. 160: footnote to essay 4.

107   F. Harrison, 'The Gospel of Industry', *Normal Society* (1918), p.183: Lecture 8.

108   Ibid.

109   Idem, 'Studies of Political Crises', in his *Thoughts on Government, Part 2* (1875), p. 44.

110   London Library Archives, Ms 1037, Harrison, 'Moral and Religious Socialism', New Year's Address at Newton Hall, 1 Jan. 1891, p. 12.

111   Ibid.

112   Ibid., p. 24.

113   Ibid., p. 19. C. Kent comments that 'although Harrison became an apologist for the Paris commune . . . he was far from being a socialist.' In fact, as Kent explains, Harrison never completely succeeded in anglicising Comtism: see idem, 'Frederic Harrison', in Baylen and Gossman (eds), *Dictionary of Modern British Radicals*, p. 393.

114   Harrison, 'Moral and Religious Socialism', p. 26.

115   Ibid., p. 48.

116   Harrison, 'The Revival of Authority: The Principle of Opinion', in his *Order and Progress* (1875), p. 368.

117   Idem, *Order and Progress*, p. 371.

118   Ibid., p. 372.

119   Ibid., p. 375.

120   Ibid., p. 376.

121 Ibid., p. 377.

122 Ibid., pp. 379–380.

123 Harrison recognised the difficulties in accommodating the pure Comtist ideal with the realities of practical politics: see Kent, 'Frederic Harrison' in Baylen and Gossman (eds), *Dictionary of British Radicals*, p. 391.

124 Harrison, *Order and Progress*, pp. 384–5.

125 Ibid., pp. 387–92.

126 Ibid., pp. 393–5.

127 Martha Vogeler comments that one of the aims of *Order and Progress* was 'to promote Positivism as a philosophy mediating between that of Mill and Carlyle, representatives here of reform and reaction respectively': Vogeler, *Harrison*, p. 119. P.D. Anthony also observes that: 'Ruskin's critical attitude to democracy is very much that of Plato. The counting of heads is not likely to secure wisdom or justice in government': Anthony, *Ruskin's Labour*, p. 30.

128 Harrison, 'Thoughts on Government', in his *Order and Progress*, pp. 48–9.

129 Idem, 'Revival of Authority', in his *Order and Progress*, p. 355.

130 Idem, 'Thoughts on Government', in his *Order and Progress*, p. 53.

131 The influence of positivism, however, continued to be felt intellectually. Its central thesis of empiricism was the dominant and enduring principle of Enlightenment thinkers and Comte's own influence on the development of sociology was considerable.

132 Royden Harrison, *Before the Socialists*, p. 333.

133 Vogeler, *Harrison*, p. 318, notes: 'In lauding Ruskin's personal philanthropy [Harrison] advances Comte's notion of altruism as the religion of the common man.'

134 Ibid: Vogeler also argues that Harrison compared Ruskin to Comte 'in their criticisms of orthodox economy, and in their insistence that only religion could provide a basis for morality.' But this, for Harrison, meant the 'religion' of humanity.

135 L.S.E. Archives, Ms 1/101, Letter from Ruskin to Harrison, dated 26 Mar. 1884.

136 Vogeler, *Harrison*, p. 59: 'much of what [Harrison] was thinking was similar to what Carlyle and Ruskin had already so dramatically written.'

137 Harrison, *John Ruskin*, p. 206.

138 Ibid., pp. 107–8.

Chapter 6
Hobson, Ruskin and New Liberalism

1 John A. Hobson, *Work and Wealth* (1914), p. 10.

2 Michael Freeden (ed.), *Reappraising J. A. Hobson* (1990), p. 8.

3 John Allett, 'The Conservative Aspect of Hobson's New Liberalism', in ibid., p. 95.

4 J.A. Hobson, *Confessions of an Economic Heretic* (1938), p. 15.

5 Ibid.

6   Ibid., p. 16.

7   Ibid., p. 19.

8   Ibid., p. 20.

9   Ibid., pp. 19–21.

10   John Allett comments: 'Hobson, like many other social observers, attributed much of this feeling of social discontent to religion's fading and a correspondent weakening of the older moral obligations and social conventions.' In Allett, 'The Conservative Aspect of Hobson's New Liberalism, in M. Freeden (ed.), *Reappraising Hobson*, p. 78.

11   Hobson, *Confessions*, p. 21.

12   Ibid., p. 22.

13   Michael Freeden comments: 'Hobson's avid assimilatory powers enabled him to synthesize the latest writing in a whole range of disciplines concerning man and society': idem, 'Hobson's Evolving Conceptions of Human Nature', in idem (ed.), *Reappraising Hobson*, p. 54.

14   Hobson, *Confessions*, p. 24. In a footnote, Hobson pointed out that this was not Mill's personal attitude and that, even as early as 1848 in his *Political Economy*, Mill 'indulged in speculations of a socialistic future'.

15   Ibid., p. 25.

16   Ibid., p. 26.

17   Alon Kadish observes that Hobson was concerned about the low demand among the working classes for Extension courses in economics. Hobson attributed this to problems of poverty and fatigue, but also, to the 'frequent domination of the local Extension committees by middle-class members': see A. Kadish, 'Rewriting the Confessions: Hobson and the Extension Movement', in Freeden (ed.), *Reappraising Hobson*, p. 163.

18   Hobson, *Confessions*, p. 28.

19   Ibid.

20   John Allett, *New Liberalism: The Political Economy of John Hobson* (1981) p. 8: Allett argues that this comment 'probably refers to the fact that the Fabians did not give serious consideration to Hobson's theory of underconsumption'.

21   Hobson, *Confessions*, p. 29.

22   Ibid., p. 30.

23   Ibid.

24   Ibid., p. 31.

25   In the widely read text, Samuel Smiles, *Self-Help* (1859), p. 2, Smiles commented: 'But there is no power of law that can make the idle man industrious, the thriftless provident, or the drunken sober.'

26   Hobson, *Confessions*, p. 32.

27   Marx and Hegel differed in their interpretations of the concept of 'contradiction', but both conceived of the movement of modern society as a dialectical process: see T. Carver (ed.), *The Cambridge Companion to Marx* (Cambridge, 1991), p. 288.

28   Hobson, *Confessions*, p. 36.

29   Freeden, 'Introduction', in Freeden (ed.), *Reappraising Hobson*, p. 9.

30 H.C.G. Matthew, 'Hobson, Ruskin and Cobden', in ibid., p. 16.

31 Hobson, *Ruskin*, p. 159.

32 Idem, *The Crisis of Liberalism* (1909; repr. 1974), p. 92.

33 Idem, *Work and Wealth* (1914), p. 16.

34 The Rainbow Circle, formed in 1894, was one of the first New Liberal groups. It took its name from the Rainbow Tavern in Fleet Street where monthly meetings were held as informal discussions. Its original members included Hobson, William Clarke, Herbert Burrows, Richard Stapely, Ramsey Macdonald, and J.R. MacDonald; but as the group began to meet on a more regular and specifically political basis, it attracted new members, including Graham Wallas, Charles Trevelyan, J.M. Robertson and Sydney Oliver.

35 L.S.E. Archives coll. misc 575/Z, Minutes of Rainbow Circle, Twelfth Session, Oct. 1905–Jun. 1906: 4 Oct. 1905.

36 Allett, *New Liberalism,* pp. 15–16.

37 Ibid., p. 19.

38 Barker, *Political Thought*, p. 222.

39 In Ruskin, *The Eagle's Nest* (7 Mar. 1872), lecture 9, section 185: 'Had Darwinism been true, we should long ago have split our heads in two with foolish thinking, or thrust out, from above our covetous hearts, a hundred desirous arms and clutching hands.'

40 In stressing this, Ruskin was drawing from the Bible, the example of the Middle Ages, and from Carlyle. It was a view also professed later by Peter Kropotkin in his *Mutual Aid* (1902).

41 Hobson, *John Ruskin,* p. 82.

42 Idem, *Work and Wealth,* p. 14.

43 Allett, 'Conservative Aspect', in Freeden (ed.), *Reappraising Hobson*, pp. 79–80.

44 Hobson, *John Ruskin,* p. 82.

45 Ibid.

46 Even the liberal theorist, T.H. Green, regarded state intervention as a last resort: see P. Thane, *The Foundations of The Welfare State* (1982), p. 15.

47 Hobson, *John Ruskin,* p. 57.

48 Ibid., pp. 58–9.

49 Hobson always insisted that Ruskin's mastery of language was central to his effectiveness as an economic critic. In his centenary address Hobson commented : 'Ruskin showed, no study has suffered more from the power of loose language to mislead thought than Political Economy.' Hobson, 'Ruskin as Political Economist', in J.H. Whitehouse (ed.), *Ruskin the Prophet and Other Centenary Studies* (1920) p. 84.

50 Hobson, *Ruskin*, pp. 60–1.

51 Ibid., pp. 61–2.

52 Matthew, 'Hobson, Ruskin and Cobden', in Freeden (ed.), *Reappraising Hobson*, p. 20.

53 Ibid., p. 21.

54 Hobson, *John Ruskin,* p. 64.

55 Ibid., p. 65.

56   Hobson observed in 1903: 'Every industrial process, whether of production, exchange, or consumption, must be reduced to terms of vital worth, human satisfaction, before its value or its contribution to the wealth of the nation can be adjudged.' Idem, 'Introduction' to Ruskin, *Unto This Last* (1903 edn), p. 13.

57   Ibid., p. 67.

58   Ibid., p. 72.

59   Mill, *Principles*, p. 2.

60   Ruskin, *Unto This Last* (1862), p. 41.

61   Hobson, *John Ruskin*, p. 74.

62   Ibid.

63   Ibid., p. 75.

64   Ibid., p. 77.

65   Ruskin, *Unto This Last* (1862), p. 156.

66   Hobson, *John Ruskin*, p. 78.

67   Ibid., p. 83.

68   Ibid., pp. 84–5. Hobson later commented: 'Ruskin was not only a humanist in the realm of industry; he was a Socialist. By this I mean that he believed that industry should be directed by the motive of social good, not of individual gain.' See Hobson, 'Ruskin as Political Economist', in idem, *Ruskin the Prophet*, p. 92.

69   Ibid., p. 86.

70   Ibid., p. 89.

71   Ibid., pp. 91–2. Yet this apparent lack of consistency in Ruskin's writing is, comments P.D. Anthony, 'misleading'. 'The whole impression of disunity was compounded by the extraordinary range of subject matter which his work encompassed.' Anthony, *Ruskin's Labour*, p. 10.

72   Hobson, *John Ruskin*, p. 93. H.C.G. Matthew observes: 'Clearly Hobson gained from Ruskin a much more sophisticated view of an organic society than the rather adversarial sense of organic *versus* individualist that he had worked out in his first books': see Matthew, 'Hobson, Ruskin and Cobden', p. 19.

73   Hobson, *John Ruskin*, p. 94.

74   Ibid., p. 96.

75   Ibid.

76   Hobson was referring to Ruskin, *The Political Economy of Art* (1857), reprinted as *A Joy Forever* (1880).

77   Hobson, John *Ruskin*, p. 98.

78   Ibid., p. 100.

79   Ibid., p. 103.

80   Ibid., p. 105.

81   Ibid., p. 106.

82   Hobson, *Confessions*, p. 42.

83   Idem, *John Ruskin,* pp. 106–7.

84   Ibid, p. 108.

85   *Letters of John Ruskin to Charles Eliot Norton*, pp. 245–6.

86 Sherburne, *Ambiguities,* p. 119.
87 Ibid., p. 120.
88 Hobson, *John Ruskin,* p. 121.
89 Ibid.
90 Ruskin, *Unto This Last* (1862), pp. 144–5.
91 Hobson, *John Ruskin,* p. 122.
92 Ibid., pp. 123–4.
93 Sherburne, *Ambiguities,* p. 179.
94 Hobson, John *Ruskin,* p. 117.
95 See J. Ruskin, 'The Nature of Gothic', in idem, *The Stones of Venice, Vol. 2* (1853).
96 Hobson, *John Ruskin,* p. 118.
97 Ibid.
98 Ibid.
99 H.C.G. Matthew, 'Hobson, Ruskin and Cobden', *Reappraising Hobson,* p. 21.
100 Matthew adds that 'Hobson's development of an analysis of the organic nature of human society was developed in a general atmosphere of liberation and intellectual experiment which characterised much of British cultural life in the 1890s and 1900s.' Idem, 'Hobson, Ruskin and Cobden', p. 21.
101 Ruskin, *Munera Pulveris* (1904 edn), p. xiv.
102 Hobson, John *Ruskin,* p. 130.
103 Ibid., p. 133.
104 Ibid., pp. 134–5. See also, J.A. Hobson, *The Social Problem* (1901), p. 29.
105 Ibid., pp. 135–6.
106 Ibid., p. 140.
107 Ruskin, *Unto This Last* (1862), p. 129.
108 Hobson, *John Ruskin,* p. 141.
109 Ibid., pp. 141–2. Hobson acknowledged, however, that this view was central to Ruskin's position. As H.C.G. Matthew points out: 'In the long run, Ruskin's argument that a truly organic society must imply the complete rejection of both profit and of interest was perhaps the more systematic.' See Matthew, 'Hobson, Ruskin and Cobden', p. 20.
110 William C. Sillar, and his brother Robert G. Sillar, in many pamphlets between 1867 and 1885, fought a futile battle against usury from a Biblical standpoint.
111 James Sherburne comments that [Ruskin's] opposition to *all* interest and rent above the original investment – seems an almost calculated provocation to critics: Sherburne, *Ambiguities,* p. 186.
112 Hobson, *John Ruskin,* p. 145.
113 Ibid., pp. 147–8.
114 Ibid., pp. 150–3.
115 Justin McCarthy, *A History of Our Own Times* (1910), Vol. 2, p. 389.
116 Hobson, *Work and Wealth,* p. 251.
117 Ruskin, *Fors* (1906 edn), Vol. 3, Letter 70, p. 411.
118 Hobson, *John Ruskin,* p. 156.
119 Ibid.

120   Ruskin, *Time and Tide* (1906 edn), Letter 13, p. 87.

121   Hobson, *John Ruskin*, p. 158.

122   Ibid., pp. 158–9.

123   Ibid., pp. 160–1. See also Hobson, *The Social Problem*, p. 198 and Idem, *The Problem of the Unemployed: An Enquiry and an Economic Policy* (1896).

124   Hobson, *John Ruskin*, p. 163.

125   Ruskin, *Time and Tide*, p. 98.

126   Hobson, *John Ruskin*, p. 165.

127   A Fabian pamphlet argued that 'Ruskin's opinions about the possession of land are in some respects remarkably modern, and although not identical with the latest socialist doctrine on this question, they come surprisingly near to the view that land held by occupying owners for agricultural purposes belongs to the category of tools, and is therefore quite properly in individual ownership.' L.S.E. Archives, Ms. BP161511/179, Edith Morley, *John Ruskin and Social Ethics* (Fabian Tract no. 179, 1926), p. 22.

128   Hobson, *John Ruskin*, p. 166. See also Idem, *The Social Problem*, pp. 188–9.

129   Hobson, *John Ruskin*, p. 167.

130   Hobson commented in 1902: 'The whole of [Ruskin's] fantastic scheme of new Feudalism is built upon the assertion of the wide and multifarious differences of human nature; and the recognition of superiority is to be the source of the reverence for authority which is the true cohesive power in his society.' Hobson, 'Ruskin and Democracy', *Contemporary Review*, Vol. 81 (Jan.–Jun. 1902), p. 109.

131   Idem, *John Ruskin*, p. 170.

132   Ibid., p. 172. See also Hobson, *The Social Problem*, p. 96.

133   Hobson, *John Ruskin*, p. 172.

134   Ibid., p. 174.

135   Ibid., p. 176. Michael Freeden observes: 'The radical circles [Hobson] moved in infused his views with strong social and collectivist, if not socialist, predilections.' Freeden, 'Hobson's Evolving Conceptions of Human Nature', in Freeden (ed.), *Reappraising Hobson*, p. 54.

136   On this last condition, Hobson cited Ruskin's close affinity with Marx.

137   Hobson, *John Ruskin*, p. 180.

138   Ibid., p. 184.

139   Ibid., p. 186.

140   Mark Frost, 'I Am a King's Man: Ruskin and the Governor Eyre Defence', *Ruskin Programme Bulletin 16, Lancaster University,* (Apr. 1988), pp. 3–6, and Gill Cockram, 'Ruskin's Anomalies', in ibid., *Bulletin* 17 (Oct. 1998), pp. 6–8.

141   It is interesting to note a comment made by Moncure Daniel Conway in his memoirs: 'I think Carlyle outgrew some of his heroes. When Germany conferred the Order of Civil Merit on him he was rather irritated by it. When I mentioned it, he said he should have been as well satisfied if they had sent him a few pounds of good tobacco . . . it was plain he had lost his old enthusiasm for Cromwell.' M. Conway, *Autobiography: Memories and Experiences of Moncure Daniel Conway* (1904), Vol. 2, p. 111.

142 Williams, *Culture and Society*, pp. 140–1.

143 Hobson, *John Ruskin*, pp. 193–4.

144 Harrison did, however, teach for a time at the Working Men's College where he was close to the Christian Socialist circle. See: Kent, 'Harrison', in Baylen and Gossman (eds), *Biographical Dictionary of Modern British Radicals*, Vol. 3, p. 390.

145 Hobson, *John Ruskin*, p. 198.

146 Ibid., p. 199.

147 Ibid., p. 204.

148 Ibid. See also Hobson, 'Ruskin and Democracy', the *Contemporary Review* (Jan–Jun, 1902), Vol. 81.

149 Ruskin, *The Eagle's Nest* (1904 edn), p. 90.

150 Hobson, *John Ruskin*, p. 209.

151 J.A. Hobson, *The Evolution of Modern Capitalism* (1894), p. 199.

152 Idem, *The Social Problem* (1901), p. 48.

153 Idem, 'Ruskin and Democracy', the *Contemporary Review*, p. 106.

154 Allett, *New Liberalism*, p. 259.

155 Many attempts were made to introduce a minimum wage in the early twentieth century but with limited success. See Thane, *Welfare State*, pp. 148–51.

156 Hobson, *John Ruskin*, p. 320.

Chapter 7
Ruskin and The Socialists

1 These extracts are taken from testimonials in the *Review of Reviews*, Vol. 33, no. 198 (Jun. 1906), pp. 568–82. They represent a small selection of the many allusions to Ruskin's works made by Labour M.P.s when invited by the editor of the *Review* to comment on 'those books which they had found most helpful in their early struggle with adverse circumstances'. Having come from homes where they 'had none of the social and educational advantages of the middle and upper classes' how was it, asked the editor, that they were nevertheless 'capable of holding their own in fair-field with the finest product of our universities'? Many authors were mentioned, but Ruskin, especially with reference to *Unto This Last*, was very prominent. It is also interesting to note that Marx was mentioned only three times.

2 E. Halevy, *A History of the English People, 1895–1905* (1939 edn), Vol. 2, p. 148.

3 See Barker, *Political Thought*, p. 208.

4 Thane, *Foundations of the Welfare State*, pp. 118–32.

5 Charles Bradlaugh, 'Socialism: Its Fallacies and Dangers', Our *Corner* (*1* Mar. 1887), p. 129.

6 Ibid.

7 Stanley Pierson, *Marxism and the Origins of British Socialism* (1973), p. xii.

8 K. Marx and F. Engels, The *Manifesto of the Communist Party* (1847; in 1948 edn), p. 21.

9 Ruskin, 'The Nature of Gothic', in Stones *of Venice* (1906 edn), Vol. 2, p. 161.

10   As quoted in Alan Davies, *To Build a New Jerusalem: The British Labour Movement from the 1880s to the 1990s* (1992), p. 15.

11   Leslie Stephen, 'Why Skilled Workmen don't go to Church', *Fraser's Magazine*, Vol. 80 (Jul. 1869), p. 112. Having turned away from Christianity himself, Stephen was not unbiased.

12   Ibid.

13   Ibid., p. 113.

14   Ibid.

15   Ibid., pp. 115–16.

16   For a discussion of the problems of liberalism in the late nineteenth century, see Robert Eccleshall, 'Liberalism' in Eccleshall and others *Political Ideologies*, pp. 71–2.

17   D. Torr (ed.), *Correspondence of Marx and Engels, 1846–95* (1934), p. 464: Letter 208, 11 Jan. 1890.

18   Pierson, *Marxism*, pp. 184–5.

19   G.J. Holyoake, *The History of Cooperation in England: Its Literature and Its Advocates* (1879), Vol. 2, p. 391.

20   For a fuller discussion of Maurice's position, see Norman, *Victorian Christian Socialists,* pp. 16–17.

21   As noted in the 1892 Kelmscott Press reprint: see William Morris, Preface to Ruskin, *The Nature of Gothic* (1892).

22   Ibid.

23   Despite his declared intention to do so, Morris never actually published *Unto This Last* by the Kelmscott Press. It was, however, through Morris's later connection with the Doves Press that an edition of *Unto This Last* was published by this company in 1907: see P. Stansky, 'Morris', in Keith Thomas (ed.), *Victorian Thinkers*, p. 405.

24   J.W. Mackail (1859–1945) was a classical scholar and lifelong friend and biographer of William Morris.

25   J.W. Mackail, *The Life of William Morris* (1899), Vol. 1, pp. 219–20.

26   A.L. Morton (ed.), *Political Writings of William Morris* (1964), p. 101.

27   Mackail, *Life of Morris*, p. 201.

28   People's History Museum, Manchester (formerly National Museum of Labour History), letter from J. Ruskin to Frederic Pickles, dated 27 Jun. 1884.

29   People's History Museum, Letter from William Morris to Frederic Pickles, dated 3 Oct. 1885.

30   Anthony, *Ruskin's Labour*, p. 200.

31   M. Morris (ed.), *The Collected Works of William Morris with Introduction by his Daughter* (1915), Vol. 23, p. 202.

32   J. Ruskin, 'The Future of England', in *The Crown of Wild Olive* (1906), p. 173.

33   See Nicholas Salmon, 'The Down-Trodden Radical: William Morris's Pre-Socialist Ideology.' *Journal of William Morris Society*, Vol. 13 (1999), pp. 27–8.

34   Anthony, *Ruskin's Labour*, p. 198.

35   Morton (ed.), *Political Writings of William Morris*, p. 243.

36   Ibid., pp. 243–4.

37   Although Morris admitted that reading J.S. Mill posthumously 'put the finishing touch to [his] conversion to Socialism', this postdated the much stronger aesthetic influence of Ruskin. See Morton (ed.), *Political Writings*, pp. 242–3.

38   Quoted in E.P. Thompson, *William Morris* (revised edn, 1976), p. 270.

39   Morton (ed.), *Political Writings of William Morris*, p. 67.

40   *Pall Mall Gazette* (19 Nov. 1883); also quoted in Cook, *John Ruskin*, Vol. 2. p. 469.

41   Thompson, *William Morris*, p. 274.

42   The size limitation of communities in order to ensure success was a central theme of Morris's utopian writings: see W. Morris, *News from Nowhere* (1924 edn) p. 81.

43   W. Morris, review of E. Bellamy, *Looking Backward*, *Commonweal* (Jun. 1889).

44   Thompson, *William Morris*, p. 779.

45   From Morris, 'How Shall We Live Then?', in *International Review of Social History*, Vol. 16 (1971), pp. 255–6.

46   Peter Stansky, 'Morris', in Keith Thomas (ed.), *Victorian Thinkers*, p. 384.

47   Morton (ed.), *Political Writings of William Morris*, p. 250.

48   Ruskin, *Fors* (1 Jan. 1871), p. 4. Letter 1.

49   Thompson, *William Morris*, p. 783.

50   Anthony, *Ruskin's Labour*, pp. 198–9.

51   'Boko on "Christianity and Socialism"', *Clarion* (6 Apr. 1901), p. 112.

52   Quoted in Holyoake, *History of Cooperation*, p. 390.

53   *The Times* (8 Oct. 1887), p. 9.

54   E. Belfort Bax (1854–1926) was the co-founder with William Morris of the Socialist League and, for a time, assisted in editing the *Commonweal*. He had a strong objection to suggestions of a compatibility between socialism and Christianity and denied evidence of any linkage between moral, ethical, or aesthetic principles and economic causes. See Baylen and Gossman (eds), *Dictionary of Modern British Radicals*, Vol. 3. pp. 78–82.

55   E. Belfort Bax, 'Religion and Socialism', *Justice* (8 Jun. 1895).

56   Ibid.

57   'George', 'Socialism and Christianity', *Justice* (11 Jan. 1896).

58   A.L. Moore on 'The Influence of Calvinism on Modern Unbelief, 1890'. Aubrey Lackington Moore (1843–1890) was a historian, theologian and a parish priest. He argued in this paper that the greatest cause of 'present day unbelief' was not science or a general increase in knowledge, 'but a higher tone of morality acting upon an immoral travesty of the gospel of Christ', as quoted in J. Moore (ed.), *Religion in Victorian Britain* (1988), Vol. 3, pp. 327, 338.

59   Peter d'A. Jones, *The Christian Socialist Revival, 1877–1914* (Princeton, 1968), p. 48.

60   Ibid.

61   William Morris remarked on the faction-ridden nature of socialism at the beginning of his *News from Nowhere*. At a meeting of the Socialist League,

he wrote, 'There were six persons present, and consequently six sections of the party were represented, four of which had strong but divergent Anarchist opinions.' See Morris, *News from Nowhere* (1924 edn) p. 1. (This text was first printed in *The Commonweal*, 1890.)

62   John Gorman, *Images of Labour* (1985), p. 108.

63   Ibid., p. 109. Gorman observes: 'Such was the spread of influence and support of the Labour Church that on 15 Jan. 1893 a service was held in the St George's Hall, Manchester, in connection with the ILP conference and was attended by 5,000 people. The chair was taken by Fred Jowett, President of the Bradford Labour Church, and speakers included Bernard Shaw, Keir Hardie, Edward Aveling and Robert Blatchford. Churches opened in Halifax, Birmingham, Barrow-in-Furness, Oldham and Leeds and at its peak the movement was active in almost thirty cities and towns.'

64   Some socialists encountered problems when trying to reconcile a basically humanitarian form of religion with lingering dogma. One particularly staunch socialist, S.G. Hobson (1870–1940), described his dilemma as a lecturer in a Labour Church: 'I had a quaint experience at the Bradford Labour Church. I was the lecturer. The proceedings opened by the audience, or congregation singing . . . [were] followed by a reading from Ruskin.' Then, wrote Hobson, he was called upon 'to engage in prayer'. To avoid this hypocrisy Hobson explained that as a Quaker he felt called to wait for inspiration. In the ensuing silence he felt he had saved himself from 'too obviously playing the hypocrite' and also 'acquired a reputation for piety'. S.G. Hobson, *Memoirs of a Modern Revolutionist* (1930), p. 41. For biographical details of S.G. Hobson, see J. Vowles in Baylen and Gossman (eds), *Biographical Dictionary of Modern British Radicals*, pp. 442–5.

65   R.W. Dale, 'George Dawson', *Nineteenth Century* (Aug. 1870), p. 44.

66   Anon., 'The Good Sermon', *Commonweal* (3 Jul. 1886), p. 110.

67   Ibid.

68   A.E. Fletcher 'Christian Ethics and Practical Politics', in A. Reid (ed.), *Vox Clamantium: The Gospel of the People by Writers, Preachers and Workers, Brought Together by Andrew Reid* (1894), pp. 124–5. A.E. Fletcher was editor of the *Daily Chronicle*.

69   It is worth noting that a National Minimum Wage was finally introduced in UK by a Labour government in 1998.

70   For further discussion of Headlam's form of socialism, see Henry Pelling, *The Origins of the Labour Party, 1880–1900* (Oxford, 1965), p. 126 and Norman, *Victorian Christian Socialists*, pp. 98–120.

71   Annie Besant (ed.), *Our Corner* (1 Apr. 1887), p. 1.

72   Jones, *Christian Socialist Revival*, pp. 106–7.

73   Stewart Headlam, *The Socialist's Church* (1907), p. 41.

74   Peter d'A. Jones, *Christian Socialist Revival*, p. 200: 'Though an avowed rationalist, Hobson's approach, which owed much to John Ruskin, was attractive to the Christian dissidents in the CSU and elsewhere, partly because his tone was heavily moral. Also many of his personal friends were religious radicals.'

75 See for example works by J.A. Hobson, *Problem of Poverty* (1891), and idem, *Problem of the Unemployed* (1896).

76 Headlam, *Socialist's Church*, pp. 79–80.

77 Thomas Shore, Jnr.,'Ruskin as a Revolutionary Preacher', *Commonweal* (26 Jun. 1886), p. 101.

78 Ruskin *Fors* (1906 edn), p. 108, Letter 6.

79 Shore, 'Ruskin as a Revolutionary Preacher', *Commonweal* (26 Jun. 1886), p. 101.

80 Ibid.

81 Shore, 'Ruskin as a Revolutionary Preacher', *Commonweal* (3 Jul. 1886), p. 109.

82 Pierson, *Marxism*, p. 22.

83 Ibid., pp. 22–3, for Pierson's additional comment that: '[Carlyle and Ruskin] shattered existing notions about the social system . . . To understand the distinctive features in the thought of these two men is to enter in some measure into the popular Socialist mentality of the nineties.'

84 Ibid., p. 36.

85 James Keir Hardie, *From Serfdom to Socialism* (1907; repr. 1974), p. 35.

86 For a discussion of Hardie's early life, his conversion to socialism, and his later influence in the movement, see A.J. Davies, *To Build a New Jerusalem: The British Labour Movement from the 1880s to the 1990s* (1992), pp. 15–36.

87 Hardie, *From Serfdom*, p. 129.

88 Hardie always insisted on the symbiotic nature of politics and religion thus he observed that the great message of the 'teachers and prophets of the nineteenth century', among whom he named Ruskin, was to show that 'all material things are but useful in so far as they serve to aid in developing character': J.K. Hardie, *Labour Leader* (Jan. 1893).

89 Hardie, *From Serfdom*, pp. 92–3.

90 Ibid., p. 94.

91 Kenneth Morgan, *Keir Hardie* (1975), p. 7.

92 Davies, *To Build A New Jerusalem,* p. 65.

93 Robert Blatchford, *Britain for the British* (1902), p. 28. In his autobiography, Blatchford commented that, in his formative period, he 'worked hard to repair [his] ignorance' by reading Ruskin and De Quincey, Dickens and Thackeray: Blatchford, *My Eighty Years* (1931), p. 59. For biographical details of Blatchford, see Baylen and Gossman (eds), *Dictionary of Modern British Radicals*, Vol. 3. pp. 96–8.

94 Mann was a trade union organiser and a revolutionary activist. Author details in ibid., Vol. 3, pp. 559–64.

95 Pierson, *Marxism*, p. 195.

96 Tom Mann, *Memoirs* (1923), p. 50.

97 Bingley is a market town in the West Riding of Yorkshire which appears to have had a very go-ahead editor on its local newspaper.

98 Ruskin, *Fors* (1906 edn), Vol. 4, p. 360.

99 Ibid., Vol. 4, p. 362.

100 Mann, *Memoirs*, p. 52.

101 Ibid.
102 Torr (ed.), *Marx and Engels: Correspondence,* p. 460: this verdict came in a letter to Sorge (7 Dec. 1889).
103 Tom Barclay, *Memoirs and Medleys: The Autobiography of a Bottlewasher* (1934), p. 64.
104 Ibid., p. 67.
105 Ibid., p. 83.
106 People's History Museum: Thomas Barclay, *The Rights of Labour According to John Ruskin* (1887).
107 Barclay, *Rights of Labour,* p. 3.
108 Ibid.
109 Ibid., pp. 13–14
110 Ibid., p. 14.
111 Ibid., p. 16.
112 Leo Tolstoy (1828–1910). Tolstoy frequently referred to Ruskin and kept translations of his works in his personal library. In 1905, Aylmer Maude observed: 'Of Ruskin Tolstoy has a very high opinion.' In A. Maude, *Tolstoy and his Problems* (1905), p. 140.
113 Royden Harrison in Carl Levy (ed.), *Socialism and the Intelligentsia, 1880–1914* (1987), pp. 38–9.
114 G.B. Shaw, *Ruskin's Politics* (1921), p. 8.
115 Ibid., pp. 8–9.
116 Ibid., p. 15.
117 Ruskin thought of himself as an old-style communist and quoted 'the Chelsea farmer' Sir Thomas More as his example: see Ruskin, *Fors* (1906 edn), Vol. 1, p. 128, Letter 7.
118 This point is stressed by Pierson, *Marxism,* p. 36.
119 Anon., 'Obituary', *Justice* (27 Jan. 1900).
120 Robert Blatchford, 'Obituary', *Clarion* (27 Jan. 1900).
121 Collingwood, *Life and Work of Ruskin,* Vol. 2. p. 153.
122 S. Ball, 'The Moral Aspects of Socialism', *Socialism and Individualism* (Fabian Socialist Series No. 3, 1908), p. 69.

Chapter 8

Conclusion: Moral Reconstruction in a Capitalist Society

1 M.K. Gandhi, *An Autobiography: Or The Story of my Experiments with Truth,* transl. from the original Gujarati by Mahadev Desai (1982), p. 274.
2 Collini, *Public Moralists,* p. 319.
3 *Palmer's Index to The Times, 1790–1905,* records some 90 entries between Jan. 1900 and Oct. 1905.
4 *The Times* (22 Jan. 1900), p. 7.
5 J.A.R. Marriott (1859–1945) was a historian, writer and a conservative M.P.
6 J.A.R. Marriott, 'Ruskin's Economics', *Cornhill Magazine,* Vol. 44 (Jan.–Jun. 1923), p. 410.

7 Ibid., p. 409.

8 H. Higgs (ed.), *Palgrave's Dictionary of Political Economy* (1926 edn), p. 748.

9 Lawrence Goldman, 'Ruskin', in Milgate, Newman and Eatwell (eds), *Palgrave's Dictionary* (1987 edn), p. 229.

10 Ibid.

11 Leslie Stephen, *National Review*, Vol. 35 (Apr. 1900), p. 248.

12 Anon., 'Obituary', *Justice* (27 Jan. 1900).

13 Anon., 'Nunquam', *Clarion* (27 Jan. 1900), p. 29.

14 Willie Henderson comments that 'Ruskin influenced a number of major economic thinkers.' Henderson includes Hobson whose Ruskinian thinking in turn influenced Keynes. As Henderson points out: 'Ruskin's ideas, preferred modes of expression and his self-presentation, have tended to keep him outside the range of writings that the economics profession call their own.' In W. Henderson, *John Ruskin's Political Economy* (2000), pp. 27–8.

15 J.A. Hobson, 'Ruskin and Democracy', *Contemporary Review*, Vol. 81 (Jan.–Jun. 1902), p. 112.

16 See above, chap. 6.

17 Hobson, 'Ruskin and Democracy', *Contemporary Review*, Vol. 81 (Jan.–Jun. 1902), p. 111.

18 Ibid.

19 Ibid.

20 M.I. Finley, *The Use and Abuse of History* (1990), p. 187.

21 See James Redmond, 'William Morris or Bernard Shaw: Two Faces of Victorian Socialism', in J. Butt and J.F. Clarke (eds), *The Victorians and Social Protest: A Symposium* (1973), p. 160.

22 H. Pelling, *Origins of the Labour Party, 1880–1900* (Oxford, 1965), pp. 10–11, observes that '[Ruskin's] essays on political economy, *Unto This Last* . . . and his *Fors Clavigera* . . . did much to encourage the growing sentiment in favour of collectivism.' Norman, *Victorian Christian Socialists*, pp. 141–2, also discusses Ruskin and collectivism.

23 Hobson, 'Ruskin and Democracy', *Contemporary Review* (Jan.–Jun. 1902), pp. 105–6.

24 Harrison, *Tennyson, Ruskin, Mill*, p. 101.

25 M. Beer, *A History of British Socialism* (1921), p. 199.

26 See G.D.H. Cole, *Guild Socialism Re-stated* (1920).

27 Penty broke with the Fabians following a disagreement over the design for the new London School of Economics. See P.D. Anthony, *Ruskin's Labour*, p. 192.

28 A.J. Penty, *A Study of the Post-Industrial State* (1917), p. 37.

29 J.C. Sherburne, *Ambiguities*, p. 24.

30 Penty, *A Study of the Post-Industrial State*, p. 79.

31 M. Beer wrote: 'According to the Board of Trade, 1913, giving particulars of rents, retail prices, and wages in 1905 and 1912, prices advanced 13.7 per cent, wages between 2 and 5.5 per cent, while the capitalists increased their income by 22.5 per cent per annum. This was a period of Labour

triumphs in Parliament, a period of Liberal social reform which was claimed by its authors to be unprecedented in the annals of legislation.' In idem. *A History of British Socialism* (1921), Vol. 1, pp. 366–7.

32   A.R. Orage, (ed.), *National Guilds: An Enquiry into the Wage System and the Way Out* (1914), p. vi. It should also be noted that this publication owed a great deal to the contribution of S.G. Hobson who was not acknowledged until the second edition of 1917.

33   Ibid., p. 16.

34   G.D.H. Cole, *A Century of Cooperation* (Manchester, 1944), p. 289.

35   Idem, *A History of Socialist Thought* (1958), Vol. 4. p. 25.

36   P.D. Anthony, *Ruskin's Labour*, p. 194.

37   Ibid.

38   Ibid., p. 198.

39   Penty, *Post-Industrialism* (1922), p. 92.

40   Ibid., p. 200.

41   Henry Pelling, *The Origins of the Labour Party: 1880–1900,* p. 31.

42   Anthony, *Ruskin's Labour*, p. 207.

43   Ibid.

44   A.J. Penty commented: 'Ruskin spent most of his life in trying to convince people that political economy is a moral science.' Penty, *A Study of the Post-Industrial State*, p. 5.

45   J.M. Ludlow, 'A Dialogue on Cooperation', *Economic Review*, Vol. 2 (Apr. 1892), p. 216: 'For one Christian Socialist in 1852, there are a dozen now.'

46   This was, for Ruskin, a weakness in the socialist philosophy and it is one which endures. In a recent private conversation, the Rev Peter Thompson, [the Anglican clergyman who introduced Tony Blair to Christian Socialism] professed to being 'a socialist because [he is] a Christian' and commented: 'Socialism does not know how to address capitalism.'

47   H.H. Lancaster, 'The Writings of John Ruskin', *North British Review* (Feb. 1862), p. 33.

48   J.A. Hobson, 'Ruskin as Political Economist', in J.H. Whitehouse (ed.), *Ruskin the Prophet*, p. 98.

SELECT BIBLIOGRAPHY

Primary Sources
Works by John Ruskin
The Library Edition of the Works of John Ruskin. 39 vols. (ed.), E.T. Cook and A.
  Wedderburn. (George Allen, 1903–12). Also on CD-Rom (Cambridge,
  1996).

Note: Numerous variant editions of Ruskin's works have been consulted and
quoted, when appropriate. This is indicated in the relevant footnotes.

Individual Works, in chronological order
Modern Painters (1843–60), in *Works*, Vols. 3–7.
The Seven Lamps of Architecture (1849), in *Works*, Vol. 8.
The Stones of Venice (1851–3), in *Works*, Vols. 9–11.
Pre-Raphaelitism (1851), in *Works*, Vol. 12.
The Harbours of England (1856), in *Works*, Vol. 13.
Inaugural Address at the Cambridge School of Art (1858), in *Works*, Vol. 16.
The Oxford Museum (1859), in *Works*, Vol. 16.
The Two Paths (1859), in *Works*, Vol 16.
Unto This Last (1862), in *Works*, Vol. 17.
Sesame and Lilies (1865), in *Works*, Vol.18.
The Study of Architecture in Schools (1865), in *Works* Vol. 19.
The Crown of Wild Olive (1866), in *Works*, Vol. 18.
Time and Tide (1867), in *Works*, Vol. 17.
The Queen of the Air (1869), in *Works*, Vol.19.
The Flamboyant Architecture of the Valley of the Somme (1869), in *Works*, Vol.19.
Lectures on Art (1870), in *Works*, Vol. 20.
Fors Clavigera: Letters to the Workmen and Labourers of Great Britain (1871–84), in
  Works, Vols. 27–9.
Aratra Pentelici (1872), in *Works*, Vol. 20.
Munera Pulveris (1872), in *Works*, Vol. 17.
Love's Meinie (1873), in *Works*, Vol. 25.
The Laws of Fesole (1877–8), in *Works*, Vol. 15.
A Joy for Ever (1880), in *Works*, Vol. 16.
Fiction, Fair and Foul (1880–1), in *Works*, Vol. 34.

The Storm Cloud of the Nineteenth Century (1884), in *Works,* Vol. 34.
On The Old Road (1885), in *Works*, Vol. 34.
Praeterita: Outlines of Scenes and Thoughts Perhaps Worthy of Memory in my Past Life
      (1885–9), in *Works*, Vol. 35.
The Story of Arachne (1894), in *Works*, Vol. 20.

Victorian Periodicals
(Helpful information on this genre is available in
W.E. Houghton (ed.), *Wellesley Index to Victorian Periodicals,*
1824–1900 (1966)).

Ainsworth's Magazine
Atlantis
Bentley's Miscellany
Bentley's Quarterly Review
Blackwood's Edinburgh Magazine
British and Foreign Review
British Quarterly Review
Contemporary Review
Cornhill Magazine
Dark Blue
Dublin Review
Dublin University Magazine
Edinburgh Review
Foreign Quarterly Review
Fortnightly Review
Fraser's Magazine
Home and Foreign Review
London Quarterly Review
London Review (1836–40)
Longman's Magazine
Macmillan's Magazine
Modern Review
Monthly Chronicle
National Review (1855–64)
New Monthly Magazine (1821–54)
New Quarterly Magazine
New Review
Nineteenth Century
North British Review
Our Corner
Oxford and Cambridge Magazine (1856)
Prospective Review
Quarterly Review
Rambler (1848–62)
Review of Reviews
Saint Paul's

Scottish Review (1882–)
Tait's Edinburgh Magazine (1832–55)
Temple Bar
Theological Review
University Magazine
Vanity Fair
Westminster Review (1824–36, 1840–1900)

Periodical Literature

(Note: articles, comments etc. are listed chronologically
by date of publication within each periodical).

Blackwood's Magazine

R.H. Patterson, 'The Economy of Capital', Vol. 95 (Mar. 1864).
G.R. Gleig, 'The Government and the Budget', Vol. 97 (Jun. 1865).
R.H. Patterson, 'Our Invisible Capital', (London Finance), Vol. 98 (Dec. 1865).
G.R. Gleig, 'The Political Crisis', Vol. 99 (Jun. 1866).
R.H. Patterson, 'Monetary Reform', Vol. 102 (Oct. 1867).

British Quarterly Review

Hannah Lawrence, '(Ruskin's) *Modern Painters* (vol. 5),' Vol. 32 (Oct. 1860).

Dublin Review

George Bowyer, 'Protestant Spiritual Destitution', Vol. 45 (Dec. 1858).
John Morris, 'Darwin, On the Origin of Species', Vol. 48 (May 1860).
M.J. Rhodes, 'Modern Principles of Government – real progress, ibid.
Purcell, 'Pugin and Turner', Vol. 51 (Feb. 1862).
W.G. Ward, 'The Labourers and Political Economy', Vol. 20 (Jan. 1873).
J.C. Hoey, 'The Fall of Mr Gladstone's Government', Vol. 22 (Apr. 1874).
J.C. Hoey, 'London Poor and London Work', Vol. 23 (Jul. 1874).
T.B. Scannell, 'The English Constitution in Theory and Practice', Vol.17 (Jan 1887).
C.S. Devas, 'Shakespeare as an Economist', ibid.
C.S. Devas, 'An Olive Branch on State Socialism', Vol. 19 (Apr. 1889).
James Britten, 'Art and the People', Vol. 21 (Apr. 1889).
Thomas Canning, 'The Labour Problem: Past and Present', Vol. 24 (Oct. 1890).
William Francis Barry, 'Labour and Capital, Limited', n.s., Vol. 3 (Apr. 1893).
Baynard Klein, 'Evolution and Ethics', Vol. 4 (Jul. 1983).
John S. Vaughan, 'The Social Difficulty', Vol. 4 (Oct. 1893).

Edinburgh Review

George Gosher, 'Seven Percent, Economic Essays', Vol. 121 (Jan. 1865).
Henry Fawcett, 'On the Social and Economical Influence of the New Gold', Vol. 2 (Jul. 1860).
J. Llewellyn Davies, 'Metropolitan Distress', Vol. 3 (Feb. 1861).
J. Llewellyn Davies, 'Political Economy and the Gospel', Vol. 7 (Jan. 1863).

Leslie, 'The Wealth of Nations and Slave Power', Vol. 7 (Feb. 1863).

Fortnightly Review

Sheldon Amos, 'Democracy in England', Vol.1 (1 Jun. 1865).

Frederic Harrison, 'The Limits of Political Economy', ibid.

John R. Wise, 'The Clouds and the Poor', Vol.1 (15 Jul. 1865).

Richard Ellerton, 'A New Franchise', ibid.

William Robinson Hopper, 'An Iron Master's View of Strikes', Vol. 1 (1 Aug. 1865).

W. Bridges Adams, 'The Political Economy of Copyright', Vol. 2 (1 Sept. 1865).

Frederic Harrison, 'Good and Evil of Trade Unionism', Vol. 3 (15 Nov. 1865).

Frederic Harrison, 'Industrial Cooperation', Vol. 3 (1 Jan. 1866).

Joseph Charles Parkinson, 'The Casual Poor of London', Vol. 3 (1 Feb. 1866).

Joseph Charles Parkinson, 'On a Uniform Poor Rate for London', Vol. 4 (1 Mar. 1866).

J.M. Capes, 'The Just Demand of the Working Man', Vol. 4 (Apr. 15 1866).

T.E. Cliffe Leslie, 'Political Economy and the Tenure of Land', Vol.5 (1 Jun. 1866).

R.H. Patterson, 'The Currency and its Reform', Vol. 6 (Dec. 1866).

W.H. Thornton, 'What Determines the Price of Labour or Rate of Wages?' Vol. 7 (May 1867).

R.H. Patterson, 'The State and the Currency', Vol. 8 (Jul. 1867).

W.H. Thornton, 'Stray Chapters from a Forthcoming Work on Labour: the Claims of Labour and its Rights', Vol. 8 (Oct. 1867).

Frederic Harrison, 'Culture: A Dialogue', (on Matthew Arnold) Vol. 8 (Nov. 1867).

A.V. Dicey, 'The Legal Boundaries of Liberty', Vol. 9 (Jan. 1868).

Edward Spencer Beesly, 'The Social Future of the Working Class', Vol. 11 (Mar. 1869).

J.S. Mill, 'Thornton on Labour and its Claims', Vol.11 (Jun. 1869).

Frederic Harrison, 'The Trades Union Bill', Vol.12 (Oct. 1869).

J.M. Ludlow, 'Old Guilds and New Friendly and Trade Societies', Vol. 12 (Oct. 1869).

Frederic Harrison, 'The Positivist Problem', Vol. 12 (Nov. 1869).

J.E. Cairnes, 'M. Comte and Political Economy', Vol. 13 (May 1870).

Frederic Harrison, 'The Romance of the Peerage', Vol. 13 (Jun. 1870).

Frederic Harrison, 'Professor Cairns on M. Comte and Political Economy', Vol. 14 (Jul. 1870).

W.T. Thornton, 'Anti-utilitarianism', Vol. 14 (Sept. 1870).

Edward Spencer Beesly, 'The International Working Men's Association', Vol. 14 (Nov. 1870).

T.E. Cliffe Leslie, 'The Political Economy of Adam Smith', ibid.

Frederic Harrison, 'Bismarckism', Vol. 14 (Dec. 1870).

Henry Fawcett, 'To What Extent is England Prosperous?' Vol. 15 (Jan. 1871).

Frederic Harrison, 'The Effacement of England', Vol. 15 (Feb.1871).

J.E. Cairnes, 'Political Economy and *Laissez-faire*', Vol. 16 (1871).

Frederic Harrison, 'The Fall of the Commune', Vol. 16 (Aug. 1871).

J.E. Cairnes, 'New Theories in Political Economy', Vol. 17 (Jan. 1872).

Frederic Harrison, 'The Monarchy', Vol. 17 (Jun. 1872).

Frederic Harrison, 'Mr Brassey on Work and Wages', Vol. 18 (Sept. 1872).

Frederic Harrison, 'On the Supposed Necessity of Certain Metaphysical Problems', Vol. 18 (Nov.1872).

Frederic Harrison, 'The Revival of Authority', Vol. 19 (Jan. 1873).

Frederic Harrison, 'The Religion of Inhumanity', Vol. 19 (Jun. 1873).

Frederic Harrison, 'Public Affairs', Vol. 20 (Oct. 1873); also Vol. 20 (Nov. 1873, Dec. 1873), and Vol. 21 (Jan. 1874).

Henry Fawcett, 'The Effect of Increased Production on Wealth and Wages', Vol. 21 (Jan. 1874).

Henry Fawcett, 'The Position and Prospects of Cooperation', Vol. 21 (Feb. 1874).

Frederic Harrison, 'Public Affairs', ibid.

Frederic Harrison, 'The Conservative Reaction', Vol. 21 (Mar. 1874).

Frederic Harrison, 'Public Affairs', Vol. 21 (Apr. 1874, also May, 1874).

Frederic Harrison, 'Mr Lewes's Problems of Life and Mind', Vol. 22 (Jul. 1874).

J. Charles Cox, 'The Power of the Labourers', ibid.

George H. Darwin, 'The Theory of Exchange Value', Vol. 23 (Feb. 1875).

John Macdonnell, 'Karl Marx and German Socialism', Vol. 23 (Mar. 1875).

W.H. Thornton, 'The Economic Definition of Wealth', Vol. 23 (Apr. 1875).

Edward Spencer Beesly, 'Positivists and Workmen', Vol. 24 (Jul. 1875).

Leslie Stephen, 'The Value of Political Machinery', Vol. 24 (Dec. 1875).

Walter Bagehot, 'The Postulates of English Political Economy', Vol. 25 (Feb. 1876).

Alfred Marshall, 'On Mr Mill's Theory of Value', Vol. 25 (Apr. 1876).

Frederic Harrison, 'Past and Present', Vol. 26 (Jul. 1871).

W. Stanley Jevons, 'The Future of Political Economy', Vol. 26 (Nov. 1876).

Henry Sidgwick, 'Bentham and Benthamism in Politics and Ethics', Vol. 27 (May, 1877).

Frederic Harrison, 'Church and State', ibid.

J.H. Bridges, 'Evolution and Positivism', Vol. 27 (Jun. 1877); part 2, Vol. 28 (Jul. 1877).

Frederic Harrison, 'The French Workmen's Congress', Vol. 29 (May 1878).

John Morley, 'An Economic Address; with some Notes', Vol. 30 (Oct. 1878).

Ralph A. Earle, 'Mr Gladstone's Policy and the New Equilibrium', ibid.

Matthew Arnold, '*Porro Unum est Necessarium*', Vol. 30 (Nov. 1878).

Henry Fawcett, 'The Recent Developments of Socialism in Germany and the United States', ibid.

Frederic Harrison, 'The English School of Jurisprudence, Part 2; Bentham's and Austin's Analysis of Law,' ibid.

T.E. Cliffe Leslie, 'Political Economy and Sociology', Vol. 31 (Jan. 1879).

Frederic Harrison, 'The English School of Jurisprudence, Part 3 concl.: The Historical Method', ibid.

John Stuart Mill, 'Chapters on Socialism', Vol. 31 (Feb. 1879).

Henry Sidgwick, 'Economic Method', ibid.

John Stuart Mill, 'Chapters on Socialism', Vol. 31 (Mar. 1879).

Moncure D. Conway, 'Thomas Paine – A Vindication', ibid.

Leonard Courtney, 'A Fair Day's Wages for a Fair Day's Work', ibid.

John Stuart Mill, 'Chapters on Socialism, Part 3, concl.', Vol. 31 (Apr. 1879).

Henry Sidgwick, 'What is Money?', ibid.

T.E.Cliffe Leslie, 'The Known and the Unknown in the Economic World', ibid.

Henry Sidgwick, 'The Wages-Fund Theory', Vol. 32 (Sept.1879).

William L. Courtney, 'Carlyle's Political Doctrines', Vol. 32 (Dec. 1879).

T.H. Farrar, 'Freedom of Land', Vol. 33 (Jan. 1880).

Frederic Harrison, 'Empire and Humanity', Vol. 33 (Feb. 1880).

Robert Giffen, 'Bagehot as an Economist', Vol. 33 (Apr. 1880).

Leslie Stephen, 'Mr Bradlaugh and his Opponents', Vol. 34 (Aug. 1880).

T.E. Cliffe Leslie, 'Political Economy in the United States', Vol 34 (Oct.1880).

Henry R. Brand, 'The Dwellings of the Poor in London', Vol. 35 (Feb. 1881).

James Bird, 'Treaties of Commerce: A Surrender of Principle', Vol. 36 (Aug. 1881).

George Tomkyns Chesney, 'Over-Production', Vol. 36 (Sept. 1881).

T.E. Cliffe Leslie, 'The History and Future of Interest and Profit', Vol. 36 (Nov. 1881).

Frederic Harrison, 'A Few Words about the Nineteenth Century', Vol. 37 (Apr. 1882).

Edith Simcox, 'Mr Morris's Hopes and Fears for Art', Vol. 37 (Jun. 1882).

Henrietta O. Barrett, 'Passionless Reformers', Vol. 38 (Aug. 1882).

J.A. Froude, 'A Lesson on Democracy', Vol. 38 (Dec. 1882.)

J. Woulfe Flanagan, 'Home Rule, Socialism and Secession', Vol. 39 (Feb. 1883).

T.W. Fowle, 'The Third Reform Bill: Why Delay it?' Vol. 39 (Feb. 1883).

G.S. Venables, 'Carlyle in Society and at Home', Vol. 39 (May 1883).

Joseph Chamberlain, 'Labourers and Artisan's Dwellings', Vol. 40 (Dec. 1883).

Violet Greville, 'Social Reforms for the London Poor (no.1); The Need of Recreation', Vol. 41 (Jan. 1884).

T.W. Brockett, 'Social Reforms for the London Poor (no. 2); The Wives and Mothers of the Working Classes', ibid.

Frederick Wedmore, 'Rational Radicalism,' ibid.

John Lubbock, 'Liberal versus Conservative Finance', Vol. 41 (Feb. 1884).

Henry Broadhurst, 'The Enfranchisement of Urban Leaseholders', Vol. 41 (Mar. 1884).

Lepel Griffen, 'The Harvest of Democracy', ibid.

Frederic W. Farrar, 'Frederick Denison Maurice', Vol. 41 (Apr. 1884).

Charles Waring, 'The Future of Industry',.Vol. 42 (Nov. 1884).

Moreton Frewen, 'Progress to Poverty', Vol. 42 (Dec. 1884).

Henry Broadhurst, 'The Ideas of the New Voters', Vol. 43, (Feb. 1885).

Frederic Harrison, 'On Positivism', ibid.

'Carlyle as a Political Teacher', Vol. 44 (Oct.1885).

W.H. Mallock, 'Wealth and the Working Classes (part 2)', Vol. 47 (May, 1887).

George Jacob Holyoake, 'The Growth of Cooperation in England', Vol. 48 (Aug. 1887).

W.H. Mallock, 'Wealth and the Working Classes', (part 3).

R.B. Haldane, 'Is a National Party Possible?' Vol. 48 (Sept. 1887).

Charles Roberts, 'The Physical Condition of the Masses', Vol. 48 (Oct. 1887).

W.H. Mallock, 'Wealth and the Working Classes', (4 concl.).

H.M. Hyndeman, 'Wealth and Ability: A Rejoinder', Vol. 48 (Nov. 1887).

J.W. Leigh, 'Labour Organisation (on Unemployment Registers)', Vol. 48 (Dec. 1887).

William G.S.S. Compton, 'Distress in London (no. 1.) Remedies', Vol. 49 (Jan. 1888).

H.E. Manning, 'Distress in London (no. 2) A Note on Outdoor Relief', ibid.

Joseph R. Diggle, 'The Abolition of School Fees: a Plea for Further Consideration', Vol. 49 (Feb. 1888).

F.W. Farrar, 'Social Problems and Remedies', Vol. 49 (Mar. 1888).

Edward Salmon, 'Domestic Service and Democracy', ibid.

William Morris, 'The Revival of Architecture', Vol. 49 (May 1888).

Frederic Harrison, '*Apologia Pro Fide Nostra* (Positivism)', Vol. 50 (Nov. 1888).

Frederic Harrison, 'What the Revolution of 1789 did', Vol. 51 (Jun. 1889).

Thomas Percy Sykes, 'The Factory Half-Timer', Vol. 52 (Dec. 1889).

Charles Bradlaugh, 'Regulation by Statute of the Hours of Adult Labour', Vol. 53 (Mar. 1890).

Roland Blennerhassett, 'Ethics and Politics', Vol. 54 (Aug. 1890).

W.H. Mallock, 'Reason Alone (Insufficient for Belief in God)', Vol. 54 (Nov. 1890).

Earnest M. Bowden, 'Scientific Sins', Vol. 55 (Jan. 1891).

W.H. Mallock, 'Public Life and Private Morals', Vol. 55 (Feb. 1891).

Oscar Wilde, 'The Soul of Man under Socialism', ibid.

J. Coulson Kernahon, 'Rossetti and the Moralists', Vol. 55 (Mar. 1891).

Mathilde Blind, 'Personal Recollections of Mazzini', Vol. 55 (May, 1891).

Florence Routledge & Emilia F.S. Dilke, 'Trades Unionism among Women', ibid.

Francis R.J. Sandford, 'Elementary Education – a Municipal Charge.'

William Smart, 'The Old Economy and the New', Vol. 56 (Aug. 1891).

Frederic Harrison, 'A Survey of the Thirteenth Century', Vol. 56 (Sept. 1891).

Frederic Harrison, 'The Emancipation of Women', Vol. 56 (Oct. 1891).

Edward Cooper, 'A National Pension Fund', ibid.

Samuel Montagu, 'Dangers of Modern Finance', Vol. 57 (Mar. 1892).

Henry Blauchamp, 'Thoughts of a Human Automaton (determinism and free-will)', ibid.

Fletcher Moulton, 'Old Age Pensions', Vol. 57 (Apr. 1892).

Lewis Pelly, 'Glimpses of Carlyle', Vol. 57 (May, 1892).

Charles Tupper, 'The Question of Preferential Tariffs', Vol. 58 (1892).

W.E.H. Lecky, 'The Political Outlook' (no. 1), ibid.

Frederic Harrison, 'How to Drive Home Rule Home', Vol. 58 (Sept. 1892).

Frank Harris, 'Profit and Loss.'

Frederic Harrison, 'Mr Huxley's Controversies', Vol. 58 (Oct. 1892).

Frederic Harrison, 'Mr Huxley's Iron Icon', Vol. 58 (Dec. 1892).

Marie Louise de la Ramee, 'The Sins of Society', ibid.

David F. Schloss, 'The Dearness of "Cheap" Labour', Vol. 59 (Jan. 1893).

Frederic Harrison, 'The Situation Abroad and at Home', Vol. 59 (Feb. 1893).

G. Bernard Shaw, 'What Mr Gladstone Ought to Do' (no. 4), ibid.

'Present Depression of Trade, The' (opinion of 27 men of business), Vol. 59 (Mar. 1893).

R.C. Billing, 'Urban Populations', ibid.

W.H. Mallock, 'The Social Remedies of the Labour Party', Vol. 59 (Apr. 1893).

Frederic Harrison, 'Rome Revisited', Vol. 59 (May, 1893).

Frederic Harrison, 'The Evolution of our Race', Vol. 60 (Jul. 1893).

Arnold White, 'The Unemployed', Vol. 60 (Oct. 1893).

Frederic Harrison, 'The Royal Road to History: an Oxford Dialogue', ibid.

William Smart, 'Is Money a Mere Commodity?' Vol. 60 (Nov. 1893).

Robert Wallace, 'The Psychology of Labour and Capital.'

Samuel A. Beckett, 'The Unemployed', Vol. 60 (Dec. 1893).

W.H. Mallock, 'Fabian Economics', Vol. 61 (Feb. 1894).

W.M.J. Williams, 'A Poor Man's Budget', Vol. 61 (Mar. 1894).

W.H. Mallock, Fabian Economics (part 2) repr. 'The So-Called Evolution of Socialism.'

Fred Hammill, 'Labour Representation', Vol. 61 (Apr. 1894).

W.H. Mallock, 'A Socialist in a Corner (Bernard Shaw)', Vol. 61 (May, 1894).

Karl Pearson, 'Socialism and Natural Selection', Vol. 62 (Jul. 1894).

Charles Maleto, 'Some Anarchist Portraits', Vol. 62 (Sept. 1894).

Karl Pearson, 'Politics and Science.'

J. Barr Robinson, 'Imaginative Currency Statistics.'

Thomas Oliver, 'Our Workmen's Diet and Wages', Vol. 62 (Oct. 1894).

Alfred R. Wallace, 'The Method of Organic Evolution', Vol. 63 (Feb. 1895).

H.G. Keene, 'Sidelights on Socialism (no. 1) Belgian Socialism', ibid.

Thomas Mackay, 'Politics and the Poor Law', Vol. 63 (Mar. 1895).

Alfred R. Wallace, 'The Method of Organic Evolution' (part 2).

Alexander Del Mar, 'The Historical Aspect of the Monetary Question', Vol. 63 (Apr. 1895).

Frederic Harrison, 'The Reaction and its Lesson', Vol. 64 (Oct. 1895).

W.S. Lilly, 'Illiberal Liberalism', Vol. 64 (Nov. 1895).

H.M. Bompass, 'The Improvement of Working Class Homes', ibid.

H.G. Keene, 'Socialism at Home and Abroad', Vol. 65 (Jan.1896).

Edward Salmon, 'From Cobden to Chamberlain', Vol. 65 (Jul. 1896).

Herbert Spencer, 'The Present Evolution of Man', Vol. 66 (Sept. 1896).

H.G. Wells, 'Human Evolution – an Artificial Process', Vol. 66 (Oct. 1896).

Mackenzie Bell, 'William Morris: a Eulogy', Vol. 66 (Nov. 1896).

'Emeritus','Democracy and Leadership', Vol. 66 (Dec. 1896).

Grant Allen, 'Spencer and Darwin', Vol. 67 (Feb. 1897).

H.G. Wells, 'Morals and Civilisation', ibid.

Claude G. Hay and Harold Hodge, 'Toryism and Toil', Vol. 68 (Sept. 1867).

W.H. Mallock, 'The Unrecognised Essence of Democracy', Vol. 68 (Sept. 1897).

Arthur A. Baurmann, 'An Apology for Unprincipled Toryism,' ibid.

A.B.C.,'The Future of Liberalism (no. 1): The Nemesis of Party' 1–11, ibid.

Edward A. Parry, 'The Insolvent Poor', Vol. 69 (May, 1898).

Walter Sichel, 'The Two Byrons', Vol. 70 (Aug.1898).

H. Heathcote Statham, 'The Truth about Ruskin', ibid.

Geoffrey Langtoft, 'Socialism and Anarchism', Vol. 74 (Oct. 1900).

Edward Dicey, 'The General Election (no. 1): The Downfall of Liberalism', Vol. 74 (Nov. 1900).

Fraser's Magazine 1830–82

J. M. Ludlow, 'Labour and the Poor', Vol. 41 (Jan. 1850).

William Whewell, *The Lamps of Architecture,* (by Ruskin) Vol. 41 (Feb. 1850).

J.A. Roebuck, 'The History of the Whig Ministry of 1830 to the Passing of the Reform Bill', Vol. 45 (Mar. 1852).

Andrew Wynter, 'The New Crystal Palace at Sydenham', Vol. 48 (Dec. 1853).

John Ruskin, *Stones of Venice* (part 1), Vol. 49 (Feb. 1854).

John Ruskin, *Stones of Venice* (part 2), Vol. 49 (Apr. 1854).

John Skelton, 'Ruskin on the Ancient and Modern Poets: Homer and Tennyson', Vol. 53 (Jun. 1856).

F.D. Maurice, 'The Denison Case', Vol. 54 (Dec. 1856).

Goldwin Smith, 'Imperialism', Vol. 55 (May, 1857).

John Skelton, 'What are the Functions of the Artist?' (On Ruskin's *Modern Painters*), Vol. 55 (Jun. 1857).

W.W.'Has Political Freedom Receded ?' Vol. 60 (Nov 1859).

John Stuart Mill, 'A Few Words on Non-Intervention', Vol. 60 (Dec 1859).

'Self-Help' (by Samuel Smiles), Vol. 61 (Jun. 1860).

Anon., 'Difficulties of Political Philosophy', ibid.

Anon., 'Political Economy in the Clouds' (on Ruskin), Vol. 62 (Nov. 1860).

John Skelton, 'Mr Ruskin at the Sea-Side: A Vacation Medley', Vol. 62 (Dec. 1860).

John Stuart Mill, 'Utilitarianism' (chaps 3–4), Vol. 64 (Nov. 1861).

John Stuart Mill, 'Utilitarianism' (chap. 5 concl.), Vol. 64 (Dec. 1861).

John Ruskin, 'Essays on Political Economy;' being a sequel to papers which appeared in the *Cornhill Magazine* (no. 1), (repr. Heavily revised, in *Munera Pulveris, Works* 17) Vol. 65, (Jun. 1862).

John Ruskin, 'Essays on Political Economy', (no. 2) Vol. 66 (Sept. 1862).

John Ruskin, 'Essays on Political Economy', (no. 3) Vol. 66 (Dec. 1862).

John Ruskin, 'Essays on Political Economy', (no. 4 concl.) Vol. 67 (Apr. 1863).

Francis Power Cobbe, 'The Rights of Man and the Claims of Brutes', Vol. 68 (Nov. 1863).

Bonamy Price, 'The Political Temper of the Nation', Vol. 69 (Feb. 1864).

Francis Power Cobbe, 'The Philosophy of the Poor Laws', Vol. 70 (Sept. 1864).

Francis Power Cobbe, 'The Indigent Class: their Schools and Dwellings', Vol. 73 (Feb. 1866).

Anon., 'France under Richelieu and Colbert (on Positivism and History)', Vol. 75 (Apr. 1867).

Anon., 'The Teaching of Mr Maurice', Vol. 75 (Jun. 1867).

T.E. Cliffe Leslie, 'Political Economy and the Rate of Wages', Vol. 78 (Jul. 1868).

W.R. Gregg, 'On the Failure of "Natural Selection" in the Case of Man', Vol. 78 (Sept. 1868).

John Skelton, 'William Morris and Matthew Arnold: A Letter from a Hermitage', Vol. 79, (Feb. 1869).

J.F.H., 'The Working Man and his Friends', Vol. 79 (Jun. 1869).

Leslie Stephen, 'The Comtist Utopia', Vol. 8 (Jul. 1869).

Leslie Stephen, 'Why Skilled Workmen don't go to Church', ibid.

Robert Williams, 'A Few Words on Utilitarianism', Vol. 80 (Jul. 1869).

Robert Williams, 'Laissez-faire', Vol. 81 (Jan. 1870).

J.A. Froude, 'Reciprocal Duties of State and Subject', Vol. 81 (Mar. 1870).

James E. Thorold Rogers, 'Capital-Labour-Profit', Vol. 81 (Apr. 1870).

Lowry Wittle, 'The Future of Labour', Vol. 82 (Sept. 1870).

J.A. Froude, 'On Progress', Vol. 82 (Dec. 1870).

Arthur Joseph Mumby, 'Primogeniture,' ibid.

John Edward Jenkins, 'The Solutions (to the Malthusian problem of population)', Vol. 83, (Apr. 1871).

Anon., 'The Working Man's Political Question', Vol. 83 (May, 1871).

Francis W. Newman, 'Malthusianism, True and False', ibid.

Thomas Wright, 'English Republicanism', signed: a working man, ibid.

'An Architect', 'On Architecture and its Relation to Modern Life', ibid.

E.B.M., 'The Commune of 1871', ibid.

Thomas Wright, 'The English Working Classes and the Paris Commune', Vol. 84 (Jul. 1871).

John S. Barker, 'Mazzini', Vol. 85 (May, 1872).

W.R. Greg, 'Strikes, Short Hours, Poor law and Laissez-faire', Vol. 86 (Sept. 1872).

Thomas Wright, 'Mis-education', Vol. 86 (Nov. 1872).

A.K.H. Boyd, 'Concerning the Disadvantages of Living in a Small Community', Vol. 86 (Dec. 1872).

G.P. Cluseret, 'Behind the Scenes at the Commune', ibid.

A.K.H. Boyd, 'Of Alienation', Vol. 87 (Jan. 1873).

J.F. Stephen, 'Liberty, Equality, Fraternity', Vol. 88 (Jul. 1873).

Abraham Hayward, 'John Stuart Mill' (on his autobiography), Vol. 88 (Dec. 1873).

T.H.S. Escott, 'Political Novels (mainly Disraeli)', Vol. 89 (Apr. 1874).

J.A. Froude, 'Party Politics', Vol.. 90 (Jul. 1874).

Robert Bell, 'Liberal Protestantism', ibid.

Richard Jefferies, 'The Labourer's Daily Life', Vol. 90 (Nov. 1874).

Mathilda Bethan- Edwards, 'The International Working Men's Association' (part 1), Vol. 92 (Jul. 1875).

J.V., 'Is Monarchy an Anachronism?' Vol. 92 (Oct. 1875).

W.M., 'Proper Uses of Wealth', ibid.

Francis William Newman, 'The Capitalist in Society' (on G.J.Holyoake's History of Cooperation) Vol. 92 (Dec. 1875).

John Ruskin, 'Modern Warfare', Vol. 94 (Jul. 1876), repr. in *Works*, Vol. 34.

W.H. Mallock, 'The Golden Ass of Apilenis', Vol. 94 (Sept. 1876).

William Allingham, 'Modern Prophets', (mainly scientists) Vol. 96 (Sept. 1897).

F.R. Conder, 'Third Class Passengers', ibid.

H., 'On the Comparitive Stupidity of Politicians', Vol. 96 (Oct. 1877).

William Morton, 'Some of the Moral Aspects of Political Economy', ibid.

Francis R. Conder, 'Working Men's Conventions', Vol. 97 (Mar. 1878).

Francis R. Conder, 'Some Remarks on the Employment of English Capital', Vol. 98 (Sept. 1878).

George Howell, 'Trade Unions: their Nature, Character and Work', Vol. 99 (Jan.1879).

G.S. 'Starvation Wages and Political Economy', ibid.

F.R. Conder, 'The Best Friend of the Working Man (the Machine)', Vol. 99 (Feb. 1879).

E.A. Ryder, 'The Crisis in Trade: its Cause and Crime', ibid.

C.E., 'Starvation Wages and Political Economy: a Reply', ibid.

Anon., 'The Failure of Altruism', Vol. 100 (Oct. 1879).

Anon., 'English Liberals and Continental Liberals', Vol. 101 (Feb. 1880).

Bonamy Price, 'What is Money?', ibid.

William L. Blackley, 'English Pauperism: its Money and Remedy', Vol. 102 (Oct. 1880).

Thomas Wright, 'Education and Boots', Vol. 102 (Nov. 1880).

Mathilda Bethan-Edwards, 'Exchange no Robbery' (part 3), Vol. 105 (Apr. 1882).

London Quarterly Review

Robert F. Horton, 'John Ruskin', Vol. 93 (3 Apr. 1900).

National Review

John Randal MacDonnell, 'The Morality of Political Economy', Vol. 14 (Apr. 1862).

North British Review

H.H. Lancaster, 'The Writings of John Ruskin', Vol. 36 (Feb. 1862).

W.G. Blackie, 'Commercial Philanthropy', Vol. 41 (Nov. 1864).

T.C. Cliffe Leslie, 'The New Gold Mines and Prices', Vol. 42 (Jun. 1865).

Louis Mallet, 'The Political Writings of Richard Cobden', Vol. 46 (Mar. 1867), repr. under his name as *The Political Opinions of Richard Cobden* (1868), and included in his 'Free Exchange' (1891).

C.E. Pritchard, 'Modern Views of the Atonement', Vol. 46 (Jun. 1867).

J.C. Shairp, 'Moral Theories and Christian Ethics', Vol. 47 (Sept. 1867).

W.R. Greg, 'The Social Sores of Britain', Vol. 47 (Dec. 1867).

Fleeming Jenkin, 'Trade Unions: How Far Legitimate', Vol. 48 (Mar. 1868).

Bonamy Price, 'Commercial Crises', Vol. 53 (Jan. 1871).

National Review 1883–1900

G.R.C. Herbert, 'Liberty and Socialism', Vol. 1 (May, 1883).

W.H. Mallock, 'The Radicalism of the Market-Place', Vol. 1 (Jun. 1883).

W.H. Mallock, 'Radicalism and the Working Classes', Vol. 2 (Sept. 1883).

Robert Cecil, 'Labourer's and Artisan's Dwellings', Vol. 2 (Dec. 1883).

William John Courthorpe, 'Johnson and Carlyle: Common Sense versus Transcendentalism.'

W.H. Mallock, 'Conservatism and Socialism', Vol. 2 (Jan. 1884).

Francis Radcliffe, 'The Plain Duty of the Opposition', Vol. 2 (Feb. 1884).

Eustace G. Cecil, 'Social Deterioration and its Remedy', ibid.

Wilfred Ward, 'A Pickwickian Positivist, (Frederick Harrison)' Vol. 4 (Oct. 1884).

Alfred Austin, 'Some Lessons from Carlyle's Life', Vol. 4 (Nov. 1884).

Percy Greg, 'The Party System (no. 1) the New Radicals', Vol. 5 (Apr. 1885).

A.J. Balfour, 'Politics and Political Economy', Vol. 5 (May, 1885).

Walter Copland Perry, 'An Apology for Jingoism', ibid.

Edward Shroder Prior, 'Mr Ruskin's Museum at Sheffield', ibid.

Hugh E. Egerton, 'A Scarce Book (Cobbett's Rural Rides)', ibid.

F.R. Conder, 'On the Remuneration of Labour in England', Vol. 5 (Jun. 1885).

W.H. Mallock, 'How to Popularise Unpopular Political Truths', Vol. 6 (Oct. 1885).

W.H. Mallock, 'The Old Order Changes', Vol. 6 (Dec. 1885).

J. Shield Nicholson, 'A Plea for Orthodox Political Economy' ibid.

Archer Gurney, 'In Correspondence: The Older System of Political Economy' Vol. 6 (Jan 1886).

Walter Armstrong, 'The Fame of Turner' Vol. 7 (Apr. 1886).

H.D.Traill, 'Hobbes and the Modern Radical.' Vol. 7 (May, 1886).

W.T. Quin, 'The Real Truth about Tory Democracy', Vol. 9 (May, 1887).

C.A. Cripps, 'Competition and Free Trade', Vol. 10 (Nov. 1887).

C.A. Cripps, 'Free Trade and the Economists', Vol. 11 (Mar. 1888).

W.H. Mallock, 'Conservatism and the Diffusion of Property', Vol. 11 (May 1888).

Alfred Austin, 'Matthew Arnold', ibid.

Golwin Smith, 'The Invitation to Celebrate the French Revolution', Vol. 11 (Aug. 1888).

H.G. Keene, 'The Disorder of the Age', ibid.

Henrietta O. Barnett, 'The Social Problem (no. 1) East London and Crime', Vol. 12 (Dec. 1888).

W.H. Mallock, 'Radicals and the Unearned Increment', Vol. 13 (Mar. 1889).

G. Rome Hall, 'The Present Feeling of the Working Classes', Vol. 13 (Jul. 1889).

W. Earl Hodgson, 'An Economic Cure for Socialism', Vol. 14 (Jan. 1890).

Guilford L. Molesworth, 'Political Economy in its Relation to Strikes', Vol. 14 (Feb. 1890).

J.A. Hobson, 'Problems of Living (no. 1): the Cost of a Shorter Working Day', Vol. 15 (Apr. 1890).

Alice Oldham, 'The History of Socialism (part 1): the Early Period, 1817–1852', Vol. 16 (Nov. 1890).

Alice Oldham, 'The History of Socialism (part 2): Anarchism– Nihilism– the Beginning of German Socialism – Ferdinand Lasalle', Vol.16 (Dec. 1890).

Alice Oldham, 'The History of Socialism (part 3 concl.): German Socialism – Karl Marx – Christian Socialists– Future of Socialism', Vol. 16 (Jan. 1891).

W.A. Appleyard, 'Matthew Arnold: Criticism of Life', ibid.

Julia Wedgwood, 'Morals and Politics', Vol. 16 (Feb. 1891).

C.A. Cripps, 'The Socialist Reaction', ibid.

H.C. Raikes, 'The Radical at Home', Vol. 17 (Mar. 1891).

George C Broderick, 'Fallacies of Modern Socialism', Vol. 19 (May, 1892).

W.A. Mallock, 'Wanted: a New Corrupt Practices Act', Vol. 20 (Sept. 1892).

W. Earl Hodgson, 'The Revival of Ethics, and of Laughter', ibid.

Charles Edwards, 'Society in Ancient Venice', Vol. 20 (Oct. 1892).

Frederick Greenwood, 'Free Trade a Variable Expedient', Vol. 20 (Nov. 1892).

W. Earl Hodgson, 'Disabilities of Democracy', Vol. 20 (Jan. 1893).

Francis R.Y. Radcliffe, 'Toryism and Progression.'

W.H. Mallock, 'A Common Ground of Agreement for all Parties', Vol. 21 (Mar. 1893).

W.H. Mallock, 'The Causes of the National Income', Vol. 21 (Apr. 1893); (May, 1893); (Jul. 1893); (Aug.1893).

E.T. Cook, 'Mr Ruskin in Relation to Modern Problems', Vol. 22 (Feb. 1894).

Leslie Stephen, 'Luxury', Vol. 23, (Mar. 1894); (Apr. 1894).

J.L. Mahon, 'The Labour Party and the General Election', Vol. 23 (Jul. 1894).

T.H. Farrer, 'Shall we Degrade our Standard of Value?' Vol. 24 (Oct. 1894).

George Lansbury, 'A Socialist View of the Government', Vol. 25 (Jun. 1895).

Thomas Mackay, 'Empiricism in Politics', Vol. 25 (Aug. 1895).

Helen D. Bosanquet, 'The Socialist Propaganda', Vol. 26 (Sept. 1895).

T.H. Farrer, 'Taking Stock of Employers' Liability', Vol. 26 (Nov. 1895).

Cosmo Monkhouse, 'The Worship of the Ugly', Vol. 27 (Mar. 1896).

Geoffrey Lushington, 'The Trade Union Triumph: Allen v Flood', Vol. 30 (Jan. 1898).

W. Wilson, 'The Policy of Jingoism', Vol. 32 (Jan. 1899).

W.H. Mallock, 'The Comedy of Christian Science', Vol. 33 (Mar. 1899).

W.A.S. Benson, 'William Morris and the Arts and Crafts', Vol. 34 (Oct. 1899).

Leslie Stephen, 'John Ruskin', Vol. 35 (Apr. 1900).

H.W. Massingham, 'The Decline of Liberalism', Vol. 35 (Jun. 1900).

H.W. Mallock, 'The Rights of the Weak', Vol. 35 (Jul. 1900).

Leslie Stephen, 'Walter Bagehot', Vol. 35 (Aug. 1900).

New Review

Lucy C. Cavendish, 'What is to be Done with the Morally Deficient?' Vol. 2 (Mar. 1890).

William Morris, 'The Socialist Ideal (no. 1): Art', Vol. 4 (Jan. 1891).

G. Bernard Shaw, 'The Socialist Ideal (no. 2): Politics', ibid.

W.H. Mallock, 'The Individualist Ideal: A Reply to (no.1): Art', Vol. 4 (Feb. 1891).

John Ruskin, 'Letters of John Ruskin to his Secretary', Vol. 6 (Mar. 1892).

W.H. Mallock, 'The Divisibility of Wealth', Vol. 8 (Apr. 1893).

Nineteenth Century

Frederic Harrison, 'A Modern Symposium' (no. 4), Vol. 1, (Apr. 1877).

Frederic Harrison, 'The Soul and Future Life', (part 1) Vol. 1 (Jun. 1877); (part 2 concl.) Vol. 1 (Jul. 1877).

John Ruskin, 'An Oxford Lecture (on Science and Religion)', Vol. 3 (Jan 1878), repr. in *Works*, 22.

Frederic Harrison, 'A Modern Symposium', (no. 4) Vol. 3 (May, 1878).

W.H. Mallock, 'Faith and Verification', Vol. 4 (Oct. 1878).

Robert Lowe, 'Recent Attacks on Political Economy', Vol. 4 (Nov. 1878).

John Ruskin, 'The Three Colours of Pre-Raphaelitism', (part 1) *Works* 34, Vol. 4 (Nov. 1878).

W.H. Mallock, 'Dogma, Reason and Morality', Vol. 4 (Dec. 1878).

John Ruskin, 'The Three Colours of Pre-Raphaelitism', (part 2 concl.).

W.H. Mallock, 'The Logic of Toleration', Vol. 5 (Jan. 1879).

George Jacob Holyoake, 'State Socialism', Vol. 5 (Jun. 1879).

W.H. Mallock, 'A Dialogue on Human Happiness', Vol. 6 (Sept. 1879).

Louise S. Bevington, 'Modern Aetheism and Mr Mallock', (part 1) Vol. 6 (Oct. 1879); (Dec.1879).

W.H. Mallock, 'Aetheistic Methodism', Vol. 7 (Jan. 1880).

Frederic Seebohm, 'Imperialism and Socialism', Vol. 7 (Apr. 1880).

W.H. Mallock, 'Altruism and the Rights of Man', Vol. 7 (May, 1880).

John Ruskin, 'Fiction: Fair and Foul' (part 1), Vol. 7 (Jun. 1880), repr. in *Works*, 34; (part 2), Vol. 8 (Aug. 1880); (part 3), Vol. 8 (Sept. 1880).

W.H. Mallock, 'The Philosophy of Conservatism', Vol. 8 (Nov. 1880).

John Ruskin, 'Fiction: Fair and Foul', (part 4), ibid.

Frederic Harrison, 'The Creeds: Old and New', ibid.

Frederic Harrison, 'Pantheism, and Cosmic Emotion' ibid.

Frederic Harrison, 'The Deadlock in the House of Commons', Vol. 10 (Sept. 1881).

John Ruskin, 'Fiction: Fair and Foul' (part 5 concl.), Vol. 10 (Oct. 1881).

Frederic Harrison, 'The Crisis of Parliamentary Government', Vol. 11 (Jan. 1882); Vol. 13 (Mar. 1883).

Samuel A. Barrett, 'Practical Socialism', Vol. 13 (Apr. 1883).

Leslie Stephen, 'The Suppression of Poisonous Opinions', ibid.

Samuel A. Barnett, 'The Universities and the Poor', Vol. 15 (Feb. 1884).

George C. Broderick, 'Democracy and Socialism', Vol. 15 (Apr. 1884).

Frederic Harrison, 'Agnostic Metaphysics', Vol. 16 (Sept. 1884).

H.M. Hyndeman, 'The Radicals and Socialism', Vol. 18 (Nov. 1885).

Samuel A. Barnett, 'Sensationalism in Social Reform', Vol. 19 (Feb. 1886).

Herbert Spencer, 'The Factors of Organic Evolution', Vol. 19 (Apr. 1886).

Frederic Harrison, 'The Two Paths: A Dialogue (on Contemporary Culture)', Vol. 23 (Jan. 1888).

H.H. Champion, 'The New Labour Party', Vol. 24 (Jul. 1888).

Frederic Harrison, 'The Sacrifice of Education', Vol. 24 (Nov. 1888).

Frederic Harrison, 'Mr Bryce's "American Commonwealth" ', Vol. 25 (Jan. 1889).

Frederic Harrison, 'Are We Making Way (with the Party System?)', Vol. 25 (May, 1889).

Frederic Harrison, 'A Breakfast Party in Paris', Vol. 26 (Aug. 1889).

Frederic Harrison, 'The New Trades-Unionism', Vol. 26 (Nov. 1889).

Herbert Spencer, 'Absolute Political Ethics', Vol. 27 (Jan. 1890).

Frederic Harrison, 'The History of Trades-Unionism', (by Sidney and Beatrice Webb).

Beatrice Webb, 'The Failure of the Labour Commission', Vol. 36 (Jul. 1894).

Frederic Harrison, 'The Centenary of Edward Gibbon', ibid.

J. Keir Hardie, 'The Independent Labour Party', Vol. 37 (Jan. 1895).

Frederic Harrison, 'Ruskin as Master of Prose', Vol. 38 (Oct. 1895).

W.H. Mallock, 'The Religion of Humanity: A Reply to Mr Frederic Harrison', ibid.

Frederic Harrison, '*Unto This Last* (by John Ruskin)', Vol. 38 (Dec. 1895).

Frederic Harrison, 'John Addington Symonds', Vol. 39 (Jun. 1896).

Frederic Harrison, 'J.S. Mill', Vol. 40 (Sept. 1896).

Algernon Charles Swinburne, 'The Well at the World's End' (by William Morris), Vol. 40 (Nov. 1896).

W.H. Mallock, 'The Buck-Jumping of Labour', Vol. 42 (Sept. 1897).

Frederic Harrison, 'On Style in English Prose', Vol. 43 (Jun. 1898).

Frederic Harrison, 'The Historical Method of J.A. Froude', Vol. 44 (Sept. 1898).

Edith May Fawkes, 'Mr Ruskin at Farnley', Vol. 47 (Apr. 1900).

John Percival, 'The Slow Growth of Moral Influence in Politics', Vol. 48 (Aug. 1900).

Oxford and Cambridge Magazine, 1856

William Morris, 'The Churches of North France', Vol. 1 (Feb. 1856).

William Morris, 'Men and Women (by Browning)', Vol. 1 (Mar. 1856).

Edward Burne-Jones, 'Mr Ruskin's New Volume (*Modern Painters* Vol. 3)', Vol. 1 (Apr. 1856).

C.J. Faulkner and Cormell Price, 'Unhealthy Employments', Vol. 1 (May, 1856).

William Morris and Edward Burne-Jones, 'Ruskin and the Quarterly', Vol. 1 (Jun. 1856).

Quarterly Review, 1824–1900

Samuel Smiles, 'Strikes', Vol. 106, (Oct. 1859), repr. as idem., *Workmen's Earnings, Strikes and Savings*, (1861).

Spencer Horatio Walpole, 'Parliamentary Reform, or the Three Bills and Mr Bright's Schedules', Vol. 106 (Oct.1859).

Spencer Horatio Walpole, 'Reform Schemes', Vol. 107 (Jan. 1860).

Thomas James Murray, 'Labourer's Homes', Vol. 107 (Apr. 1860).

Samuel Smiles, 'Workmen's Earnings and Savings', Vol. 108 (Jul. 1860).

Robert Cecil, 'Democracy on its Trial', Vol. 110 (Oct. 1861).

J.R. Lichfield, 'Life, Enterprise, and Peril in Coalmines', Vol. 110 (Oct. 1861).

T.E. Kebbel, 'Modern Political Memoirs', Vol. 112 (Oct. 1862).

Robert Cecil, 'Four Years of a Reforming Administration', Vol. 113 (Jan. 1863).

Alfred Hill, 'Cooperative Societies', Vol. 114 (Oct. 1863).

Samuel Smiles, 'Workmen's Benefit Societies', Vol. 116 (Oct. 1864).

Robert Cecil, 'The Church in her Relations to Political Parties', Vol. 118 (Jul. 1865).

J.H. Themenheere, 'The Children's Employment Commission', Vol. 119 (Apr. 1866).

John Percy Murray, 'Coal and Smoke', ibid.

Robert Cecil, 'The Reform Bill', ibid.

Samuel Smiles, 'Iron and Steel', Vol. 120 (Jul. 1866).

James Davies, 'Curious Myths of the Middle Ages', Vol. 122 (Apr. 1867).

Robert Lowe, 'Trades Unions', Vol. 123 (Oct. 1867).

J.R. Mozley, 'Mr John Stuart Mill and his School', Vol. 133 (Jul. 1872).

H. Evershed, 'Exhaustion of the Soil of Great Britain', Vol. 134 (Jan. 1873).

R.H.I. Palgrave, 'History of British Commerce', ibid.

John Wilson, 'Liberty, Equality, Fraternity: John Stuart Mill', Vol. 135 (Jul. 1873).

H.H.M. Herbert, 'Lessons of the French Revolution,' ibid.

Victorian Newspapers

Bingley Telephone
Christian Life
Christian Socialist
Clarion
Daily News
Justice
Labour Leader
Manchester Examiner and Times
Pall Mall Gazette
Saturday Review
The Times, 1804–1905

Other Primary Sources

T. Barclay, *Memoirs and Medley: The Autobiography of a Bottlewasher* (1934).

——, *The Rights of Labour According to John Ruskin* (Jul.1887).

E. Bellamy, *Looking Backward* (Commonweal, 1889).

R. Blatchford, *Britain for the British* (1902).

——, *My Eighty Years* (1931).

T. Carlyle, *Carlyle's Letters to Ruskin: A Finding . . . with some Unpublished Letters* (ed.) Charles Richard Sanders (Manchester, 1958).

W G. Collingwood, *The Life and Work of John Ruskin* (both 1873 and 1893 edns.).

E.T. Cook, *Studies in Ruskin* (1890).

M.K. Gandhi, *An Autobiography* (1982).

P. Geddes, *John Ruskin: Economist* (Edinburgh 1884).

J. Gray, *Lecture on Human Happiness* (1825).

J.K. Hardie, *From Serfdom to Socialism* (1907).

F. Harrison, '*Apologia pro Fide Mea*: Introductory', in idem, *The Creed of a Layman*: *Apologia pro Fide Mea* (1907).

——, *Autobiographic Memoirs* (1911).

——, *John Ruskin* (1902).

——, *Order and Progress* (1875).

——, 'Moral and Religious Socialism', New Year's Address at Newtown Hall 1 Jan. 1891.

——, *Normal Society* (1918).

——, *Realities and Ideals* (1908).

——, *Tennyson, Ruskin, Mill and Other Literary Estimates* (1899).

S. Headlam, *The Socialist's Church* (1907).

J.A. Hobson, *Confessions of an Economic Heretic* (1938).

——, *John Ruskin Social Reformer* (1898).

——, *Problems of Poverty* (1891).

——, *Problems of the Unemployed* (1896).

——, 'Ruskin and Democracy', published in *The Contemporary Review* (Jan.–Jun. 1902).

——, *The Crisis of Liberalism* (1909).

——, *The Evolution of Modern Capitalism* (1894).

——, *The Social Problem* (1901).

——, *Work and Wealth* (1914).

G.H. Holyoake, *The History of Cooperation in England: Literature and Advocates* (1879), 2 vols.

J.W. Mackail, *The Life of William Morris* (1889).

T. Mann, *Memoirs* (1923).

K. Marx, *Capital* (1867–94), (1957 edn with introduction by G.D.H. Cole), 2 vols.

Marx and Engels *The Manifesto of the Communist Party* (1847, 1948 edn).

T. Malthus, *Essay on the Principles of Population* (1798).

M. Mather, *John Ruskin: His Life and Teaching* (1901).

J. McCarthy, *A History of Our Own Times* (1910), 2 vols.

J.S. Mill, *Principles of Political Economy* (1848).

W. Morris, Preface to Kelmscott Press reprinting of 'The Nature of Gothic' (1892).

W. Morris, *News from Nowhere* (1924), first pub. in *Commonweal* (1890).

May Morris (ed.), *The Collected Works of William Morris with Introduction by his Daughter, May Morris (1915)*, vol. 23.

Letters of Charles Eliot Norton: with Biographical Comment by his Daughter Sara Norton and M.A. DeWolfe Howe (1913), 2 vols.

R. Owen, *Report to the County of Lanark (1821)*, in Gregory Claeys (ed.), *Selected Works of Robert Owen* (1993), Vol. 1.

W. Paley, *Natural Theology* (1802).

T. De Quincey *Collected Writings*, Vol. 9 (Edinburgh, 1890).

A. Reid, (comp.), *Vox Clamantium: The Gospel of the People by Writers, Preachers and Workers, Brought Together by Andrew Reid* (1894).

S. Smiles, *Self Help* (1859).

A. Smith, *An Enquiry into the Nature and Causes of the Wealth of Nations* (1776).

Norman St John-Stevas (ed.), *The Collected Works of Walter Bagehot* (1986) Vol. 14.

W. Thompson, *An Inquiry into the Principles of the Distribution of Wealth Most Conducive to Human Happiness* (1824).

D. Torr (ed.), *The Correspondence of Marx and Engels 1846–95* (1934).

A.Toynbee, 'Are Radicals Socialists?' In his *Lectures on the Industrial Revolution of the Eighteenth Century in England* (1884; repr. 1923).

Unpublished Primary Sources

L.S.E. Archives, Ms Harr. 1/101, Letters from Ruskin to Frederic Harrison.

Minutes of Rainbow Circle 1905–6.

People's History Museum, Ms Pic 42, Ruskin letter to Mr Frederick Pickles, Jun. 1884;

Ms Pic 37, Letter signed by William Morris dated 3 Oct. 1885.

Ruskin Library, Lancaster University, Ms 1–26, John Ruskin Diaries 1861–3;

Ms 33, Diaries of John James Ruskin, 1845– 64.

Selected Secondary Sources

J. Abse, *John Ruskin, the Passionate Moralist* (1980).

J. Allett, *New Liberalism: The Political Economy of J.A. Hobson* (1981).

P.D. Anthony, *John Ruskin's Labour* (1983).

L.M. Austin, *The Practical Ruskin: Economics and Audience in the Late Work* (Baltimore, 1991).

E. Barker, *Political Thought in England, 1848–1914* (rep. 1930).

J. Batchelor, *John Ruskin. No Wealth but Life* (2000).

Q. Bell, *Ruskin* (1963, 1978).

M. Beer, *A History of British Socialism* (1921).

G. Best, *Mid-Victorian Britain, 1851–75* (1973).

Dinah Birch, *Ruskin's Myths* (Oxford, 1988).

——, *Ruskin and the Dawn of the Modern* (Oxford 1999).

J.L. Bradley (ed.), *Ruskin: the Cultural Heritage* (1984).

J.L. Bradley and Ian Ousby (eds), The Correspondence of John Ruskin and Charles Eliot Norton (Cambridge, 1987).

A. Briggs, *Victorian Cities* (1968).

——, *Victorian People* (1965).

C. Bryant, *Possible Dreams, A Personal History of the British Christian Socialists* (1996).

J. Butt and J.F. Clarke (eds), *The Victorians and Social Protest. A Symposium* (1973).

G. Claeys, *Machinery, Money and the Millennium* (Oxford, 1987).

——(ed.), *Selected Works of Robert Owen* (1993).

K. Clark, *Ruskin Today* (1967).

——, *The Gothic Revival* (1964).

G.D.H. Cole, *A Century of Cooperation* (Manchester, 1944).

——. Cole, *A History of Socialist Thought* (1958).

——. Cole, *Persons & Periods: Studies* (1938).

——. Cole & R. Postgate, *The Common People, 1746–1946* (1946).

S. Collini, *Public Moralists: Political Thought and Intellectual Life in Britain, 1850–1930* (Oxford, 1991).

A. Davies, *To Build a New Jerusalem: The British Labour Movement from the 1880s to the 1990s* (1992).

P. Dawson, *The People's Ruskin, A Collector's Guide to the Cheap Editions 1882–1914* (Sussex 1999).

J.S. Dearden (ed.), *Facets of Ruskin:* Some Sequicentennial Studies (1970).

A.V. Dicey, *Lectures on the Relation between Law and Public Opinion in Britain in the Nineteenth Century* (1914).

I. Donnachie, *Robert Owen: Owen of New Lanark and New Harmony* (Tuckwell Press, East Lothian, 2000).

J.T. Fain, *Ruskin and the Economists* (1956).

M.I. Finley, *The Use and Abuse of History* (1990).

M. Freeden (ed.), *Reappraising J.A. Hobson* (1990).

J. Gorman, *Images of Labour* (1985).

W.H. Greenleaf, *The British Political Tradition* (Cambridge, 1983), Vols 1–4.

E. Halevy, *A History of the English People 1895–1905: Epilogue* (Middlesex, 1939) Vols 1–3.

M. Hardman, *Ruskin and Bradford: An Experiment in Victorian Cultural History* (Manchester, 1986).

R. Harrison, *Before the Socialists. Studies in Labour and Politics, 1861–81* (1965).

W. Henderson, *John Ruskin's Political Economy* (2000).

T. Hilton, *John Ruskin: The Early Years* (Bath, 1995).

——, *John Ruskin: The Later Years* (Bath, 2000).

E.J. Hobsbawm, *The Age of Revolution 1789–1848* (1962).

J.D. Hunt, *The Wider Sea: A Life of John Ruskin* (1982).

R. & E. Jay (eds), *Critics of Capitalism: Victorian Reactions to Political Economy* (Cambridge, 1985).

P.D.A. Jones, *The Christian Socialist Revival, 1877–1914* (Princeton, 1968).

W. Kemp, *The Desire of My Eyes: The Life and Work of John Ruskin* (New York, 1990).

D. Knoop and G.P. Jones, *The Medieval Mason* (repr. 1967).

D. Larg, *John Ruskin* (Edinburgh 1932, 1935).

M. Levin, *The Condition of England Question: Carlyle, Mill, Engels* (1998).

C. Levy (ed.), *Socialism and the Intelligentsia, 1880–1914* (1987).

S.F. Markham, *A History of British Socialism* (1930).

D. McLellan, *Karl Marx: The Legacy* (1983).

J.R. Moore (ed.), *Religion in Victorian Britain, Vols 1–4* (Manchester, 1988).

K. Morgan, *Keir Hardie* (1975).

A.L. Morton (ed.), *Political Writings of William Morris* (1984).

E.R. Norman, *The Victorian Christian Socialists* (1987).

A.R. Orage, ed. *National Guilds: An Enquiry into the Wage System and the Way Out* (1914).

H. Pelling, *The Origins of the Labour Party, 1880–1900* (Oxford, 1965).

A.J. Penty, *A Study of the Post-Industrial State* (1917).

S. Pierson, *Marxism and the Origins of British Socialism* (1973).

R. Quinault and N.B. Harte (eds), *Land and Society in Britain, 1700–1914* (1996).

C.E. Raven, *Christian Socialism, 1848–54* (1920).

J.D. Rosenburg, *The Darkening Glass: A Portrait of Ruskin's Genius* (1963).

G. Rosser in *Essays in Criticism*, No. 154 (Jan. 1997).

G.B. Shaw, *Ruskin's Politics* (1921).

J.C. Sherburne, *John Ruskin: Or the Ambiguities of Abundance* (Mass., 1972).

J. Spear, *Dream of an English Eden: Ruskin and his Tradition in Social Criticism* (Columbia, 1984).

P. Stansky, In *Victorian Thinkers: Carlyle, Ruskin, Arnold, Mill* (Oxford, 1983).

G. Stedman Jones, *'Utopian Socialism Reconsidered'* (Ruskin College Position Papers, 30 Nov.–2 Dec. 1979).

P. Thane, *Foundations of the Welfare State: Social Policy in Modern Britain* (Essex, 1982).

E.P. Thompson, *The Making of the English Working Class* (1963).

——, *William Morris: Romantic to Revolutionary* (1977).

N. Thompson, *The People's Science: The Popular Political Economy of Exploitation and Crisis 1816–34* (Cambridge, 1984).

D. Thomson, *England in the Nineteenth Century* (1961).

A. Vidler, *The Church in an Age of Revolution: 1789 to the Present Day* (1968).

M. Vogeler, *Frederic Harrison: The Vocation of a Positivist* (Oxford, 1984).

A.M.C. Waterman, *Revolution, Economics and Religion: Christian Political Economy, 1798–1883* (1991).

M. Weiner, *English Culture and the Decline of the Industrial Spirit 1850–1980* (1981).

M. Wheeler, *Ruskin's God* (Cambridge, 1999).

——(ed.), Ruskin and Environment (Manchester, 1995).

——(ed.), *Time and Tide: Ruskin and Science* (1996).

J.H. Whitehouse, *Ruskin Centenary Address* (8 Feb. 1919).

R. Williams, *Culture and Society* (1958).

D. Winch, *Riches and Poverty: An Intellectual History of Political Economy in Britain, 1750–1834* (1996).

J. Wolff, *The Social Production of Art* (1985).

G. Young, *Portrait of an Age: Victorian England* (Oxford 1936).

INDEX